John Wyatt is Emeritus Professor of Neonatal Paediatrics, Ethics and Perinatology, University College London, and Faraday Associate at the Faraday Institute for Science and Religion, Cambridge. He has a special interest in the interface between medical ethics, technology and Christianity, and co-led a research project on the social, ethical and theological implications of advances in artificial intelligence and robotics based at the Faraday Institute. He is the author of *Dying Well*, *Right to Die: Euthanasia, assisted suicide and end-of-life care* and *Matters of Life and Death: Human dilemmas in the light of the Christian faith* (all published by IVP in 2018, 2015 and 2009 respectively).

Stephen N. Williams is Honorary Professor of Theology at Queen's University, Belfast, and was a participant in the research project based at the Faraday Institute, Cambridge. His books include *The Election of Grace: A riddle without a resolution?* (Eerdmans, 2015), *The Shadow of the Antichrist: Nietzsche's critique of Christianity* (Baker Academic Press, 2006) and *Revelation and Reconciliation: A window on modernity* (Cambridge University Press, 1995).

John Wyatt is Emeritus Professor of Neonatal Paediatrics, Ethics and Perinatology, University College London, and Faraday Associate at the Faraday Institute for Science and Religion, Cambridge. He has a special interest in the interface between medical ethics, technology and Christianity, and co-led a research project on the social, ethical and theological implications of advances in artificial intelligence and robotics based at the Faraday Institute. He is the author of *Dying Well, Right to Die: Euthanasia, assisted suicide and end-of-life care* and *Matters of Life and Death: Human dilemmas in the light of the Christian faith* (all published by IVP in 2018, 2015 and 2009 respectively).

Stephen N. Williams is Honorary Professor of Theology at Queen's University, Belfast, and was a participant in the research project based at the Faraday Institute, Cambridge. His books include *The Election of Grace: A riddle without a resolution?* (Eerdmans, 2015), *The Shadow of the Antichrist: Nietzsche's critique of Christianity* (Baker Academic Press, 2006) and *Revelation and Reconciliation: A window on modernity* (Cambridge University Press, 1995).

THE ROBOT WILL SEE YOU NOW

Artificial intelligence and the Christian faith

Edited by
John Wyatt and Stephen N. Williams

First published in Great Britain in 2021

Society for Promoting Christian Knowledge
36 Causton Street
London SW1P 4ST
www.spck.org.uk

British Library Cataloguing-in-Publication Data
A catalogue record for this book is available from the British Library

ISBN 978-0-281-08435-7
eBook ISBN 978-0-281-08436-4

Typeset by Fakenham Prepress Solutions
First printed in Great Britain by Jellyfish Print Solutions
Subsequently digitally reprinted in Great Britain

eBook by Fakenham Prepress Solutions

Produced on paper from sustainable sources

Contents

Part 2
THEOLOGICAL FRAMEWORKS AND RESPONSES

Part 3
ETHICAL AND SOCIAL ISSUES

Contributors

Nigel Cameron is President Emeritus, Center for Policy on Emerging Technologies, Washington, DC.

Crystal L. Downing is Marion E. Wade Professor in Christian Thought at Wheaton College, Illinois, USA.

Andrew Graystone is an independent author, broadcaster and journalist, and Fellow of St John's College, Durham University.

Noreen Herzfeld is Professor of Theology and Computer Science at the College of St Benedict/St John's University, Minnesota, USA.

Christina Bieber Lake is Clyde S. Kilby Professor of English at Wheaton College, Illinois, USA.

Victoria Lorrimar is Lecturer in Systematic Theology at Trinity College, Queensland, Australia.

Nathan Mladin is Senior Researcher at Theos think tank in London.

Vinoth Ramachandra is International Secretary for Dialogue and Social Engagement, International Fellowship of Evangelical Students, and is based in Sri Lanka.

Peter Robinson is Professor of Computer Technology at the University of Cambridge Computer Laboratory.

Robert Song is Professor of Theological Ethics at Durham University.

Andrzej Turkanik is Executive Director of the Quo Vadis Institute, Salzburg, Austria.

Foreword

In *The Robot Will See You Now*, John Wyatt and Stephen N. Williams have produced a challenging and thought-provoking book on the nature of artificial intelligence (AI) and its implications for Christian thinkers in a range of spheres. The very title evokes the prospect of a patient entering a consulting room to be examined, not by a flesh-and-blood human doctor but by a machine equipped to diagnose and prescribe. This immediately prompts ideas of utopia or dystopia – or both. The utopian vision would look to the possibility that such inanimate devices could compensate for the shortage of medical staff and their inability to know of all the possible diagnoses, while the dystopian response would shrink from the idea of a mere machine tinkering with something so delicate as the human body. Rather than 'delicate', I might better have said 'personal', because a leitmotiv running through the excellent essays in this volume is the question of what it is to be a person, created in the image of God. The Turing test would suggest that if we could not distinguish between the diagnoses and prescriptions from a human or a robotic physician, then the latter should be regarded as possessing human 'intelligence', but that again opens up the question of what it is we mean when we use the word 'intelligence'. Readers will have to decide for themselves whether the Turing test remains the gold standard here.

This book is timely because, as the various writers concur, we are confronted already with the reality of phenomena such as 'surveillance capitalism' – amassing information on us from social media, online purchases, 'virtual personal assistants', public CCTV and other sources of information about our habits and activities, from which extraordinarily accurate and, some would say, intrusive conclusions may be drawn about our thoughts and attitudes. It is the application of AI to mass data that enables governments and corporations to achieve these spectacular and potentially sinister results. So, consideration of the impact of AI on our lives is not a matter of purely philosophical or theological speculation: it is both practical and urgent.

The shape of the book is especially helpful, drawing on a number of contributors who provide complementary insights from their respective specialist fields. Most focus on what the Christian response should be to AI now and in the future, but this book can be profitably read by non-Christians and people of no faith, as it touches on matters of human nature and autonomy that affect us all. It eschews easy answers and often raises difficult questions but, in doing so, renders us all a service. From the ever-present danger of reductionist thought to the implications of lethal autonomous weapon systems (LAWS), from the vital concern for human dignity to consideration of the highly contested nature of consciousness – not to mention many other dimensions of AI – these essays cover an impressive range of aspects of the implications for AI that will, there is no doubt, affect all our lives. Some reading this book will be especially struck by recalling that the word 'robot' is the Czech word for 'slave': while not necessarily accepting the proposition that intelligent machines should deserve the equivalent of human rights, we are forced to look back at our unhappy record of exploiting human beings as if they were in fact machines. What price the dignity of labour and what constitutes exploitation?

Thus, the richness of this volume is far greater than might appear from a superficial consideration of its subject-matter. The complementarity of the essays is itself an asset. To the extent that different contributors duplicate references to common sources, this serves only to strengthen the whole – rather as shining lights from different angles on to the same gemstone serves to reveal its full potential. I defy anyone to come away from this book without being moved and challenged – unless, that is, the reader is a robot. But that is another story.

++*Justin Cantuar*
Lambeth Palace, London

Editorial introduction

JOHN WYATT AND STEPHEN N. WILLIAMS

Artificial intelligence (AI) is in the air that we breathe. When we undertake a credit-card transaction, turn right when instructed by the GPS, or click on an item specially recommended for us, we do not usually have a sustained awareness that we are dealing with AI or ruminate on ethical issues that arise in connection with our interactions. AI just seems to be a step on the path of a technologically advanced society, as natural a part of our social environment as colour televisions became for an earlier generation and telephones for a generation before that.

Yet there are forms of and prospects for AI, with which we are now becoming familiar, that make it a matter for public reflection and urgent debate. Concern for the created and social order lies at the heart of Christian thought and commitment, even though Christians have often neglected their responsibilities in this respect. The word 'created' signals our commitment to belief in a Creator God who has placed humans within an order. It is an order marred and disarranged by human wrongdoing but one that is conducive to human well-being and flourishing, if we can find and walk in the way of wisdom. Our aim in this volume is to make a modest start with respect to AI.

To change metaphor, we are very conscious that we have only scratched the surface with the chapters that follow. This applies not only to the treatment of a given topic within these chapters but also to the restriction in the topics covered. For example, the area of AI and law is rapidly burgeoning, and it is only spatial constraints – certainly not a judgement that it is relatively unimportant – that account for the omission of a chapter on it in this book. Similarly, we do not have a separate chapter on the military and security applications of AI, although the topics are raised on more than one occasion. Evaluating military technology is undoubtedly of the first ethical importance, but it involves moral discussion of that most serious of issues, the whole question of war, and this raises profound moral quandaries that are independent of questions surrounding AI.

As it is, our volume is divided into three parts, starting with cultural and historical accounts, proceeding to theological essays, and finally dealing with a number of ethical and social issues raised by AI and robotics. The chapters are all designed to exhibit and encourage informed, serious thought, but they are not meant to be academic treatments, accessible only to academic specialists or specialists in the field of AI. This would defeat the whole purpose of this book, which is to inform and engage a 'lay' readership willing and eager to wrestle with questions and issues concerning AI that have a social impact, whether direct or indirect.

Although the authors are Christians who reflect on AI from a Christian point of view, their accounts often presuppose no Christian or religious conviction whatsoever. We also trust that, where they offer religious responses, these responses will be of interest and use to those who do not share the authors' commitments. 'Christianity' is such a massive tent today that it is worth saying that we are trying to define it neither too narrowly, in accordance with just one church or theological tradition, nor so broadly that it is detached from any recognizable connection with what the major Christian traditions have in common.

Although the range and incidence of disagreement is small, the contributors do not always agree and the editors have not attempted to disguise this. Each contributor was charged with taking his or her independent line, but some had participated together in workshops hosted by the Faraday Institute in Cambridge. As editors, we realized from the beginning that there would be some overlap in the matters touched on; indeed, it would be strange and a little worrying if a number of contributors did not ponder, in connection with their assigned topic, the implications of humankind being in the image of God, a key Christian conviction. However, we have sought to ensure that the overlap is minimal and, where it happens, positively helpful. As editors, we have either ourselves occasionally inserted or asked authors to insert a sentence or footnote referring to other contributions in this collection.

AI encompasses a wide range of phenomena and we always have to be on our guard against lazily failing to make distinctions about all the things which come under that heading, ranging from a strictly mathematical or scientifically based sub-discipline or sub-field in computer science to talk of superintelligences that might take over the world. At the heart of society's preoccupation with AI, there apparently lie two things. One is the nature of machine intelligence and how we should understand that in relation to human intelligence or, more widely, to the ways and doings of humankind. The other involves the social consequences of the practical incursion of AI into a number of domains, such as employment and health care. These two preoccupations are often, although not always, connected. In assembling these essays, we have naturally had those concerns at the forefront of our minds, although we have not confined ourselves to the narrowly conceptual and social.

This volume originated in a research project entitled 'Human identity in an age of nearly human machines: the impact of advances in robotics and AI technology on human identity and self-understanding', based at the Faraday Institute, Cambridge, in 2015–18. We are extremely grateful to the Templeton World Charity Foundation, which provided funding for the project, for the contribution of Dr Beth Singler, who acted as Research Associate, and for the staff of the Faraday Institute who supported this work. We are also very grateful to the Quo Vadis Institute, which provided additional financial support to enable this book to become a reality, and to Alison Barr of SPCK for her encouragement and enthusiastic support.

Introduction: a computer technology perspective

PETER ROBINSON

'What hath man wrought!' exclaimed the headline above David Lawrence's editorial for the *United States News*[1] in the immediate aftermath of the destruction of Hiroshima and Nagasaki by atomic bombs. It could almost apply to the world of artificial intelligence. What have we done? The same question could be asked of the technologists who pioneered the Industrial Revolution late in the eighteenth century. Their technology has allowed humankind to inflict climate change on the whole planet. As we see these effects 200 years later, we might be tempted to ask, 'What have they done?'

The timescales are very different. It has taken 200 years to see the effects of increasing carbon dioxide concentrations in the atmosphere, and the changes have been so slow that they were easily overlooked or even ignored. The consequences of atomic warfare were immediately apparent, so the public reaction was more forceful. AI has developed at a slower rate. It is 70 years since Maurice Wilkes and his team built the world's first practical computer, 65 years since John McCarthy coined the term 'artificial intelligence', 40 years since the Japanese launched their fifth-generation computer project, 25 years since IBM's Deep Blue beat the world champion at chess, and 10 years since products using AI entered the domestic market. Has the progress been so slow that

1 David Lawrence, founder of the *United States News* (later the *U.S. News and World Report*), writing on 17 August 1945; see <www.usnews.com/news/special-reports/the-manhattan-project/articles/2015/09/28/editorial-from-1945-what-hath-man-wrought>, accessed 8 February 2021.

we are falling into a trap every bit as serious as man-made climate change?

AI, atomic power and the Industrial Revolution are just the latest examples of technologies that pose these questions. They go back to prehistoric times, with ploughshares being beaten into swords, wheeled carts being turned into chariots, and fire used for destruction as well as warmth. The fallen nature of humankind makes it only too easy to find unhelpful uses for new technologies. The eminent mathematician G. H. Hardy wrote, 'I have never done anything "useful". No discovery of mine has made, or is likely to make, directly or indirectly, for good or ill, the least difference to the amenity of the world.'[2]

Hardy could not have been more wrong. His work in number theory, the purest of pure mathematics, is central to all modern cryptography used to secure communications in banking and commerce, by the military to control weapons and in billions of mobile phone conversations every day. Few technologies are devised with malicious intent, but most technologies can be turned to malicious use. So it is with AI.

Before embarking on the chapters that follow, it would be worth exploring the distinctions between information technology, AI and robots. Information technology combines computing and communications to automate operations that could be undertaken by people. Computing makes them faster and possibly more accurate, while electronic communication allows them to be geographically dispersed. Banking is an obvious example. Computers automate the work of bank clerks writing in ledgers, and communication allows banking services to be provided remotely, perhaps through automatic teller (cash) machines. Satellite navigation uses computing and communications to automate the determination of a location that would previously have been undertaken using a sextant and

2 G. H. Hardy, Sadlerian Professor of Mathematics at the University of Cambridge, in *A Mathematician's Apology* (Cambridge: Cambridge University Press, 1940), 49.

chronometer. Neither is an example of 'artificial intelligence' in its strict sense.

AI is simply the display by a machine of any cognitive process that we would expect to be done by a person. It has become more widespread in the past ten years, with dramatic increases in the processing power and memory storage of computers, combined with data that can be used to characterize models by machine learning. The combination of these three allows systems to be built that identify patterns in data and use them to make predictions about the real world in new contexts. An important characteristic is that the systems rely on probabilistic modelling to allow their outputs to identify what is likely rather than absolute. Of course, this means that they should be treated with some caution. Banking systems have also grown to use these techniques. When a withdrawal is made from an automatic cash machine that is for an unusual amount or in an unusual location, the conflict with the system's model of a particular customer can be used to prevent fraud. The transaction may be genuine but the calculation shows it to be unlikely, which can give rise to difficulties when it is refused.

The term 'artificial intelligence' is widely used for marketing, scaremongering or, perhaps, simply to describe something that we think computers can't do yet but might do at some point in the indeterminate future. Working computer technology instead has terms such as 'language processing', 'speech understanding', 'computer vision' and so on.

Practical applications of AI are now mainly implemented using forms of machine learning, that is, the statistical analysis of large bodies of data to characterize mathematical models, which can predict a person's probable response to novel stimuli. The analysis is computationally demanding, but computers have doubled in speed every two years from 700 instructions/second on the EDSAC in 1949 to 700 billion instructions/second on a modern (2021) desktop computer, while the cost has decreased at a similar rate. Memory density has increased and its cost has decreased even more steeply over the same period. Finally, the growing use of computers in every aspect of our daily lives has allowed the collection of the data needed to construct the models. Even social media have played their part, collecting information about their users that can be used to predict their behaviour.

This processing is simply mathematical modelling, but it allows computers to simulate aspects of human understanding and behaviour. Many people have confused this simulation with emerging sentience and speculate that the machines are exhibiting nascent intelligence akin to that in humans. Taken to an extreme, this leads to the idea of 'artificial general intelligence' in which the machines evolve faster than humans and become the dominant species. As the physicist Stephen Hawking wrote:

> The development of full AI could spell the end of the human race. Once humans develop AI, it will take off on its own and redesign itself at an ever-increasing rate. Humans, who are limited by slow biological evolution, couldn't compete and would be superseded.[3]

As we shall see in the following chapters, the theme of machines surpassing their human inventors has run through science fiction from ancient Jewish golem mythologies, through Talos protecting Crete several centuries before Christ, Mary Shelley's *Frankenstein* in 1818, Karel Čapek's *R.U.R.: Rossum's Universal Robots* in 1920, to the proliferation of novels accompanying the twentieth-century scientific revolution. This takes us to our third item: robots. A recurrent theme is of humanoid robots, made to serve humankind,

3 Stephen Hawking, quoted by Rory Cellan-Jones in 'Stephen Hawking warns artificial intelligence could end mankind' (BBC News, 2 December 2014), <www.bbc.co.uk/news/technology-30290540>, accessed 8 February 2021.

turning on their creators. There is a fascination with machines made in the image of human beings. They have a physical resemblance to human form and are often inherently malicious. The character of these robots perhaps says more about their creators than it does about technology. The fact is that most robots today are simply machines undertaking mechanical tasks that require strength, precision or attention to detail in a repetitive process.

Vint Cerf, widely regarded as 'the father of the Internet', helpfully characterizes robots more widely:

> In most formulations, robots have the ability to manipulate and affect the real world. Examples include robots that assemble cars (or at least parts of them). Less facile robots might be devices that fill cans with food or bottles with liquid and then close them up. The most primitive robots might not normally even be considered robots in normal parlance. One example is a temperature control for a home heating system that relies on a piece of bi-metal material that expands differentially causing a circuit to be closed or opened depending on the ambient temperature.
>
> I would like to posit, however, that the notion of robot could usefully be expanded to include programs that perform functions, ingest input and produce output that has a perceptible effect.[4]

Even with this broader definition, Cerf is not concerned at the prospect of sentient robots overthrowing the human race. However, he is worried that flawed software could pose a real threat to humans. 'If there are bugs in the software and some device is operating

4 Vint Cerf, President of the American Association for Computing Machinery, writing in the January 2013 issue of the *Communications of the ACM*: 'What's a robot?', <https://cacm.acm.org/magazines/2013/1/158758-whats-a-robot/fulltext>, accessed 8 February 2021.

autonomously with regard to that software, the bugs can cause bad things to happen.'[5] Programmers' carelessness or incompetence has already led to catastrophic accidents. These programs are the robots that pose a genuine threat.

The Boeing 737 MAX debacle presents an interesting case study. Boeing introduced the 737 passenger jet in 1967. Over the following 50 years, the design was modified to expand its capacity, fit increasingly modern engines and improve its control systems, while retaining the principal features of the airframe. The 737 MAX was introduced in 2017 as the fourth generation of an enormously successful design. It used a new type of engine to improve fuel economy, which, unfortunately, was too large to replace the earlier engines directly. The new engines had to be mounted differently, which rendered the aircraft inherently unstable. Boeing solved this problem by adopting a technique used in the design of military aircraft, in which computers maintain the correct pitch of the plane. The Maneuvering Characteristics Augmentation System (MCAS) detected that the plane was pulling up and forced the pilots' controls down.[6] Poor software engineering practices allowed a faulty reading from a single sensor to override the pilot without warning. This became apparent only after two fatal accidents leading to the deaths of 346 people.

Poor programming led to instability in automatic stock trading systems, which exacerbated the 2007–8 financial crisis in the wake of concerns about bad debts affecting bank solvency.[7]

---

5 Nextgov report on an address by Vint Cerf at the Italian embassy in April 2016; see Mohana Ravindranath, 'Vint Cerf: buggy software is scarier than a robot takeover' (Nextgov, 26 April 2016), <www.nextgov.com/emerging-tech/2016/04/vint-cerf-buggy-software-greater-threat-rogue-robots/127808>, accessed 8 February 2021.

6 Michael Laris, 'Changes to flawed Boeing 737 MAX were kept from pilots, Defazio says', *Washington Post* (19 June 2019), <www.washingtonpost.com/local/trafficandcommuting/changes-to-flawed-boeing-737-max-were-kept-from-pilots-defazio-says/2019/06/19/553522f0-92bc-11e9-aadb-74e6b2b46f6a_story.html>.

7 United States Senate Permanent Subcommittee on Investigations report, *Wall Street and the Financial Crisis: Anatomy of a financial collapse* (13 April 2011), <http://hsgac.senate.gov/public/_files/Financial_Crisis/FinancialCrisisReport.pdf>.

These two examples also illustrate a second factor alongside flawed software that 'can cause bad things to happen': motivation. Both Boeing and the banks were motivated by profit. Boeing wanted to retain the same pilot certification for the 737 MAX while fitting more efficient engines. This required them to retain the same basic airframe despite the new engines rendering it inherently unstable. Stability would be maintained by the automatic software. Unfortunately, indicators of failure in the sensors used by the software were a chargeable option on the aircraft, so not all airlines bought them. In the same way, stock-market players were motivated by the additional margins that could be earned by automatic high frequency trading.

It is important to point out that aeroplane control and automatic trading rely only marginally on AI. However, AI lies at the heart of social media. The companies' motivation is financial: the sale of advertising requires users to continue clicking through links on their sites, which is achieved by tailoring the presentation to engage each individual user. This, in turn, is achieved by inferring their interests and offering them more of the same. (Incidentally, that is why social media are so effective in amplifying people's political prejudices.) Finally, the systems encourage users to share information with their friends, so recruiting them into an ever-expanding audience for advertisements. The financial motivation is met by increasing advertising, engagement and growth.[8] Given that aim, they are very competent.

Lethal autonomous weapon systems (LAWS) also raise questions of motivation and the gravity of their effects raises questions of competence. They increasingly rely on AI, delegating decisions on targeting and even tactics to computer systems. Legal decisions, medical diagnoses and medical interventions also rely on AI. Civilian as well as military decisions may be delegated to

8 *The Social Dilemma*, a drama documentary released by Netflix in 2020, <www.netflix.com/gb/title/81254224>.

computers. These are serious matters concerning liberty and even life. In her chapter, Noreen Herzfeld usefully cites Amish questions directed at any new technology: does it provide tangible benefits? How does it affect our relationships?[9]

Professional practitioners are paid well because they are expected to be well trained and to use their skills wisely. The rewards are substantial not least because the responsibilities are also substantial. Software engineering in general and AI in particular are no different. Their practitioners are expected to keep to higher ethical standards of motivation and competence.

I conclude by returning to David Lawrence. The headline for his editorial was a deliberate play on Balaam's declaration, 'What hath God wrought!' in Numbers 23.23 (AV). A modern translation would be, 'See what God has done!' The context is that God's will cannot be deflected by human endeavours. But it remains the case that humans are still perfectly capable of inflicting pain on themselves by trying to deflect God's will.

Nuclear power is a clear example of a technology that has the potential to do great good as well as great harm. Nine years after the bombing of Hiroshima and Nagasaki, Lewis Strauss, then the Chairman of the United States Atomic Energy Commission, declared, 'It is not too much to expect that our children will enjoy in their homes electrical energy too cheap to meter.'[10] That might have been hyperbole, but nuclear power has undoubtedly been a great blessing, despite the dreadful spectre of nuclear war. The more powerful the technology, the more wisdom required in its use.

So it is with computer technology in general and AI in particular. Both have the potential to do great good and great harm. The same is true of robots. They serve well by undertaking dangerous, repetitive

---

9 Ch. 8 of this volume: 'Surrogate, partner or tool: how autonomous should technology be?'

10 Lewis Strauss, addressing the National Association of Science Writers on 16 September 1954; see <www.nrc.gov/docs/ML1613/ML16131A120.pdf>, accessed 8 March 2021.

or delicate tasks and, possibly, in health care (although the risks of abdicating human responsibility to machines is a concern). But their ability to deceive could lead to great harm. Computing professionals will be at the forefront of those who make such choices, guided by their ethical principles of motivation and competence. Many other professionals will be making similar choices in their specialities. The role of the Christian professional is to apply those principles in pursuing God's will.

A number of writers in this volume highlight the fact that God created humankind in his image to rule over the earth, and to enjoy relationships with him and with one another. We must be careful when we delegate that rule to automatic computer systems or when we forget the importance of those relationships.

As David Lawrence's editorial concluded:

> For at last it has been demonstrated to all of us that only by following His guidance in our daily conduct as individuals and as nations can we hope to fulfil our true mission as the children of God on earth. It is the only road left now – the road of mutual forbearance. It is the way to survival and human happiness.[11]

11 See note 1.

Part 1

WHAT IS GOING ON? CULTURAL AND HISTORICAL ANALYSIS

1

Science fiction, AI and our descent into insignificance

CHRISTINA BIEBER LAKE

Although it was written just over 200 years ago, Mary Shelley's *Frankenstein* is as relevant today as ever. At the very least, it set the trajectory for the genre that it arguably birthed: science fiction, referred to in academic circles as SF. Indeed, Shelley's 'hideous progeny' includes the replication and proliferation within SF of one of the novel's main concerns: the loss of control of our creations. As the Industrial Revolution was building up steam in England, the prescient 19-year-old was asking readers to consider whether it was possible to go too far with the desire to create a race of beings – whether humanoid or robotic – to serve as the final chapter of our triumphant control over nature.

In spite of her warnings (and those of generations of SF novelists to follow), many contemporary theorists and practitioners think that such control is the evolutionary destiny of the human race. Ray Kurzweil may be the most prominent of these. He celebrates what he calls 'the age of spiritual machines', and eagerly awaits the year 2043, his predicted date for the Singularity: when machines exceed human intelligence and we 'gain power over our fates', including our mortality.[1]

That the utopian desire for such control, and concerns about it, are as pertinent now as they were explains the continuing popularity of SF novels and films in technologically advanced nations.

1 Ray Kurzweil, *The Singularity Is Near: When humans transcend biology* (New York, NY: Viking, 2005), 9. See also Ch. 9 of this volume: Victoria Lorrimar, 'The future of humanity'.

But it would be a mistake to assume that the fear of the loss of control of our creations is still SF's primary concern. Indeed, a close look at the range of SF as it developed through the mid twentieth and into the twenty-first century reveals that as our technology has advanced, our primary fears have changed. Where once we worried that we were overreaching the God-given limits of human existence, we now worry that there is no God and there are no limits. What we had experienced as exhilarating terror now devolves into numbing despair, for if there is no God, there is also nothing special about human existence. The fear that artificial intelligence will take our jobs is just the tip of the iceberg. Our real worry is not that AI will render us obsolete and insignificant, but that it will prove that we never were significant to begin with.

The purpose of this chapter is to trace that transition through some exemplary SF texts to illustrate how our race towards the Singularity is changing our view of human nature, and to highlight the theological perspectives that the Church needs to reassert in response.

The three orders of simulacra

The theorist Jean Baudrillard wrote his most significant work in the 1980s, just as Apple had planted its seeds of dominance and well before the word 'Internet' came into household use. First published in French in 1981, Baudrillard's book *Simulacra and Simulation* reads today like an eerie premonition of my recent struggle to elbow past a teenager with a selfie stick, who was standing with her back turned towards the *Mona Lisa*. Using the USA (especially California) as his exemplary case, Baudrillard argues that we are living in the 'simulacra of simulation', a world of images that are themselves copies of copies. The real has been replaced by simulated images; 'signs of the real' have been substituted for the real. The substitution is total: the simulacrum serves only to reveal that the real never actually existed. Baudrillard argues that this is what iconoclasts actually feared: 'That deep down God never existed, that only the simulacrum ever existed, even that God himself was never anything but his own simulacrum – from this came their urge to destroy the images'.[2] But we are far past iconoclasm, says Baudrillard. It's the end of metaphysics. We are no longer even looking for the really real. Our backs are turned towards the *Mona Lisa*, and we do not experience this as loss.

When Baudrillard turns his attention to SF, he argues that its development can be mapped on to what he calls the three orders of simulacra, with the 'simulacra of simulation' being the final order. They are so densely constructed that I will parse them a bit.

The first order of simulacra are simulacra that are 'natural' and which exist as a hopeful, inherently conservative effort to restore 'nature as made in God's image'.[3] In this pre-modern order, simulations (models, works of art and so on) represent the dream of utopia as somewhere else, such as a return to Eden. They represent an imaginary vision that seems hopelessly separated from the world as we know it. This is utopia as transcendence.

The second order of simulacra are those that are meant to be productive of a new industrial order. They are utopian and share with a progressive society the 'Promethean aim of a continuous globalization and expansion'.[4] Second-order simulacra are more materialistic; they are the product of a society committed to progress, production and the dream of control. They project an alternative real world that we believe we can actually build. These simulacra support the idea that robots should rise to power because they would necessarily create a better society than flawed humans.[5] Only this second order corresponds with SF proper, and most classical SF celebrates this dream of robotic control (as we will see).

2 Jean Baudrillard, *Simulacra and Simulation*, tr. Sheila Faria Glaser (Ann Arbor, Mich.: University of Michigan Press, 1995), 4.

3 Baudrillard, *Simulacra*, 121.

4 Baudrillard, *Simulacra*, 121.

5 In Baudrillard's cryptic formulation, the 'projected hypostasis of the robot' (*Simulacra*, 122).

Baudrillard's third order of simulacra is 'the simulacra of simulation', in which any image is a copy of a copy of a copy, as I mentioned above. Baudrillard calls this total substitution of the simulated for the real 'hyperreality'.[6] In an information economy, the value of images has almost completely replaced the value of things. The simulated world has not only replaced the real one; it has also erased any trace of origins. Hyperreality seems like an extreme concept only until we ponder the dizzying number of contemporary manifestations, many appearing well after Baudrillard's time: Instagram celebrities, Internet pornography, fake news, Deepfake videos, 'Zoom University' and the increasing use of virtual reality interfaces. The third order of simulacra consists of digital images that are completely abstracted from the real. It is 'stuff' become information – the world translated into zeroes and ones, and then manipulated. The model for this type, argues Baudrillard, is the 'cybernetic game' or virtual reality as game.[7] If you have seen the films *The Matrix* or *Ready Player One*, you have seen hyperreality in action.

For the rest of this chapter, I will both show how SF illustrates how we moved from a society characterized by second-order simulacra to one characterized by third-order simulacra, and help us to ponder the implications of that move.

I, Robot

I am introducing these concepts to provide structure for the huge change in SF. But we should not think (to disagree somewhat with Baudrillard) that issues pertaining to second-order simulacra, or the dream of robot control, have somehow disappeared. In contemporary SF, we often get a mix of second- and third-order simulated images. The best example of this that I can think of is HBO's

6 Baudrillard insists that only this world of simulacra – virtual reality – 'can still truly interest us' (*Simulacra*, 127).

7 Baudrillard, *Simulacra*, 121.

Westworld. Whereas the original *Westworld* (a camp 1973 film, created after Michael Crichton's novel) was concerned primarily with the classic SF issue of robots going on a vengeful rampage, the Jonathan Nolan and Lisa Joy version takes a leap into the world of hyperreality, in which everything is a copy of something that never existed to begin with. Indeed, the robots don't even start taking over and killing guests until the end of season two. Season one is exemplified by the conversation between one of the guests (the people who go to Westworld to be entertained by humanoid robots) and one of the hosts (the humanoid robots of the amusement park). When the guest asks the host, 'Are you one of them or are you real?', the apparent host replies, 'If you can't tell the difference, does it matter?'

Before SF became hyperreal (third-order simulacra), it was interested in exploring the ramifications of robot control (second-order simulacra). As I intimated above, many SF writers fall on the utopian side of that projection, and some on the dystopian side, but the theological issues it raises are largely the same.

Let's start with the dystopian side because it is a lot more fun. Since the *Frankenstein* die was cast, SF has been in love with its murderous robots. It is important to note that writers must anthropomorphize the robots to make them want to seek revenge. It has become commonplace for viewers and readers to accept that an AI that becomes self-aware would want to destroy its creators completely. So, we end up with HAL, the creepy computer in *2001: A Space Odyssey*; the Terminator film franchise, because, of course, self-aware machines would want to obliterate humanity; *Battlestar Galactica* and its successful twenty-first-century reboot; and pretty much any Michael Crichton novel. *Prey* may be the most interesting of these because, instead of individuated positronic robot brains, it imagines what experts call 'distributed cognition' that enlivens a swarm of nanobots. Killer nanobots, of course.

But most classic or early SF writers do not share this dystopian view of the robot or AI. The most exemplary of the utopian novels is Isaac Asimov's *I, Robot*, published in 1950. Set in 2057, the plot revolves around the creation of thinking machines that have been programmed to follow the three rules of robotics:

> First Law
> A robot may not injure a human being or, through inaction, allow a human being to come to harm.
>
> Second Law
> A robot must obey the orders given it by human beings except where such orders would conflict with the First Law.
>
> Third Law
> A robot must protect its own existence as long as such protection does not conflict with the First or Second Law.[8]

On one side, there are programmers and visionaries who think that the robots cannot endanger humanity because of these three laws, and, on the other, are the folks who feel nervous about giving up human control. It becomes clear that the only time the robots go 'insane' and malfunction is when they face situations in which the laws are in conflict with one another.

This insistence on robots following rules helps to clarify the most noticeable difference between utopian robot/AI novels and dystopian ones. It turns on the question of why and how the robots are anthropomorphized. In *I, Robot*, the machines are given seemingly human characteristics only when they emerge out of necessity. That is, the machines have what can be considered human emotions or behaviour *only* when it is required for them to keep perfectly their directives. Most notably, they lie or obscure the truth when they determine that humans would be more harmed by knowing the

8 Isaac Asimov, *I, Robot* (New York, NY: Del Rey, 2008), 37.

truth. They view themselves as superior (display arrogance) only because they are superior and it is necessary for humans to understand that to accept their rule.

If this sounds like a robotic version of Plato's suggestion that society should be ruled by philosopher kings, that is precisely the point. Because they perfectly execute decisions based only on reason and logic, the robots are ideal leaders. Empathy is (supposedly) not required when your first directive is to 'not injure a human being' or fail to act to protect one.

In the novel's conclusion, because the robots prove their consistency over time, the opponents of robot rule end up where Asimov wanted them: admitting that human beings never had any control to begin with. They finally recognize that we have always been determined by our limited understanding, flawed motives and failed reasoning. The novel's main proponent of robot rule – humorously named Susan Calvin – finally convinces her interlocutor of the new utopian era that we will enter:

> 'But you are telling me, Susan, that the "Society for Humanity" is right; and that Mankind *has* lost its own say in its future.'
>
> 'It never had any, really. It was always at the mercy of economic and sociological forces it did not understand – at the whims of climate, and the fortunes of war. Now the Machines understand them; and no one can stop them, since the Machines will deal with them as they are dealing with the Society, – having, as they do, the greatest of weapons at their disposal, the absolute control of our economy.'
>
> 'How horrible!'
>
> 'Perhaps how wonderful! Think, that for all time, all conflicts are finally evitable. Only the Machines, from now on, are inevitable!'[9]

9 Asimov, *I, Robot*, 224.

Although Asimov is not centrally motivated by the question of the difference between robots and humans, the novel assumes that what makes us human is our flaws. Because we are small, limited and imprisoned in our weak bodies, we cannot or will not follow the most reasonable rules to allow all humanity to flourish. But the robots have evolved beyond those flaws. Because they know more and see more, their rule will be superior to any human rule. They will keep us from the petty conflicts that have plagued us.

I happened to read *I, Robot* at the precise time I was teaching on Julian of Norwich's *Revelations of Divine Love.* The experience was uncanny and sharpened the theological issues at stake. Whereas Julian insists that 'all things shall be well' under the omnipotent and omniscient care of a loving God, Asimov assumes that God does not exist. For Asimov, omniscience is still the key to benevolent rule, but that rule is best when it is running in the background, unnoticed. All will be well in Asimov's version of the future because of the development of what is called 'the Brain' – a kind of super robot, an interconnected intelligence. Robot rule after the Singularity arrives will be better than even the best manifestations of Christendom because there is no need for our humility. More intelligent than we are, the robots will work out how to manipulate our basest desires to create the best of all possible worlds for humanity. They will take the place of God.

Simulacra and simulation

To try to locate the exact cause of the transition from Baudrillard's second-order (robot rule) to his third-order (hyperreality) simulacra is to set out on a fool's errand. Here are just a few candidates: the transition from an industrial economy to an informational economy; the increasing power of the technological revolution, especially its digital advances; the role of television in the Vietnam conflict; Watergate; and the advent of social media. All these contribute to our simulated world, our distrust of the idea of the real.

As is often the case, SF anticipated the advent of hyperreality, and was primarily troubled by it. In the USA, there has never been a more disturbed – and disturbing – prophet of the hyperreal than the SF novelist, Philip K. Dick. While most Westerners have never read a single one of his novels, they most certainly have been invited into his paranoias. His 1968 novel *Do Androids Dream of Electric Sheep?* was translated into the cult classic film *Blade Runner* (1982). The Netflix television series *The Man in the High Castle* (2015–19) was also derived from one of his novels. There are many more.

There is no space here for a full analysis of what is kept and lost when *Do Androids Dream?* is translated into *Blade Runner*, but one core concept remains: anxiety over AI (in the form of androids) is experienced as the terrifying thought that humans may not be fundamentally different from machines. Thus *Blade Runner* begins with an agent of the Tyrell Corporation trying to determine whether a new employee (Leon Kowalski) is human or android. Because the cybernetic technology used to create androids is extremely sophisticated, the only way the agent can do this is by asking a series of emotionally charged questions meant to catch the android displaying unhuman behaviour.

Astute viewers will note immediately that this interview is a Turing test in action. The development of the Turing test in the 1950s was and is essential to the project of AI and the question it raises of what it means to be human. The test puts a human subject (the tester) in one room, a second human in a different room and a computer in a third room. The three entities can communicate only via typed question-and-answer exchanges. The 'test' is to see whether the human tester can discern which is the human and which is the AI. If the tester cannot tell the difference, this outcome is interpreted as a marker of advanced AI. As N. Katherine Hayles has argued, the development and deployment of this test is not neutral.[10] To use

10 N. Katherine Hayles, *How We Became Posthuman: Virtual bodies in cybernetics, literature, and informatics* (Chicago, Ill.: University of Chicago Press, 1999).

this test as the arbiter of machine intelligence is to assume that an entity's ability to identify information patterns (thinking), and not its material instantiation (embodiment), is what 'counts', as it were, in being alive. In other words, the development of the test itself is a step towards erasing the difference between human intelligence and machine intelligence. It is also necessarily a gnostic step, but without any spiritual content. It describes persons as mere 'ghosts in the machine'. Our brains are more essential to who we can become than are our bodies, which often only get in the way.

Philip K. Dick's novels heighten the fear we experience when we begin to suspect that the idea that we are our brains means that all human decisions can also be reduced to zeroes and ones, to patterns and pattern recognition. *The Simulacra* (first published in 1964) is one of many novels that explore this fear.[11]

The Simulacra contains a particularly prescient vision because, in it, the government of what used to be the USA proves to be a nearly total simulation, set up to manipulate citizens according to the will of a hidden cabal. The president (given the German title *der Alte* because of Dick's invented alternative post-Second World War global history) is known to be just a figurehead. The real leader of the state is his wife, Nicole Thibodeaux. Because of her charisma, beauty and aura, Nicole has immense power. She goes through a series of these figurehead spouse presidents, but she herself never loses energy, beauty or political power. During the course of this unnecessarily convoluted plot, it is revealed that the figurehead spouse presidents have all been androids – simulacra. But it is also later revealed that Nicole is herself a simulation of sorts. She is merely one of a series of look-alike actresses that each replace the previous Nicole seamlessly. Since everything is manipulated on camera, no one notices. When we recognize that Dick contrived this scenario before the election of the former actor Ronald Reagan

11 Philip K. Dick, *The Simulacra* (Boston, Mass.: Mariner Books, 2011).

to the US presidency – and the advent of the Trump and Fox News echo chamber – it is truly chilling.[12]

Dick's work highlights the fact that although many of our fears about robots taking over remain (we don't want to lose control), the primary fear here is the pointlessness of even attempting to change a society in which the true sources of power are completely buried. The simulated has replaced the real. Politics is reduced to a fight over whose simulated reality – which dream – is the most appealing to a capitalistic mass culture, not a fight over truth or justice. Ideology is a constructed façade, not a genuine expression of different approaches to solving problems. In short, there is no possible way to speak truth to simulacra. What this means is that Dick did nothing less than anticipate the epistemological crisis of the technologically advanced world.

What else is theologically at stake in a simulated world? My own misreading of a sentence of Baudrillard's might best make the point. In a chapter called 'Value's last tango', Baudrillard argues that higher education has become a simulated performance. This situation produces the 'terror of value without equivalence', meaning that we know and are terrified by the fact that there's no there *there*: that the value of a university degree is a construct and not the equivalent to the value of any real knowledge.[13] But I accidentally read the sentence as the 'terror of value without significance'. And seen from a theological perspective, that's the real terror here. When we submit to the idea that the constructed image of ourselves is all we have, that we are only what we can sell, we have given up on any idea of the inherent dignity of human life. We have abandoned the idea that any particular human life has significance because all humans are made in the image of God. Instead, we are reduced to manipulating

---

12 For an illustration of this echo chamber, see Brian Stelter, *Hoax: Donald Trump, Fox News, and the dangerous distortion of truth* (New York, NY: One Signal Publishers/ Atria Books, 2020).

13 Baudrillard, *Simulacra*, 155.

Instagram images of ourselves for the public. In short, if we actually look deeply at our world of hyperreality, we are terrified that we, too, amount only to zeroes and ones – with the emphasis on the zeroes.

But what was a cause of anxiety for Philip K. Dick is not a cause of anxiety for everyone. Indeed, when it comes to AI, most contemporary SF writers seem to have acquiesced in the hyperreal world of simulacra and have even pitched it as the way to a new utopian freedom. If reality is a construct, these novels suggest, then let's just roll up our sleeves and construct it the way we want to and move forward.

The best example of this perspective can be seen in Iain Banks's Culture novels. Beginning with *Consider Phlebas*, Banks has imagined a universe in which many, but not all, planetary societies have agreed to be ruled by AI (called 'Minds' in the Culture), and thus have achieved the elimination of war and scarcity. But it is very important to note that the Culture represents a step beyond the robot rule that Asimov illustrated in *I, Robot* and many other novels. Advancement of the Culture requires a kind of assimilation to its values, which includes acceptance of total human insignificance. If this sounds similar to the Borg from *Star Trek*, the comparison is apt – but also comes up short. Whereas the writers of *Star Trek* saw this kind of assimilation into a collective as terrifying, Banks sees it as liberating, a kind of ultimate *deus ex machina*: the moment in ancient plays when a machine representing deity swoops in and saves the players from their foibles. If humans are no different from the cyborgs/androids that are a part of the Borg Collective, why should we fear being assimilated into their protective cube (starship)?

A novel that illustrates this fundamental change in perspective is Banks's *The Player of Games*.[14] Written in 1997, it is the second book of the Culture series, a series that grew to seven novels (and many more related novels) before Banks's death in 2013. In many ways, its

14 Iain M. Banks, *The Player of Games* (New York, NY: Orbit, 2008).

focus on game playing makes it the most theologically revealing. The protagonist is a human citizen of the Culture, Gurgeh, who is known across the galaxy as a master game player. But Gurgeh is bored – and without his boredom there would be no story. Since the Culture has achieved ultimate safety, satiety and peace for its citizens through advanced technology, Gurgeh has nothing to do but play more games, to try to find more intellectual challenges. So the Culture uses him and his skills; it tricks him into playing a game in a non-Culture society called the Empire. From the Culture's perspective, the Empire is still one of the crudely religious societies that insists on its old, high-risk and violent traditions to determine rulers. The Culture means to school them, and it does – by manipulating Gurgeh to play and win at the Empire's traditional high-stakes games.

The novel has a complicated plot that would take far too long to reiterate here. But what's important to note is that Banks's conception of the utopian Culture takes the post-human to its logical end. In a world where all problems have been solved and humans can live as long as they want to, there is literally nothing to do. Life itself has become the ultimate simulation – the ultimate game. A person's body, perfectly protected because of technology (there are sensing robots that unfailingly catch you if you go rock climbing and fall), is too meaningless even to be considered a nuisance. In the Culture, you can change your gender at will, have any experience you want and go anywhere you want (in sentient ships). It is complete techno-gnostic freedom, with nothing actually at stake.

With our existence here reduced to information patterns housed in a fleshy prosthesis, and no god but what we create, we have a choice. We can choose either to despair at our human insignificance and fight a losing battle against it or to affirm the joy of play. Go with the flow; fully enter the simulation. Play to win, but don't worry about losing because it's just a game after all. In *The Player of Games*, it eventually turns out that even the narrator is an AI. This AI proclaims about Gurgeh:

> the point of the game was to win; he had been forgetting that. Nothing else mattered; nothing else hung on the outcome of the game either. The game was irrelevant, therefore it could be allowed to mean everything, and the only barrier he had to negotiate was that put up by his own feelings.[15]

This paradoxical formulation makes sense only to atheists like Banks. Because the game of life is inherently irrelevant, we simply choose to allow it to mean everything. The plot of our individual lives is just part of a continuing game. The only thing to do is to keep on playing. In the similar television series *Devs*, when the protagonist discovers that he can experience everything he wants from inside a simulation, he proclaims to his co-workers: 'I just need you to help me keep it turned on.'[16]

This is the emergence of AI as the complete immersion in hyper-reality. The simulated has replaced the real. When the machines guide us into their digital utopia, the only challenge will be to keep the power on. Origins and births are irrelevant in this world, for there is and can be no final *telos* (that is, destiny).

But there is a substantial fissure in this utopian vision, a fissure that Banks's work reveals, however unwittingly. I have argued elsewhere that the novel as a genre is inherently theological because it focuses its gaze on particular humans that it thereby values.[17] The storyteller mimics God by looking on God's creation and calling it good. Banks knows that if human beings really believed that their lives here are lived as pawns on a chessboard, then no one would actually care enough to read his work. Neither, for that matter, would an AI bother to tell a human's story. Although I cannot

15 Banks, *The Player of Games*, 343.

16 'Episode #1.8', *Devs*, SF television series, created and written by Alex Garland (DNA Films, FX Productions, Scott Rudin Productions, 2020), Hulu, broadcast 16 April 2020.

17 Christina Bieber Lake, *Beyond the Story: American literary fiction and the limits of materialism* (Notre Dame, Ind.: University of Notre Dame Press, 2019).

argue the point here, it seems to me that we read novels because we suspect that the novelist's gaze on his or her characters resembles the loving, attentive gaze that God has on us. We read novels because we suspect that our decisions here do matter. We want to see how certain decisions work out before we make them ourselves.

It is for this reason that the Church's best response to the human as a player of games is to insist that each particular human being has been made in the image of God and set on a journey of discovery in this life. It is a journey towards the discovery of our human significance *and* our insignificance. As Blaise Pascal explains:

> it is dangerous to show man too clearly how much he resembles the beast, without at the same time showing him his greatness. It is also dangerous to allow him too clear a vision of his greatness without his baseness. It is even more dangerous to leave him in ignorance of both.[18]

Like God looking in on his servant Job, I believe that the novelist cares about decisions made by his or her characters because the stakes are actually high for them. And they are for us, too. SF can play with as many scenarios of human insignificance as it wants to but, in the end, the novelist's own, human-centred point of view will belie that perspective. Furthermore, as Henri de Lubac argues, when we look intently and truthfully at human beings, we also see God. Because we are made in the image of God, 'Every creature is, in itself, a theophany. Everywhere we find traces, imprints, vestiges, enigmas; and the rays of divinity pierce through everywhere.'[19] We can create robots and use them to argue away our humanity, but as long as human beings still walk the earth, we will bear an imprint of the divine.

---

18 Quoted in Warren S. Brown, Nancey Murphy and H. Newton Malony, *Whatever Happened to the Soul? Scientific and theological portraits of human nature* (Minneapolis, Minn.: Fortress Press, 1998), 87.

19 Henri de Lubac, *The Discovery of God* (Grand Rapids, Mich.: Eerdmans, 1996), 88.

2

Out of the machine: cinema and science fiction

CRYSTAL L. DOWNING

During the reign of Caesar Augustus (27 BCE – 14 CE), a decree went out that all the world should be enrolled (Luke 2.1), guaranteeing Bethlehem as the location where God took on flesh to save humanity from sin. During the same reign, the Roman poet Horace wrote *Ars Poetica* (*c.*19 BCE), which notes how Greek gods came to earth in the flesh to save humanity. The gods Horace described, however, were actors that appeared on theatrical stages. As described in Aristotle's *Poetics* (*c.*335 BCE), a crane-like machine would lower on to the stage an actor representing a deity who saves the protagonist. This god 'out of the machine' or 'from the machine' – *deus ex machina* in Horace's Latin – would either resolve the conflict or transport the character to safety. A machine providing salvation, in the sense of mediating it, has thus long been part of dramatic fiction, serving as an apt metaphor not only for science-fiction cinema but also for robots that appear on screen. In what follows, I explore the various meanings and nuances that lie behind the phrase *deus ex machina*.

This chapter explores the close connection between cinematic machines and science fiction, before considering robots in movies. It then looks in depth at *Ex Machina* (2014), a film about the making and marring of artificial intelligence machines. The chapter culminates with theological reflections inspired not only by the apostle Paul's allusion to one of the most famous Greek advocates of the *deus ex machina* convention but also by the work of Dorothy

L. Sayers, a lover of cinema whom C. S. Lewis identified as one of the four most important influences on his spiritual life. In a book Lewis recommended to others called *The Mind of the Maker* (first published in 1941), Sayers explores the Christian significance of creativity, including the creativity that generates, in her words, 'robots and Frankenstein monsters'.[1] To help illustrate her theory, the chapter closes with comments about the relevance of *deus ex machina* to one of the most famous films about AI, *Matrix Revolutions* (2003).

Creating lifelike movement on film

Reminiscent of Frankenstein constructing a humanoid creature that could move, Thomas Edison and his assistant William Dickson were the first to construct and market images of human movement. By 1893, the year of Sayers' birth, their customers could put coins into box-like machines called kinetoscopes in order to watch, through peepholes on top, moving images inside. Although kinetoscope movies were only about twenty seconds long, one amazed reporter described seeing a filmed man in the machine as though he were witnessing the impressive movement of a robot: 'It bowed and smiled and waved its hands and took off its hat with the most perfect naturalness and grace. Every motion was perfect.'[2] It was like a god out of a machine.

In 1895, the technology of cinema took a leap forward when French brothers Auguste and Louis Lumière developed a machine that could both film movies and project them on a wall, thus freeing recorded human movement from kinetoscope coffins. In history, 28 December 1895 goes down as the first time people paid

1 Dorothy L. Sayers, *The Mind of the Maker* (New York, NY: HarperCollins, 1979), 64. Sayers' work is also explored in this volume by Andrzej Turkanik in Ch. 13, 'Art, music and AI: the uses of AI in artistic creation'.

2 Quoted in Patrick Robertson, *Film Facts* (London: Billboard, 2001), 5.

money to gather together as a viewing audience for a movie. A reporter who attended that screening in a Parisian café described the Lumière machine as though it would someday achieve what Frankenstein could only imagine:

> When these apparatuses are made available to the public, everybody will be able to photograph those who are dear to them, no longer as static forms but with their movements, their actions, their familiar gestures, capturing the speech on their very lips.[3]

And he ends his statement with a comment not that far removed from Frankenstein's motivation: 'Death will no longer be absolute.'[4] The journalist thus implies that salvation from death is made possible from out of a machine: *deus ex machina*. Ironically, Louis Lumière dismissed the power of the machine, famously stating that 'cinema is an invention without a future'.[5]

Cinema, of course, did have a future and it was advanced by the science-fiction genre. Whereas the Lumière brothers strung together shots of everyday events for their viewing audiences, their fellow Frenchman Georges Méliès created fictional narratives for the screen, stories enhanced by some of the earliest known 'special effects', such as stop-motion photography, which created the illusion of something disappearing or turning into something else on screen. Although his initial narrative film, with multiple scenes, was produced in 1899, Méliès's most famous work is *A Trip to the Moon* (1902). Often described as the first ever science-fiction movie, Méliès's iconic film shows astronomers rocketing to the moon and exiting their ship like gods out of a machine.

---

3 Quoted in David A. Cook, *A History of Narrative Film*, 2nd edn (New York, NY: W. W. Norton & Co., 1990), 13.

4 Cook, *A History of Narrative Film*, 13.

5 Quoted in James Monaco, *How to Read a Film: The art, technology, language, history, and theory of film and media*, rev. edn (Oxford: Oxford University Press, 1981), 20.

Science fiction as a distinct film genre

Science fiction didn't become a popular film genre until after the Second World War, with plots usually taking one of three forms:

1 trips *to* outer space;
2 invasions *from* outer space;
3 monsters created by new technology.

Fed by fears over the atomic bomb, 'Science fiction films of the fifties', as James Monaco summarizes, 'were fascinating psychoanalytic documents: paranoid fantasies of moving blobs, invading pods, reified ids, and metamorphoses.'[6] The genre was so popular in the USA that, according to David A. Cook, 'virtually every film-releasing organization in the country, from the largest studio to the sleaziest distributor, was involved'.[7] Usually low budget, often made in less than a week, the movies had telling titles: *The Creature with the Atom Brain* (1953), *The Magnetic Monster* (1953), *The Attack of the Crab Monsters* (1956), *I Married a Monster from Outer Space* (1958).[8]

One science-fiction movie from the post-war era actually retells the story of Frankenstein, who, having been disfigured by the Nazis, purchases an atomic reactor to energize a creature made in his image. However, unlike Mary Shelley's *Frankenstein*, in which the humanoid creation takes revenge on the scientist, the 1958 movie establishes that the atomic reactor is the real threat, destroying both creature and creator with a blast of radioactive steam. Starring the famous Boris Karloff and futuristically titled *Frankenstein 1970*, the 1958 film was itself constructed in eight days.

The science-fiction genre was revolutionized a decade later with the release of *2001: A Space Odyssey* (1968), which, unlike

6 Monaco, *How to Read a Film*, 255.

7 Cook, *A History of Narrative Film*, 522.

8 Cook, *A History of Narrative Film*, 522–3.

Frankenstein 1970, took more than three years to make. Stanley Kubrick, the director, employed not only technologically sophisticated special effects but also cinematic techniques associated with European art cinema. For the film's opening sequence, he created 'one of the boldest graphic matches in narrative cinema' by depicting an ape discovering the hammer-like utility of a bone, which it triumphantly throws into the air.[9] After capturing the horizontal bone framed by the sky, the shot then cuts to the image of a spaceship filling the exact same location on the screen: a graphic match of shape and size that suggests the evolution of humans from primitive-tool users to high-tech space explorers.

Later in the film, we see the next stage of evolution: tools now using humans. HAL, a spaceship computer, overrides its human programming to take control away from the astronauts to protect its own system. Rather than a mere conveyor of godlike technology, the *machina* has itself become *deus*. Indeed, the film ends with theological implications, showing an astronaut, having been overthrown by AI, now floating through space in the form of a foetus, soon to be born again: a rebirth propelled by the evolution of technology itself.

Robots out of control

The evolution of technology informs another kind of science-fiction plot: movies about robots. The silent *Metropolis* (Fritz Lang, 1927) shows beleaguered workers operating machines underground to sustain wealthy industrialists above. In order to catch rebels, the city's leader forces an inventor to give a robot the face of a well-known working-class woman. Passing for flesh and blood, the robot incites rebellion and the destruction of the machines, which floods

9 David Bordwell, Kristin Thompson and Jeff Smith, *Film Art: An introduction*, 11th edn (New York, NY: McGraw-Hill Education, 2017), 252. For the film's parallels with European art cinema, see Kristin Thompson and David Bordwell, *Film History: An introduction*, 3rd edn (New York, NY: McGraw-Hill, 2010), 478.

the underground city. The distraught workers burn the 'woman' at the stake, which exposes that she is merely a machine.

Most likely influenced by *R.U.R.: Rossum's Universal Robots*, the 1920 Czech play that introduced the word 'robot' to the world, *Metropolis* anticipates AI films to follow. The droid C3PO, introduced in the first Star Wars film (*Star Wars: A New Hope*, George Lucas, 1977), looks remarkably similar to the *Metropolis* robot before the inventor endows it with female features. C3PO's comical fastidiousness, however, reflects the influence of a different genre on *Star Wars: A New Hope*: the old-fashioned western, with clear-cut distinctions between good guys and bad guys. Spaceship pilot Han Solo (played by Harrison Ford) even dresses like a cowboy, gun holster and all, clearly distinguishing him from another science-fiction role he later played: Rick Deckard in *Blade Runner* (Ridley Scott, 1982). Influenced by 1940s film noir, which destabilizes distinctions between good and evil, *Blade Runner* is filled with moral ambiguity, especially concerning AI 'replicants'. Created as service personnel, replicants are hard to distinguish from humans, their AI so sophisticated that the newest model doesn't even realize she is a machine. Deckard, hired to destroy replicants that defy their programming, falls in love with the humanoid robot.

Like *Metropolis*, *Blade Runner* was a box office failure that is now considered a classic. Both force viewers to grapple with what it means to be human, as well as to think about the control of machines, in both senses of 'control'. What happens when humans lose control of the robots they create? Will robots someday control human behaviour, like 'gods out of the machine'? These questions inform *Ex Machina* (Alex Garland, 2014), to which we now turn.

Manipulating *Ex Machina*

'One day the AIs are going to look back on us the same way we look at fossil skeletons on the plains of Africa. An upright ape living in dust with crude language and tools, all set for extinction.' Slyly alluding to the opening sequence of Kubrick's *2001: A Space Odyssey*, the makers of *Ex Machina* put these words in the mouth of Nathan Bateman (Oscar Isaac), a creator of sophisticated androids. As though alluding to the Dionysian origins of Greek theatre and the *deus ex machina* tradition, the film shows Bateman going on alcoholic binges and using lifelike female robots to gratify his sexual appetites. In the apt words of Christina Bieber Lake, Bateman has become 'a womanizing male god like Zeus'.[10] Indeed, as one *Ex Machina* character puts it, AI reflects 'the history of the gods', with Nathan later confirming, 'I'm not a man; I'm a god.' One might describe his sense of divine creativity as *machina ex deo*: robot machines 'from' the god.

We see Bateman through the eyes of Caleb Smith (Domhnall Gleeson), a computer programmer selected to complete a Turing test on Bateman's most recent AI product, Ava (Alicia Vikander). In the process, Caleb is forced to consider how much a robot reflects the mind of its maker, symbolized in the film by numerous reflections off glass. The opening shot displays bodies reflected on glass office partitions as they walk left to right. It soon cuts to a close-up on one worker's face, signalling that this is our protagonist. Staring at his glass computer screen, Caleb almost seems to look into our eyes – as though we are on the other side of his screen, just as he is on the other side of our movie screen. Subliminally, we become aware of two sides of a partition: the inside versus the outside of a machine.

Soon, sparkling lights from the computer screen reflect off Caleb's face, making him look like a robot with an electrical short. Later, Caleb is indeed aligned with Bateman's robot Ava, whose multiple reflections in her glass cell sometimes include images of Caleb watching her, destabilizing distinctions between inside and outside, between human and AI. The ambiguity is enhanced by Ava's glass body parts, which reveal computerized mechanisms

10 Christina Bieber Lake, 'Children of a lesser (but incredibly tech-savvy) god', *The Cresset*, vol. 78, no. 5 (June 2015), 34.

underneath a persona far more endearing than that of the alcoholic and abusive Bateman. The title *Ex Machina*, then, suggests not only intelligent behaviour coming 'from' or 'out of' a lifelike machine but also the possibility of that machine stepping away 'from' its deterministic programming, 'out of' the mechanistic control of its godlike creator. To capture this double meaning, the filmmakers add another visual motif, one with biblical precedents.

Let my robot go

When Moses demands of Pharaoh, 'Let my people go!', and then leads the enslaved people out of Egypt, the word 'hand' is repeated more than forty times (Exodus 6—18). In most cases, Moses raises his hand, either as he calls for another plague on Egypt or to help the Israelites conquer enemies in the wilderness. It therefore seems appropriate that *Ex Machina* employs a hand motif as Ava seeks to escape enslavement.

Caleb first notices the power of Ava's hand after the Turing test. Pressing its hand against the glass wall of its prison, Ava causes the lights of the whole facility to shut down. Soon thereafter we see Caleb pressing his hand against glass on a door, echoing what we see several robots doing in the film. Which hand is in control? The issue of control is symbolized in a scene when Caleb sits facing Nathan, who lies in a drunken stupor on a couch. The camera films from behind the couch towards Caleb, so that all we can see are Nathan's hands waving above the back of the couch, with Caleb's upper body appearing immediately beyond them. At one point, Nathan's fingers wiggle directly in front of Caleb's stationary form, as though to indicate the latter is merely a puppet manipulated by the former.

Caleb's worry about Nathan's control intensifies when he sees a comely housekeeper pull sheets of artificial skin from her body. It is a revelation similar to the one in *Metropolis*, when workers discover a beautiful woman is nothing more than a robot. Frightened that he has lost the ability to distinguish real humans from androids, Caleb cuts open his arm to make sure that his skin does not hide artificial programming as well. Bright lights sparkle off his face, reminiscent of the computer reflections in the film's opening scene. After shedding his own blood, Caleb punches his hand against a mirror, spreading his blood on the glass, as though in despair over his inability to distinguish flesh and blood from the AI machines that so effectively reflect human thoughts, actions and emotions.

Because Ava is much more charming than Nathan, Caleb decides he must save the robot from Nathan's manipulations. Quite deliberately, the filmmakers caused Caleb to fly to Nathan's retreat in a helicopter that lowers him down to earth, as if he were a saviour lowered 'from the machine' in Greek drama. In his role as *ex machina* rescuer, he takes action after seeing Ava press both hands against the glass walls of her cell while mouthing, 'Help me.' The 'it' has become a 'she' for him. When Nathan encounters the freed robot, he raises his hand against her but, this time, Ava's hand succeeds in killing her creator. Ironically, she leaves Caleb locked in a room, his hands ineffectually banging on glass. Reflecting her creator, Ava has manipulated others to achieve self-serving ends. (The word 'manipulation', of course, like 'manage' and 'manoeuvre', comes from a Latin root that means 'hand'.) Ava proceeds to board the helicopter waiting to transport Caleb back to the city, symbolizing her appropriation of the *deus ex machina* role.

Ex Machina ends as it begins, with reflections on glass of human bodies walking left to right. But this time, overlaid on top of the reflections is the stationary image of Ava, now in female clothing and a wig, blending in with walkers on a city street. As in *Blade Runner*, we are forced to ask whether advances in AI will someday allow robots to exercise control over human behaviour. Will androids become the next instantiation of godlike behaviour that comes from a machine, of *deus ex machina*? The very title of the film forces us to ask that question.

Godlike behaviour: from *deus ex machina* to *imago Dei*

The apostle Paul knew about the theatrical convention Horace called *deus ex machina*. A citizen of the Hellenized university town of Tarsus (Acts 21.39), Paul was familiar with the work of Euripides, a Greek playwright so famous for his *deus ex machina* endings that Aristophanes parodied them in one of his plays. Paul actually quotes from a play by Euripides while recounting his experience on the road to Damascus to King Agrippa in Caesarea (Acts 26.14).[11]

Paul's goal, of course, was to communicate that he followed a God who differed from the Greek gods: an incarnate God who offered salvation to humanity not 'from' thrilling theatrical machines but from the sacrifice of his flesh. On the stage of the world, as Paul explained to the Philippians, God Incarnate 'made himself nothing, taking the very nature of a servant, being made in human likeness' (Phil. 2.7, NIV84). Unlike actors pretending to be gods as they are lowered down to the stage in classical Greece, and unlike androids made in human likeness in our own era, Christ Jesus 'became obedient to death – even death on a cross' (Phil. 2.8, NIV84): an incarnate God who rose from the dead three days later.

Familiar with Paul's epistles as well as classical drama, Dorothy L. Sayers argued that each bloody event of Greek tragedy is 'mere domestic incident' compared with the founding event of Christianity, when 'a number of quite commonplace human beings, in an obscure province of the Roman Empire, killed and murdered God Almighty'.[12] Proclaiming that 'the greatest drama ever staged

11 The italicized phrase in the following verse is from Euripides' *The Bacchae*: 'Saul, Saul, why persecutest thou me? it is hard for thee *to kick against the pricks*' (Acts 26.14, AV).

12 Dorothy L. Sayers, 'Introduction', *The Man Born to Be King: A play-cycle on the life of our Lord and Saviour Jesus Christ* (Grand Rapids, Mich.: Eerdmans, 1943), 5.

is the official creed of Christendom',[13] Sayers emphasizes, rather than *deus ex machina*, a different Latin term, *imago Dei*, taken from the opening chapter of Genesis in the Vulgate Bible: 'So God created humankind in his image, in the image of God [*imago Dei*] he created them; male and female he created them' (Gen. 1.27, NRSV).

Many androids, of course, are created in the image of their makers. Sayers herself acknowledged a parallel between the making of robots and the *imago Dei*. Mentioning *Rossum's Universal Robots* in a 1930 detective novel,[14] Sayers argues in *The Mind of the Maker* that 'stories which tell of attempts to manufacture robots and Frankenstein monsters bear witness' to what she calls a 'strange desire': the 'desire to create something that shall have as much free will as the offspring of procreation'.[15] This, of course, does not match the robot-maker's desires in *Ex Machina*, perhaps because Nathan Bateman is like an ancient Greek god: primarily interested in servicing his own needs and appetites.

The *imago Dei* celebrated by Sayers, in contrast, is about creativity itself, humans fulfilling the *imago Dei* whenever they are genuinely creative rather than merely self-serving. After all, the God described in the first chapter of Genesis is not lawgiver, judge or redeemer. The God presented at the start of the Bible is a Creator: a Maker who regarded each act of creation 'good' in and of itself, creating humans to reflect that image of creativity. For Sayers, then, the human 'mind of the maker' is one that creates something new – whether book, movie or robot – allowing it to stand on its own rather than to service the maker's selfish interest in money, fame or status.

Even more outrageously, Sayers establishes that the *imago Dei* fulfilled by human creativity is actually Triune – like the God

---

13 Dorothy L. Sayers, 'The greatest drama ever staged is the official creed of Christendom', *Creed or Chaos?* (Bedford, NH: Sophia Institute, 1974), 3–9.

14 Dorothy L. Sayers with Robert Eustace, *The Documents in the Case* (New York, NY: Harper & Row, 1987), 204.

15 Sayers, *The Mind of the Maker*, 64.

of Christianity. Paralleling Father, Son and Holy Ghost, human creativity comprises three inseparable components: Idea, Energy and Power. Since Sayers herself used the making of robots for an analogy, her theory could be summarized as follows: Idea is the robot as originally conceptualized by a maker; Energy is putting the robot together, according to the original Idea – incarnating it, as it were; and Power is manifest in the way the robot affects others, including the creator herself as she may change the design in the process of making the robot. Originally exploring her idea about Creative Idea, Creative Energy and Creative Power in a play called *The Zeal of Thy House*, Sayers has one of her characters explain: 'These three are one, each equally in itself the whole work, whereof none can exist without other; and this is the image of the Trinity.'[16] Like God's work of creation outlined in Genesis, human creativity occurs over a span of time, with Idea, Energy and Power co-substantial in the act of creation, fulfilling the *imago Dei*.

Although many theologians have praised Sayers' watershed understanding of the *imago Dei*, others have found it disturbing. If creativity is inherently good, how do we respond to creations by despicable people such as Nathan Bateman? *Ex Machina*, however, provides its own answer. Rather than celebrating the inherent goodness of creation, Nathan creates robots to serve his own interests – much as when filmmakers make science-fiction movies not out of love for creation, but to reap financial rewards, sometimes extorting sexual favours in the process (as the Me Too movement has so chillingly exposed). Significantly, Sayers makes a distinction between genuine creativity and self-serving merchandising while praising C. S. Lewis's science-fiction novels: 'Lewis has a remarkable gift for inventing imaginary worlds which are both beautiful and plausible – very unlike the dreary mechanisms of

16 Dorothy L. Sayers, *The Zeal of Thy House*, in *Four Sacred Plays* (London: Gollancz, 1948), 103.

the space-fiction merchants.'[17] This explains why she also valued the fiction of Lewis's friend J. R. R. Tolkien, who created plausible 'imaginary worlds' as well. Tolkien, in fact, called his work 'sub-creation',[18] a concept that closely parallels Sayers' sense of the *imago Dei*, wherein makers desire their hobbits or robots to have as much free will in their created world as the offspring of procreation have in our own.

Sayers would consider it no coincidence that two science-fiction movies about robots, *Metropolis* and *Blade Runner*, although now considered works of film art, were box office failures. They didn't pander to contemporary tastes to make money. Significantly, film scholars call one form of such pandering *deus ex machina*: ending a movie with implausible happiness, all tension either resolved or surmounted to please paying audiences.

Ending with *deus ex machina*

In *Ars Poetica*, Horace mentions *deus ex machina* as a warning, cautioning writers against artificially contrived endings, like those of Euripides. Influencing English literary criticism since the translation of *Ars Poetica* in 1566, Horace's phrase is so well known that movies themselves sometimes reference it. One famous science-fiction film, the third in the Wachowskis' famous Matrix franchise, actually contains a machine named Deus Ex Machina.

The first film in the series, *The Matrix* (1999), introduces a virtual reality system named the Matrix that makes humans oblivious to the fact that their perceptions are controlled by machines that have taken over the world. Hence, rather than robots rebelling against their makers, like the imprisoned Ava in *Ex Machina*, *The*

17 Sayers to Barbara Reynolds, 21 December 1955, in Barbara Reynolds (ed.), *The Letters of Dorothy L. Sayers*, vol. 4 (Cambridge: Dorothy L. Sayers Society, 2000), 264.

18 J. R. R. Tolkien, 'On fairy-stories', in C. S. Lewis (ed.), *Essays Presented to Charles Williams* (Grand Rapids, Mich.: Eerdmans, 1966), 67.

Matrix shows imprisoned humans rebelling against the machines that control their understanding of reality. In the third film, *Matrix Revolutions* (2003), the protagonist Neo (Keanu Reeves) recruits a leader of the machines, called Deus Ex Machina, to help human rebels defeat a mutual enemy. At the end of the movie, as though alluding to a play by Euripides, Neo is carried away to safety by a machine: *deus ex machina*!

Neo's love interest, a human rebel named Trinity, is not saved with him. She, of course, is a very different Trinity from that celebrated by Dorothy L. Sayers in *The Zeal of Thy House* and *The Mind of the Maker*. One could argue, in fact, that the Matrix movies earned millions of dollars and many awards because *deus ex machina* meant more to the filmmakers than the *imago Dei*. Overflowing with numerous allusions to multiple religious mythologies, the franchise panders to people who love to extract spiritual meanings, picking and choosing references that best support their preferred religious assumptions. *Matrix Revolutions* pandered, as well, to the marketplace, opening 'simultaneously on 8,000 screens in the USA and 10,000 screens in 107 other countries', all openings 'synchronized to start at the same minute across all time zones'. The authors of *Film Art* describe it as a 'stroke of showmanship' rather than as an example of artistic integrity.[19]

That does not mean that financially successful works are inevitably inferior. The machines of the Matrix franchise, including Deus Ex Machina, are fascinating to contemplate. It means, instead, that Sayers would rather we regard our film watching as part of a Trinitarian *imago Dei*: we as viewers contribute to the Power of cinema by recognizing and celebrating its creativity rather than wallowing in crowd-pleasing screen marvels or extracting unwarranted evangelistic messages from science-fiction movies. Sayers

19 Bordwell, Thompson and Smith, *Film Art*, 38.

actually addresses the impetus behind science fiction in an essay she wrote while composing *The Mind of the Maker*:

> The delusion of the mechanical perfectibility of man through a combination of scientific knowledge and unconscious evolution has been responsible for much heartbreak. It is, at bottom, far more pessimistic than Christian pessimism [about evil], because, if science and progress break down, there is nothing to fall back upon.[20]

Rather than endorsing *deus ex machina*, whether that of Greek drama or of contrived movie endings, or through high-tech robots dramatized on screen, Sayers proclaimed:

> It is the dogma that is the drama – not beautiful phrases, nor comfortable sentiments, nor vague aspirations to loving-kindness and uplift, nor the promise of something nice after death – but the terrifying assertion that the same God who made the world lived in the world and passed through the grave and gate of death [only to rise again].[21]

Whereas Trinity is fatally wounded in *Matrix Revolutions*, the Trinity of Christian faith is very much alive, honoured, even if unconsciously, every time we celebrate the creative mind of a filmmaker.

20 Sayers, 'Creed or chaos?', *Creed or Chaos?*, 46.

21 Sayers, 'The dogma is the drama', *Creed or Chaos?*, 25.

3
Behind artificial intelligence

STEPHEN N. WILLIAMS

'The story of artificial intelligence', said Hubert Dreyfus, 'might well begin around 450 BC', with Plato.[1] In the middle of the 1960s, Dreyfus, a teacher of philosophy at the Massachusetts Institute of Technology (MIT) who subsequently went on to become Professor of Philosophy at the University of California, Berkeley, was landed or landed himself in the middle of a professional and personal storm on account of his critique of what was happening in the world of artificial intelligence. Although AI has moved on considerably since he was writing, it remains rewarding to study his critique. However, its rights and wrongs then and now do not concern us here. Our interest lies in the deep historical context in which he located the basis and problem of AI. Dreyfus held that, for all their philosophical differences, Plato and Aristotle both elevated human rational processes to a misplaced kind of primacy in the constitution of human beings. Accordingly, they established a philosophical trajectory that enabled some of the thinkers involved one way or another in the scientific revolution of the seventeenth century to emphasize thought as calculation. This is a vital notion for AI. Machines, such as those later devised in the course of developing AI, 'might have remained overgrown adding machines, had not Plato's vision, refined by two thousand years of metaphysics, found in them its fulfilment'.[2] Plato's missteps included

---

1 *What Computers Still Can't Do: A critique of artificial reason* (Cambridge, Mass.: MIT Press, 1992), 67. This was a fresh edition of *What Computers Can't Do*, first and second editions of which were published in 1972 and 1979 respectively.

2 Dreyfus, *What Computers Still Can't Do*, 72.

1 separating the intellect from the body, believing that the body gets in the way of intelligence and reason;
2 viewing human knowledge as something that can be stated in explicit definitions and is subject to rules;
3 seeking to overlay all human life, including action and not just thought, with a rational structure, represented in theory.

As long as a supposition 'that the world must be represented as a structured set of descriptions' informs AI, it is aligned with what Plato sought: 'A world in which the possibility of clarity, certainty and control is guaranteed; a world of data structures, decision theory, and automation.'[3]

We do not need to make an informed judgement on Dreyfus's historical reading of the philosophical background of AI to agree that we need, at least, to examine the influence of a tradition of philosophical investigation, which stretches back to long before the birth of Christ, if we are to appreciate the intellectual roots of AI. Identifying a philosophical tradition, in order to grasp the intellectual roots of AI, is only one way of doing it; approaching the story of AI as a story of the human imagination takes us even further back than Plato.[4]

From a strictly technological point of view, of course, AI was born in the twentieth century; the designation came into currency in the 1950s, by courtesy of the mathematician John McCarthy. McCarthy was the co-founder of a conference or workshop held in 1956 at Dartmouth College, New Hampshire, USA, which is commonly credited with having brought the notion of AI on to the world stage. The conference was avowedly set up to explore

---

3 Dreyfus, *What Computers Still Can't Do*, 211.

4 For example, see Pamela McCorduck, *Machines Who Think: A personal inquiry into the history and prospects of artificial intelligence*, 1st edn (San Francisco, Calif.: W. H. Freeman & Co., 1979).

> the conjecture that every aspect of learning or any other feature of intelligence can in principle be so precisely described that a machine can be made to simulate it. An attempt will be made to find how to make machines use language, form abstractions and concepts, solve the kinds of problems now reserved for humans, and improve themselves.[5]

Among those who wrote the proposal was Marvin Minsky, the technical consultant for Stanley Kubrick's *2001: A Space Odyssey*, also by formation a mathematician, who would later take up a position at MIT, and is renowned as a pioneer in the field of AI. Minsky described AI as 'the science of making machines do things that would require intelligence if done by men'.[6]

Whatever 'intelligence' does in fact involve in the human (or, for that matter, the non-human) being, and whatever the merits or demerits of using the language of 'AI' in various contexts, distinctions are commonly drawn with regard to it, although not always drawn in the same way. For example, we encounter talk of 'weak', 'narrow' and 'strong' AI or the more specific vocabulary of artificial general intelligence (AGI) as opposed to artificial superintelligence (ASI), the former corresponding to, the latter significantly exceeding, human cognitive capacities.[7] 'AI' may refer to a range of things from a sub-discipline of computer science to humanoid robots. But what lies behind talk of 'AI' or machine intelligence? Is it the notion that humans are machines? And is such a notion born of philosophical ideas that go as far back as Dreyfus takes us?

---

5 J. McCarthy, M. L. Minsky, N. Rochester and C. E. Shannon, 'A proposal for the Dartmouth Summer Research Project on Artificial Intelligence, August 31, 1955', *AI Magazine*, vol. 27, no. 4 (2006), 12.

6 Quoted in Daniel Crevier, *AI: The tumultuous history of the search for artificial intelligence* (New York, NY: Basic Books, 1993), 9.

7 Comparison with Peter Robinson's reference to AGI (p. 4) indicates how the terminology may be used in different ways. See the Index of subjects for other references to AGI and ASI.

The English computer scientist Alan Turing has often earned the appellation 'the father of AI', not because he had great direct influence on the participants at the Dartmouth conference but because he posed questions on the back of his work in the field of computer science, including explicitly the question of machine intelligence, which he was addressing years before the conference. In his most famous, but not first, paper to broach this question, Turing asked whether machines could think, discussed objections to the idea and found none of them compelling.[8]

What exactly is it or would it be for a machine to think? Assuming, for a moment, a working knowledge of what a machine is, we are pushed back to the question: what is thinking? If Turing has been called the father of AI, the English philosopher Thomas Hobbes (1588–1679) has been called its grandfather. It is too much of a stretch for us to visit Plato and Aristotle in a short chapter, but we must go back to Hobbes. In his *Elements of Philosophy* (1656), he said, 'By RATIOCINATION, I mean *computation*,' thus, as one author puts it, 'prophetically launching AI'.[9] Although Hobbes is best known as a political philosopher, his view of reason is rightly judged to be 'one of his best claims to historical distinction' by a biographer who describes his great work of political philosophy, *Leviathan*, as a 'Bible for Modern Man' because it captures the spirit of modern thought comprehensively.[10] In its 'Introduction', Hobbes observes that 'life is but a motion of limbs . . . For what is the *heart*, but a *spring*; and the *nerves*, but so many *strings*; and the *joints*,

8 'Computing machinery and intelligence', published in 1950; see B. Jack Copeland (ed.), *The Essential Turing: Seminal writings in computing, logic, philosophy, artificial intelligence, and artificial life plus the secrets of Enigma* (Oxford: Clarendon Press, 2004), 441–63. This essay includes brief and very superficial observations on theology (449–50). Other essays by or discussions featuring Turing that bear on artificial intelligence are gathered together in this volume (353–506).

9 John Haugeland, *Artificial Intelligence: The very idea* (Cambridge, Mass.: MIT Press, 1989), 23. Hobbes could define 'ratiocination' in other ways, too.

10 A. P. Martinich, *Hobbes: A biography* (Cambridge: Cambridge University Press, 1999), 124 and 225.

but so many wheels, giving motion to the whole body . . . ?'[11] And what is thought but motion in the brain? Hobbes was a materialist: nothing exists that is not embodied, hence thoughts are embodied. Talk of thoughts as motions in the brain is literal, and the rational computation that goes on in the brain is also quite literally computation – addition and subtraction. (For Hobbes, multiplication and division are forms of addition and subtraction.) 'When a man *reasoneth*, he does nothing else but conceive a sum total from *addition* of parcels, or conceive a remainder from *subtraction* of one sum from another.'[12] AI may be seen as a branch of cognitive science – broadly speaking, the science of mind – and the notion of reason as calculation was there at its modern origins.

Hobbes heads up our story not only because he exercised a major direct and explicit influence on AI researchers but also because his philosophy shows the influence of early modern science in a way also displayed in the work of a younger contemporary, whose influence on the range of disciplines that constitutes the modern science of mind was second to none. I refer to René Descartes (1596–1650), often (since we are in the business of assigning paternity and grandpaternity) called the 'father of modern philosophy' and sometimes 'the father of modern mathematics'. The early modern scientist who influenced both Hobbes and Descartes along the lines of interest to us is the great Galileo Galilei (1564–1642) himself. Just how Galileo's influence on Hobbes worked in detail is a matter of disagreement. What cannot be contested is Hobbes's admiration for Galileo, whom he regarded as 'the greatest philosopher of all time', 'philosopher' here meaning 'natural philosopher', roughly equivalent to 'scientist'.[13] In

11 *Leviathan, with selected variants from the Latin edition of 1688*, ed. Edwin M. Curley (Indianapolis, Ind.: Hackett, 1994), 3 (emphasis original). The language 'artificial' and 'automata' also appears at this juncture but we should not swiftly extrapolate from current usage to what Hobbes had in mind with his terminology.

12 Hobbes, *Leviathan*, 22; emphasis original.

13 A. P. Martinich and K. Hoekstra, *The Oxford Handbook of Hobbes* (Oxford: Oxford University Press, 2016), 107.

his dedicatory epistle to a part of the *Elements of Philosophy* (the part 'On the body'), he tells us that Galileo 'was the first that opened to us the gates of Natural Philosophy Universal, which is the knowledge of the Nature of Motion'. Although Hobbes adopted Galileo's science of motion and sought to apply it to the mind, the detail of the science itself need not concern us (and there is some disagreement on the precise conceptual connection between Galileo and Hobbes at this point). However, Hobbes had a wider indebtedness to Galileo, who inspired him with the conception of philosophy as 'written in this grand book, the universe, which . . . cannot be understood unless one first learns to comprehend the language and read the letters in which it is composed . . . the language of mathematics'.[14] Galilean science inspired Hobbes to apply Galileo's understanding of motion in mathematical terms to the world of thoughts.

Enter Descartes. While he approached issues of common interest differently from Galileo, he, like Hobbes, felt the impact of Galileo, and, like Hobbes, he fastened on to the mathematical theme, taking up Galileo's interest in a mathematical physics. Descartes is an important figure in the deep modern intellectual background of AI. On the face of it, his influence tugs in the opposite direction from AI and, more widely, from what broadly makes for the modern science of mind. Descartes is the most celebrated proponent of dualism in the history of Western philosophy: the belief that reality is composed of both material substance and a quite different, non-material, substance – mind. Thinking is the activity of mind. The body is a machine. A machine cannot think. But in depicting the body as a machine, Descartes took an important and controversial step forward. He had critics who believed that the logic of his position left his view of mind open to the objection that mental operations work in exactly the same way as bodily operations, because the mind, even if it is distinct from the body, is thoroughly embodied. Descartes was so

14 Martinich and Hoekstra, *The Oxford Handbook*, 110 n. 21.

successful in explaining the mechanism of the body in material terms that he opened a door through which he himself never walked, the door to regarding the mind in material terms, in terms of a machine.

In 1747, Julien Offray de La Mettrie (1709–51) wrote a volume titled *L'homme machine*, later to be celebrated as the first clear statement of what the title announced.[15] A slender and rather shallow work, it was just one of a number of contributions of French Enlightenment thinkers who subsequently took a similar line and developed a purely materialist understanding of human beings. Within this materialist outlook, they talked of humans in terms of machines. The roots of the atheistic materialism that they paraded in their work were anchored in the scientific and intellectual developments of the seventeenth century. Although de La Mettrie dissented from Descartes's dualism, he lauded Descartes's account of the body's functioning as a machine. He was not alone among French materialist philosophers in drawing on Descartes's researches and reflections on the physiology of both the animal and the human body to reach, in contrast to Descartes, a materialist conclusion about the nature of the mind. *Treatise on Man* by Descartes was a major source here. In the *Treatise*, Descartes supposed 'the body to be nothing but a statue or machine made of earth' and made by God, unlike the marvellous artificial machines – 'clocks, artificial fountains, mills and other such machines' that are man-made.[16] 'Machine', in Descartes's time, referred to a wider range of constructions than it does today (and Descartes was fascinated by cutting-edge contraptions), but that does not affect our reading of what he says about body and mind.

Commentators disagree on how Descartes uses the terminology that we translate into English as 'mind' and 'soul'; the two words are often used interchangeably but sometimes there appears to be

15 *Man a Machine*, tr. Gertrude C. Bussey (Chicago, Ill.: Open Court, 1912).

16 *Treatise on Man*, in *The Philosophical Writings of Descartes*, vol. 1, tr. John Cottingham, Robert Stoothoff and Dugald Murdoch (Cambridge: Cambridge University Press, 1985), 99. See also, in the same volume, the fifth part of Descartes's more famous *Discourse on Method*.

a distinction. Descartes's denial that animals had souls, and his affirmation that their bodies, like the human body, were susceptible to purely mechanical explanation, was massively significant. He substituted a corporeal and mechanical explanation of animal life for what most people of that time thought of as functions of some kind of soul in the animal – not the rational soul that is the human mind, but certainly an animated principle of non-mechanical life, present in animal appetites, inclinations and feelings.

Descartes's detachment of soul or mind from body caused contemporaries to challenge his understanding of humans long before de La Mettrie came on the scene. Descartes, they said, had completely failed to show how the human mind was exempt from the laws governing the human body. 'How do you demonstrate that a body is incapable of thinking? . . . [H]ow do you know that you are not a corporeal motion, or a body which is in motion?' asked the weighty Marin Mersenne.[17] By the time Descartes had explained both animal life and how human passions work in the human body, it seemed to many discussants completely gratuitous to posit an immaterial mind or soul: what was there left to explain that could not be explained in purely material terms? As another heavyweight philosophical peer, Pierre Gassendi, put it to Descartes:

> To prove that your [that is, human] nature is different (that is, incorporeal, as you maintain), you ought to produce some operation which is of quite a different kind from those which brutes perform . . . and this you do not do.[18]

We could explore the conceptual link between Descartes and AI in more specific and narrower, but still very significant, terms in relation

17 *The Philosophical Writings of Descartes*, vol. 2, tr. John Cottingham, Robert Stoothoff and Dugald Murdoch (Cambridge: Cambridge University Press, 1984), 88. (We cannot be quite certain that Mersenne penned these particular lines.)

18 *Philosophical Writings*, vol. 2, 188.

to language, meaning and mathematics, particularly by attending to his innovations in seventeenth-century algebra and the beginning of what has been called 'algebraic thought'. However, for the purposes of picking up the mathematical and logical side of our story, we move on to the contribution of a thinker of quite extraordinary intellectual power and range, the 'universal genius' Gottfried Wilhelm Leibniz (1646–1716). Descartes approached science by trying to search out abstract mathematical relations in order to understand the natural world, but it was Leibniz who extended the mathematical approach to logic. In 1948, Norbert Wiener, Professor of Mathematics at MIT, introduced readers to the field of cybernetics, which is distinct from AI but features in its background story.[19] He observed that if he 'were to choose a patron saint for cybernetics out of the history of science', he 'should have to choose Leibniz'.[20] He is not the only Wiener to have something to say about Leibniz. Introducing a selection of Leibniz's writings, Philip Wiener observed that it was only in the past generation that scientists have applied a symbolic logic – to which Leibniz made a great contribution – 'to relay-switch circuits, punch-card systems, and calculating machines', applying it apparently unaware 'that the immortal spirit of Leibniz is gazing with rewarding delight on their embodiment of his visions'.[21]

What visions were those? Visions of outstanding breadth. Against the background of recent bloody strife in Europe, the Thirty Years War (1618–48), which appeared to make a mockery of Christian religion as a force for peace and unity, Leibniz – himself a sincere Christian believer – pursued the dream of a grand unification of

19 The title of his volume explains the field: *Cybernetics or Control and Communication in the Animal and the Machine* (Cambridge, Mass.: Technology Press, 1948).

20 Norbert Wiener, *Cybernetics*, 20. Wiener also described Leibniz as 'the intellectual ancestor' of the ideas that he set out in *The Human Use of Human Beings: Cybernetics and society* (Boston, Mass.: Houghton Mifflin, 1950; repr. 1989), 19, although he also indicated material divergence from Leibniz. Wiener has been described as 'America's second Leibniz'.

21 Gottfried Wilhelm Leibniz, *Selections*, ed. Philip P. Wiener (New York, NY: Scribner, 1951), xxxiii.

knowledge. In its pursuit, he 'was the first who formulated the role of mathematics in the following way. Mathematics offers an instrument to automatize the intellectual work of humans.'[22] Leibniz wanted to produce a calculus of reason that could represent concepts in a universal script which took a logical form, the logical form consisting of numerical characters. Very early in his life, Leibniz sought a method for analysing concepts that was universal and mathematical. He did so in a study that owed some of its inspiration to the medieval thinker Ramon Llull (1232–1316), a figure of independent interest to historians curious about the roots of computer science in symbolic logic. Leibniz persisted beyond his early years in his aspiration to produce a symbolic logic ordered in mathematical (embracing geometric and algebraic) terms.

Although there are different interpretations of the detail of what Leibniz was up to, it was a comprehensive ambition in relation to human thought. As the earlier reference to concepts indicates, Leibniz's interest in reasoning, logic and mathematics was integrated into an interest in language, and it all bears fruit in an attempt to make philosophical thinking, as much as possible, mechanical. This was as far as can be from being a matter of mere indulgence in abstract thought. Leibniz would have welcomed, in principle, the ambition of any third-millennial thinkers aspiring to create AI, whose calculative capacities are put at the service of solving vital social and global problems. John McCarthy showed himself to be an heir to the Leibnizian dream when he said: 'The only reason we have not yet succeeded in formalizing every aspect of the real world is that we have been lacking a sufficiently powerful logical calculus. I am currently working on that problem.'[23]

---

22 Juraj Hromkovič, 'Alan Turing and the foundation of computer science', in Giovanni Sommaruga and Thomas Strahm (eds), *Turing's Revolution: The impact of his ideas about computability* (Cham: Springer International, 2015), 274.

23 Quoted in Joseph Weizenbaum, *Computer Power and Human Reason: From judgment to calculation* (Harmondsworth: Pelican, 1984), 201. This volume was first published in 1976 but a new preface was subsequently added to it.

What was promised in Leibniz moved towards fulfilment in George Boole (1815–64), Professor of Mathematics at Queen's College, Cork. Leibniz's quest for a formal logic, the syntax of which corresponded to the laws of thought, was significantly furthered in a work that Boole wrote in 1854, bearing the significant title *An Investigation of the Laws of Thought on Which Are Founded the Mathematical Theories of Logic and Probabilities.* Mathematics had always incorporated logic, as you have to demonstrate logically how you have reached mathematical conclusions. What Boole did was to scrutinize the logic itself and try to understand it mathematically. He sought to describe logical processes algebraically. This not only launched mathematical logic; it was also the basis for the design of computers. Humming along at high speed, computers needed a mathematical language for logical operations. Boole provided its rudiments. His book *The Mathematical Analysis of Logic* (1847) expounded logic as a branch of mathematics. As Desmond McHale points out:

> By enlarging the horizons of mathematics so enormously, Boole . . . highlighted a topic that has come to influence virtually every aspect of present-day life – the storage and processing of information, which in turn has led to the development of computer science.[24]

Boole thought that if we could understand logic, we could understand thought, and if we could understand thought, we were understanding how the human mind works.

Bertrand Russell once observed that Boole's *Laws of Thought* was 'the work in which pure mathematics was discovered', although he later said that he had not meant it literally.[25] Applied to technology, the mathematics provided the basis from which computer science

24 Desmond McHale, *George Boole: His life and work* (Dublin: Boole Press, 1985), 71.

25 McHale, *George Boole*, 130.

eventually developed. If we were to follow our story through the nineteenth century to the twentieth, we would encounter a rich and influential array of thinkers (including Russell himself) and ideas – who and which are standard in textbooks on philosophy, including the philosophy of mathematics and logic – that would bring us right up to the era of AI. Of course, schematizing mathematical logic does not entail viewing humans as thinking machines. However, if we have reason to view the mind as operating according to laws that may be logically formalized, then the prospect of the thinking machine appears on the horizon and awaits technological development to close in on the prospect, although the prospect is certainly not inevitable if we distinguish logical calculation from thought.[26] We must underline what was said previously: AI has moved on considerably since its earliest days, but the story behind AI – or the segment of the story told here – is worth telling. The idea of thinking machines is central both to AI's history and to its continuing development.

We began by referring to a philosopher, Hubert Dreyfus, who took us to the distant past, to Plato on rationality. We end by referring to a computer scientist contemporary of Dreyfus, with whom he interacted, Joseph Weizenbaum, whose volume on *Computer Power and Human Reason* repays reading, as does Dreyfus's work, irrespective of the years that have rolled on since in the development of AI.[27] We have focused our attention on the background to AI by asking about machines that think and answering by introducing the question of humans as machines. Dreyfus, however, indicated a background to our background, and Weizenbaum also believed that we need to grasp the broader question of the nature of reason to understand the phenomenon of AI well. Not long after the earliest edition of Dreyfus's work, Weizenbaum, then the Professor of Computing Science at MIT, took up, like Dreyfus, the question of reason and specifically picked out

26 I am indebted to Dr David Glass of the School of Computing at the University of Ulster for relevant comments on this point.

27 See note 23.

'instrumental' reason, while asking, 'What is it about the computer that has brought the view of man as a machine to a new level of plausibility?'[28] This is reason deployed in the service of a specific end but not rooted in the deep reason that should be possessed by human beings and thus 'not authentic human rationality'.[29] Weizenbaum expressed early a worry about the way the 'computing machine represents an extreme usurpation of man's capacity to act as an autonomous agent in giving meaning to his world'.[30] The basic question underlying what is happening in computer technology was 'whether or not every aspect of human thought is reducible to a logical formalism, or, to put it into the modern idiom, whether or not human thought is entirely computable'.[31] The consequence of equating rationality with logicality and with computability is that the moral question of human obligation and responsibility is occluded because we have lost touch with rational depths.

The subtitle of Weizenbaum's work, *From judgment to calculation*, recalls Hobbes's 'reason as calculation'. Weizenbaum praised the insight of another thinker, Max Horkheimer, a member of the celebrated Frankfurt School of social theory, who also took a long view in *Eclipse of Reason*. Presciently, shortly after the end of the Second World War and before the public computer revolution, Horkheimer lamented the instrumental use of reason so that 'thinking itself [has] been reduced to the level of industrial production', and that the intellectual roots of such great concepts as justice and equality have been buried and lost, with no objectivity to which reason can attach them.[32] Reason, said Horkheimer, 'is declared incapable of determining the ultimate aims of life and must content

28 Despite mutual agreements and sympathies, both Weizenbaum and Dreyfus acknowledged differences in their respective approaches.

29 Weizenbaum, *Computer Power*, 253.

30 Weizenbaum, *Computer Power*, 9.

31 Weizenbaum, *Computer Power*, 12.

32 Weizenbaum, *Computer Power*, 249–52.

itself with reducing everything it encounters to a mere tool'.[33] Even if informed readers of their work will part company with them, Dreyfus, Weizenbaum and Horkheimer did well to train the spotlight on reason in the early days of, or before the inception of, AI. We shall surely not arrive at an informed judgement on the philosophy of AI without probing some of its deep background.

A Christian, theological reading of that background is not only possible in principle but important in practice. Christian faith, as we readily discover on reading the Christian Scriptures, is centred on an interpretation of history. If I have not offered a theological reading here, it is because we have to know something of that history first. In taking the trajectory that I have, the suggestion is not that we understand AI best by concentrating exclusively on the intellectual forces that enabled or aided its arrival. Economic and cultural forces are equally important as social forces, as are intellectual ones. But 'AI' is a technology that takes its name from an intellectual idea – that of the possibility of an artificial or machine intelligence. Economic forces put us in the practical position of having to ask the question about the possibility of thinking machines; cultural forces will often explain why we are disposed to answer that question in one way rather than another. But the question invited by AI about the nature of personhood and mind is, for Christians, obviously a theological question. It is a question that is most effectively addressed when we understand something of the intellectual forces that have helped to carve out the modern world in which AI is, by now, so conspicuously and ubiquitously embedded.

33 I am quoting directly here from Max Horkheimer, *Eclipse of Reason* (New York, NY: Oxford University Press, 1947), 92. Like Dreyfus, Horkheimer comments on Plato, connecting him with what he calls the 'philosophical technocracy' of nineteenth-century thinkers who were called 'positivists', who thought 'that the way to save humanity [was] to subject it to the rules and methods of scientific reasoning' (59–60).

4

Being human in a world of intelligent machines

JOHN WYATT

What does it mean to be human? The age-old quest for an objective and authoritative perspective on our own human identity seems to have a new urgency in the twenty-first century. And there is little doubt that this urgency is stimulated in part by growing popular awareness of the power and potential of artificial intelligence. This chapter aims to review a range of recent trends in popular and academic thinking about humanity that seem to have been accentuated by the ubiquity of AI.

What is the human? A question that could previously have been dismissed as abstract, speculative and irrelevant to the realities of everyday life has emerged into popular culture. Paperbacks such as *Sapiens: A brief history of humankind* and *Homo Deus: A brief history of tomorrow* from the popular historian Yuval Noah Harari have taken on cult status, selling tens of millions of copies worldwide. In 2016, more than 200 million people watched the Go contest between the AI program AlphaGo and Lee Sedol, the human world champion of Go, with the event framed as an ultimate test as to whether 'AI has become more intelligent than human beings'.[1]

---

1 See, for example, Alan Boyle, 'AlphaGo vs. Lee Sedol: odds are shifting in $1 million man-vs.-machine Go match' (GeekWire, 14 February 2016), <www.geekwire.com/2016/alphago-lee-sedol-whos-underdog-in-google-ai-million-go-match>, accessed 8 March 2021.

The centrality of intelligence

Max Tegmark, an influential physicist who is President of the Future of Life Institute, claims that

> [t]he conventional wisdom among AI researchers is that intelligence is ultimately about information and computation, not about flesh, blood or carbon atoms. This means that there's no fundamental reason why machines can't one day be at least as intelligent as us.[2]

He argues elsewhere:

> Everything we love about civilization is a product of intelligence, so amplifying our human intelligence with artificial intelligence has the potential of helping civilization flourish like never before – as long as we manage to keep the technology beneficial.[3]

And Stephen Hawking echoed the same idea:

> Intelligence is central to what it means to be human. Everything that our civilization has achieved is a product of human intelligence, from learning to master fire, to learning to grow food, to understanding the cosmos. I believe there is no deep difference between what can be achieved by a biological brain and what can be achieved by a computer. It therefore follows that

---

2 Max Tegmark, *Life 3.0: Being human in an age of artificial intelligence* (London: Penguin, 2017), ch. 2, Kindle 926.

3 Max Tegmark, 'Benefits and risks of artificial intelligence' (Future of Life Institute, n.d.), <https://futureoflife.org/background/benefits-risks-of-artificial-intelligence>, accessed 10 February 2021.

> computers can, in theory, emulate human intelligence – and exceed it.[4]

There's a simple logic here – everything humans have achieved is a product of intelligence. This can also now be reproduced in information-processing machines that are continually increasing in power and complexity. Therefore, machines will ultimately be capable of reproducing everything that humans have achieved, and more. Demis Hassabis, the human prodigy behind the Google company DeepMind, is on record as stating that his goal is to 'solve intelligence and then use that to solve everything else'![5]

Of course, the word 'intelligence' is in reality far more slippery and ambiguous than it seems at first glance. A moment's reflection shows that to define everything that human civilization has achieved as a product of 'intelligence' is highly misleading. What is the common factor in a musical symphony, a great cathedral, the wordless emotional intelligence in a human relationship, a mathematical theorem, the activities of a stock-market trader, a profound novel about human loss, the text of the Bible, a scientific research paper, a cave drawing or the work of a mime artist? The word 'intelligence' seems to expand to become synonymous with all the glorious variety and eccentricity of human achievements over the centuries.

The only 'intelligence' we have any deep understanding of is that of human beings. The very concept of machine intelligence is immediately problematic, similar to common ideas of machines 'perceiving', 'knowing', 'understanding' and 'choosing'. It seems obvious that the apparent intelligence of machines cannot be

---

4 From a speech given at the launch of the Leverhulme Centre for the Future of Intelligence, 19 October 2016; see University of Cambridge, '"The best or worst thing to happen to humanity" – Stephen Hawking launches Centre for the Future of Intelligence' (19 October 2016), <www.cam.ac.uk/research/news/the-best-or-worst-thing-to-happen-to-humanity-stephen-hawking-launches-centre-for-the-future-of>, accessed 10 February 2021.

5 Tom Simonite, 'How Google plans to solve artificial intelligence', *MIT Technology Review*, 31 March 2016.

the same as human intelligence, the form of intelligence that we recognize as characteristic of an embodied, biological organism. Our understanding of and interaction with the world are inextricably intertwined with our embodied mammalian nature, and the web of social relationships we find ourselves in, as much as our abstract cognitive abilities. It seems axiomatic that machine 'intelligence' can never completely replicate human intelligence, although machines can undoubtedly perform some tasks at a level that far exceeds our human capacity.

Are human beings machines?

A fascinating collection of articles published in 2015 and entitled *What to Think about Machines that Think*[6] provides a spectrum of perspectives from contemporary luminaries. The physicist Sean Carroll expounds the classic materialist perspective:

> When asked for my thoughts about machines that think, I can't help but reply: 'Hey, those are my friends you're talking about.' We are all machines that think, and the distinction between different types of machines is eroding.[7]

In the same collection, the psychologist Steven Pinker points to the attraction of computational metaphors for moderns who are wedded to materialism:

> Thomas Hobbes's pithy equation of reasoning as 'nothing but reckoning' is one of the great ideas in human history . . . The cognitive feats of the brain can be explained in physical

6 John Brockman (ed.), *What to Think about Machines that Think: Today's leading thinkers on the age of machine intelligence* (New York, NY: Harper Perennial, 2015).

7 Sean Carroll, 'We are all machines that think', in Brockman (ed.), *What to Think*, Kindle 1256.

> terms: To put it crudely (and critics notwithstanding), we can say that beliefs are a kind of information, thinking a kind of computation, and motivation a kind of feedback and control. This is a great idea because it completes a naturalistic understanding of the universe, exorcising occult souls, spirits, and ghosts in the machine. Just as Darwin made it possible for a thoughtful observer of the natural world to do without creationism, Turing and others made it possible for a thoughtful observer of the cognitive world to do without spiritualism.[8]

For Pinker, this represents an exhilarating liberation from metaphysics. We don't need to worry that there might be something non-material or spiritual hidden behind the mystery of our humanity – for example, in the strange miracle of human consciousness or in our universal sense of moral responsibility. We can now accept that every aspect of our humanity is explicable by scientific materialism.

Metaphors and reality

Of course, there is a certain truth behind the dogmatic statement that we are 'machines that think'. There are indeed aspects of our human functioning that are similar to those of mechanical devices which humans have designed and created. In other words, the machine is a useful metaphor for certain aspects of our humanity. Machine metaphors have been extremely fruitful in academic disciplines such as human physiology, molecular biology, cognitive neuropsychology, computational neuroscience and so on. But there is a critical difference between a fruitful metaphor and an ontological definition, a description of core reality. It may be helpful to say that, in some aspects, a human being is like a computer, but to say that a human being is a computer is incoherent.

8 Steven Pinker, 'Thinking does not imply subjugating', in Brockman (ed.), *What to Think*, Kindle 630.

Metaphors have profound and pervasive effects on cultures, and the 'information-processing machine' seems to have become a distorting lens through which many of us understand our own humanity. We are 'hard-wired', 'suffering from information overload' or 'programmed for failure'. The dualism of software and hardware seems to provide an obvious and fertile conceptual framework for understanding ourselves. The hardware (often dismissively referred to as 'wetware') is the physical material that our brains are composed of. The software is the 'information' expressed in the hardware – thoughts, memories, perceptions and emotions.

And within this dualistic paradigm, it seems that it is software that carries ultimate significance. Hardware is something that is disposable, recyclable, modifiable, but the disembodied software is the most precious aspect of all existence – pure information. In the previous chapter, reference was made to the suggestion that Platonic thought has found new resonances in the age of AI. What really matters is the non-material: information, beauty, meaning, significance and consciousness.

One expression of this is the growing enthusiasm for preserving people's digital identity beyond the grave. As an example, when Roman Mazurenko was killed in a road accident, his close friend, the tech entrepreneur Eugenia Kuyda, built an artificially intelligent chatbot to replicate Roman's personality, based on text messages and emails that had passed between them. 'I found myself sharing things with the bot that I wouldn't necessarily [have told] Roman when he was alive,' said Eugenia. This experience led to the creation of the AI chatbot Replika, which offers 'a safe space for you to talk about yourself every day'. As Eugenia put it, 'Those unconditional friendships and those relationships when we are being honest and being real . . . are so rare, and becoming rarer . . . so in some way the AI is helping you to open up and be more honest.'[9]

9 Eugenia Kuyda, interviewed by Eddie Mair in an episode titled 'I talk to my dead friend', *The Eddie Mair Show*, BBC Radio 4, broadcast 16 February 2018.

Anthropomorphism and simulated relationships

In the 1960s, the distinguished computer pioneer Joseph Weizenbaum, who was based at the MIT Artificial Intelligence Laboratory, built a simple text-based program, ELIZA,[10] which was designed to replicate the stereotyped responses of a non-directional psychotherapist. The program became popular with many of his co-workers; Weizenbaum's own secretary reportedly asked him to leave the room so that she and ELIZA could have a confidential conversation. Weizenbaum was both surprised and disturbed by ELIZA's hold over people, later writing in his influential 1976 volume *Computer Power and Human Reason*:

> I had not realized . . . that extremely short exposures to a relatively simple computer program could induce powerful delusional thinking in quite normal people . . . This reaction to ELIZA showed me more vividly than anything I had seen hitherto the enormously exaggerated attributions an even well-educated audience is capable of making, even strives to make, to a technology it does not understand.[11]

What became known among computer scientists as 'the ELIZA effect' lies behind the extraordinary success of AI chatbots and devices such as Amazon's Alexa, Google Home and Apple's Siri. The tech companies are engaged in an intense competition for their conversational devices to be present in every home, every workplace and every vehicle. In 2018, Amazon reported that there were hundreds of thousands of developers and device makers building

10 Weizenbaum named the program ELIZA after Eliza Doolittle, a character in George Bernard Shaw's play *Pygmalion*.

11 Joseph Weizenbaum, *Computer Power and Human Reason: From judgment to calculation* (New York, NY: W. H. Freeman & Co., 1976), 7.

Alexa 'experiences', contributing to more than 70,000 'skills' (individual topics that Alexa is able to converse about), and there are more than 28,000 different versions of Alexa-connected smart devices now available.[12] It seems likely that interactions with apparently human-like and 'emotionally intelligent' bots will become increasingly commonplace within the next ten years.

In a later chapter, I will discuss the implications of anthropomorphic technology for health and social care. But we cannot avoid wider questions about the impact of machine-simulated relationships on our self-understanding. Can they perhaps play a helpful role for those grieving the loss of a loved one, or those merely wishing to have an honest and self-disclosing conversation with a simulated reflection of themselves? Or could synthetic relationships with AIs somehow interfere with the messy process of real human-to-human interactions, and with our understanding of what it means to be a person?

There is no doubt that the commercial use of powerful anthropomorphic technology opens us up to new forms of commercial manipulation and even psychological abuse. As the journalist David Polgar put it:

> Human compassion can be gamed. It is the ultimate psychological hack; a glitch in human response that can be exploited in an attempt to make a sticky product. That's why designers give AIs human characteristics in the first place: they want us to like them.[13]

---

12 Paul Cutsinger, 'Alexa gets smarter every day, thanks to you: 2018 Alexa developer year in review', *Alexa Blogs* (19 December 2018), <https://developer.amazon.com/blogs/alexa/post/38bb01ef-ac9b-49ec-9e2c-fcb0b51a8b31/2018-highlights-for-alexa-skill-builders>, accessed 10 February 2021.

13 David Ryan Polgar, 'Is it unethical to design robots to resemble humans?', *Quartz* (22 June 2017), <https://qz.com/1010828/is-it-unethical-to-design-robots-to-resemble-humans>, accessed 10 February 2021.

Machines as moral agents

The topic of 'AI ethics' or 'machine ethics' has become a major preoccupation for many academics and technical specialists. But the focus of this growing industry is entirely anthropocentric. The question is how to programme intelligent machines so that they act in the best interests of human beings. Asimov's fictional three laws of robotics became the simplistic forerunner of complex mathematical algorithms intended to ensure that autonomous machines behave in 'ethical' ways – in accordance with human interests and human 'values'.

But a number of recent thinkers are challenging this preoccupation. In the words of Matthew Calarco:

> the genuine critical target of progressive thought and politics today should be *anthropocentrism* as such, for it is always one version or another of *the human* that falsely occupies the space of the universal and that functions to exclude what is considered nonhuman (which, of course, includes the immense majority of human beings themselves, along with all else deemed to be nonhuman) from ethical and political consideration.[14]

In other words it is argued that our human way of being should not be regarded as the supreme touchstone by which all other beings are assessed.

The pioneering roboticist Rodney Brooks recognized the problem, which he discussed in a book written in 2002:

> We will use (robots) as slaves just as we use our dishwashers, vacuum cleaners, and automobiles today. But those that we make

14 Matthew Calarco, *Zoographies: The question of the animal from Heidegger to Derrida* (New York, NY: Columbia University Press, 2008), 10; quoted in David J. Gunkel, *The Machine Question: Critical perspectives on AI, robots, and ethics* (Cambridge, Mass.: MIT Press, 2012), 48; emphasis original.

> more intelligent, that we give emotions to, and that we empathize with, will be a problem. We had better be careful just what we build, because we might end up liking them, and then we will be morally responsible for their well-being. Sort of like children.[15]

Kate Darling, a researcher at the MIT Media Lab, performed studies in which groups of volunteers were given small robotic dinosaurs to interact and play with. The volunteers were then asked to tie up, strike and 'kill' their robots, even though the bots 'whimpered' while being broken. Darling reported that many of the participants refused to 'hurt' the robots, and expressed a sense of discomfort when the robots whimpered while they were being smashed.[16]

Darling uses this kind of evidence to argue that it may be necessary to extend some level of rights or legal protections to robots in general and to social robots in particular. Even if social robots cannot formally be regarded as moral subjects, Darling argues that we perceive robots differently from other objects. 'Violent behaviour toward robotic objects *feels* wrong to many of us, even if we know that the "abused" object does not experience anything.'[17]

Philosopher David Gunkel raises similar questions in his books *The Machine Question* and *Robot Rights*.[18] Instead of an 'essentialist' understanding of personhood, in which certain claims about the intrinsic nature of a being must be met before it can be considered a person, he argues that we should move towards a socially constructed understanding of personhood. A person is what we all agree is a person.

---

15 Rodney A. Brooks, *Flesh and Machines: How robots will change us* (New York, NY: Random House, 2002), 195.

16 Kate Darling, 'Extending legal protection to social robots: the effects of anthropomorphism, empathy, and violent behavior towards robotic objects', in Ryan Calo, A. Michael Froomkin and Ian Kerr (eds), *Robot Law* (Cheltenham: Edward Elgar, 2016), 213–31.

17 Darling, 'Extending legal protection to social robots', 223; emphasis added.

18 Gunkel, *The Machine Question*, see note 14; *Robot Rights* (Cambridge, Mass.: MIT Press, 2018).

'What we should be arguing about', R. G. A. Dolby writes in an article entitled 'The possibility of computers becoming persons',

> is not the possibility of machine souls or machine minds, but whether robots could ever join human society. The requirement that must be met by a robot is that people are prepared to treat it as a person. If they are, they will also be prepared to attribute to it whatever inner qualities they believe a person must have.[19]

In other words, it is argued that personhood should not be decided on the basis of the possession of some hidden metaphysical properties. Rather, it is something that is socially constructed, negotiated and conferred.

Consciousness and moral 'patiency'

Is consciousness necessary before we should accept that a machine has moral 'patiency' (the ability to suffer that is viewed as morally relevant)? And, if so, how can we ever know whether a machine is genuinely conscious or not? David Levy argues that

> if a machine exhibits behaviour of a type normally regarded as a product of human consciousness (whatever consciousness might be), then we should accept that that machine has consciousness. The relevant question therefore becomes, not 'Can robots have consciousness?', but 'How can we detect consciousness in robots?'[20]

But this raises further complex questions, as Wallach and Allen point out:

---

19 R. G. A. Dolby, 'The possibility of computers becoming persons', *Social Epistemology*, vol. 3, no. 4 (1989), 321–36.

20 David Levy, 'The ethical treatment of artificially conscious robots', *International Journal of Social Robotics*, vol. 1, no. 3 (2009), 209–16.

> If bots might one day be capable of experiencing pain and other affective states, a question that arises is whether it will be moral to build such systems – not because of how they might harm humans, but because of the pain these artificial systems will themselves experience. In other words, can the building of a bot with a somatic architecture capable of feeling intense pain be morally justified?[21]

But how will we ever know whether a machine is genuinely capable of suffering or whether it has consciousness? Martine Rothblatt envisages that committees of experts in relevant disciplines, such as computer science, psychology and neuroscience, will be created to interrogate software programs that are behaving in ways which might be considered conscious. A consensual decision would be taken on whether they should be regarded as moral agents.

Rothblatt continues:

> Of course an expert judgment of consciousness is not the same thing as a fully objective determination of consciousness. After all, juries can and have gotten it wrong; they have deemed defendants as lacking in criminal intent whereas, in fact, they most certainly had such malevolent intent . . . However, when objective determinations are impossible, society readily accepts the wisdom of alternative appraisals of peers or experts, and accepts as inevitable that errors in judgment will sometimes occur.[22]

Gunkel concludes:

---

21 Wendell Wallach and Colin Allen, *Moral Machines: Teaching robots right from wrong* (Oxford: Oxford University Press, 2009), 209.

22 Martine Rothblatt, *Virtually Human: The promise – and the peril – of digital immortality* (New York, NY: St Martin's Press, 2014), 57.

> Should machines like AIs, robots, and other autonomous systems be granted admission to the community of moral subjects, becoming what would be recognized as legitimate moral agents, patients, or both? This question cannot be answered definitively and finally with a simple 'yes' or 'no.' The question will need to be asked and responded to repeatedly in specific circumstances. But the question needs to be asked and explicitly addressed rather than being passed over in silence as if it did not matter.[23]

Our human future

Some futurists, such as the distinguished astronomer Martin Rees, see the advent of AI as presaging the extinction of our species. Rees writes:

> There are chemical and metabolic limits to the size and processing power of organic ('wet') brains. Maybe we're close to these limits already. But no such limits constrain silicon-based computers (still less, perhaps, quantum computers): For those, the potential for further development could be as dramatic as the evolution from monocellular organisms to humans. So, by any definition of *thinking*, the amount done by organic, human-type brains (and its intensity) will be swamped by the cerebrations of AI . . . Abstract thinking by biological brains has underpinned the emergence of all culture and science. But this activity – spanning tens of millennia at most – will be a brief precursor to the more powerful intellects of the inorganic, post-human era.[24]

23 Gunkel, *The Machine Question*, 272.

24 Martin Rees, 'Organic intelligence has no long-term future', in Brockman (ed.), *What to Think*, Kindle 706.

In his bestselling book *Life 3.0: Being human in the age of artificial intelligence*, Max Tegmark defines all earthly life as 'self-replicating information-processing systems':

> Life 1.0 is simple and biological: it is *unable to redesign either its hardware or its software during its lifetime.*
>
> Life 2.0 is human and biological: it can *redesign much of its software (through culture), but not its hardware.*
>
> Life 3.0, which doesn't yet exist on earth, although it is nearly here, is non-human and post-biological or technological: it can *dramatically redesign not only its software but its hardware as well.*[25]

The grand narrative that is now being promoted by many techno-optimists is a significant development from the older and very familiar Darwinian story of the progressive emergence of human life from the primeval swamp. Instead of humanity as the ultimate goal and purpose of the entire evolutionary process, we must recognize that we are merely a temporary (although essential) staging post on the way to the true goal of the cosmos, which is the emergence of 'post-biological life'. Our true children will be our 'mind children', the intelligent machines that will soon outstrip their primitive creators and spread across the cosmos.

A recurring theme is the promise of breaking out from the constraints and limitations of human biology, which seems increasingly unsuited to the modern technological age. Human biology restricts us in every direction, especially when we consider the prospect of spreading beyond Planet Earth into the cosmos. But the intelligent machine is able to break out into an unlimited future. There appear to be no physical limits to the potential power of

25 Tegmark, *Life 3.0*, ch. 1, Kindle 457; emphasis added.

information-processing machines, and technological hardware can be replicated and modified indefinitely. At long last, we will have broken free from the confines of our own human nature.

The science writer Pamela McCorduck expresses the recurrent trope of humankind come of age and fulfilling its destiny through AI:

> For all the imaginary deities we've petitioned throughout history who have failed to protect us – from nature, from one another, from ourselves – we're finally ready to call on our own enhanced, augmented minds instead. It's a sign of social maturity that we take responsibility for ourselves. We are as gods, Stewart Brand famously said, and we may as well get good at it.[26]

However, the breezy techno-optimist narrative that emerges particularly from the West Coast of the USA is often haunted by dystopian fears. Here is Tegmark again:

> It appears that we humans are a historical accident and aren't the optimal solution to any well-designed physics problem. This suggests that a superintelligent AI with a rigorously defined goal will be able to approve its goal attainment by eliminating us.[27]

In a striking postscript to his book *Life 3.0*, Tegmark describes the emotional impact of visiting an exhibition about robotics at the London Science Museum.

> I very rarely cry but that's what I did on the way out – and in a tunnel full of pedestrians, no less, en route to the South Kensington tube station. Here were all these people going about their lives blissfully unaware of what I was thinking. First, we

26 Pamela McCorduck, 'An epochal human event', in Brockman (ed.), *What to Think*, Kindle 1193.

27 Tegmark, *Life 3.0*, ch. 7, Kindle 4590.

> humans discovered how to replicate some natural processes with machines . . . Gradually we started realising that our bodies were also machines. Then the discoveries of nerve cells started blurring the borderline between body and mind. Then we started building machines that could outperform not only our muscles, but our minds as well. So in parallel with discovering what we are, are we inevitably making ourselves obsolete? That would be poetically tragic. This thought scared me.[28]

Conclusion

In the history of Christian theology, it seems that it is often the advent of profound external challenges to orthodox beliefs that lead to further creative development and deepening of the understanding of the 'faith that was once for all delivered to the saints' (Jude 1.3). The first four centuries after Christ were characterized by a ferment of intellectual challenges to orthodoxy, leading to profound and lasting advances in theological understanding. Might it be possible that the twenty-first century provides a comparable range of profound challenges to orthodox understandings of human embodiment, personhood, relationships, morality and future hope? The ubiquity and effectiveness of various forms of machine intelligence have created a distorting lens through which our humanity is being perceived in new ways. The dangers seem obvious: the denaturing and deconstruction of the most precious realities of our human lives – compassion, empathy, friendship, moral responsibility and consciousness. But perhaps this time in history represents a unique opportunity for creative thought and engagement as a Christian community, to deepen and enrich our understanding of what it means to be human, of the extraordinary possibilities of the tools we are creating and of the strange new world in which we find ourselves.

28 Tegmark, *Life 3.0*, ch. 8, Kindle 5272.

5

AI and robots: some Asian approaches

VINOTH RAMACHANDRA

Technological artefacts capable of autonomous decision-making and action are increasingly interwoven into the social fabric of advanced industrial societies. The scope of their application continues to expand with human-to-machine, and even machine-to-machine, interactions supplementing or replacing entirely human-to-human interactions. We ask Amazon's Alexa or Apple's Siri, rather than family or friends, for recommendations on music or restaurants; we request help from chatbots and we play with robotic toys.

Many ancient societies, Eastern and Western, have been fascinated by self-propelling devices representing natural plants and animals. In the third century BCE, engineers in Hellenistic Alexandria, Egypt, were building mechanical robots. Accounts of similar machines in China date from around the same period, when a mechanical orchestra was made for the emperor.[1]

In her book, *Gods and Robots*,[2] Adrienne Mayor recalls how, in their legends and mythologies, Ancient Greek, Roman, Indian and Chinese societies envisaged artificial life, automata and human enhancements. Chinese chronicles tell of emperors fooled by realistic androids and describe artificial servants crafted in the second

1 See 'Automaton', *Britannica*, <www.britannica.com/technology/automaton#ref188963>, accessed 11 February 2021.

2 Adrienne Mayor, *Gods and Robots: Myths, machines, and ancient dreams of technology* (Princeton, NJ: Princeton University Press, 2018).

century CE by the female inventor Huang Yueying. In one Indian legend, presumably reflecting ancient trade links between India and the Hellenistic world, the Buddha's precious remains were defended by robot warriors, copied from Greco-Roman designs for real automata. In India, automatons or mechanical beings that could move on their own were called *bhuta vahana yanta*, 'spirit movement machines' in Pali and Sanskrit. According to the story, it was foretold that the robots guarding the Buddha's relics would remain on duty until a future king distributed those relics throughout his realm.

In recent years, Korean filmmakers have gone beyond this with the story *Chunsangui Pijomul* (*The Heavenly Creature*), one of three episodes in the 2012 science-fiction anthology Inryu Myeongmang Bogoseo (usually known in English as Doomsday Book). Far from robots being regarded as friendly human servants, these stories question the usefulness and highlight the danger of technology, and the possibility of automata in a high-tech age taking over humankind. In *The Heavenly Creature*, In-myung is a robot that lives in a Buddhist monastery, becomes a Buddhist, and somehow achieves independence from the humans who created it and escapes their control. The robot eventually attains enlightenment/nirvana. The robot-Buddha generates various reactions among humans: the Buddhist community venerates the enlightened robot; the corporation that invented it, however, decides to exterminate it out of fear, because the robot-creation no longer responds to the commands of its human creators, and it has achieved something (Buddhist enlightenment) that they have not.[3]

Japan has long been at the cutting-edge of the robotics industry and, today, robots (including social/humanoid robots) are in wider

3 See Falkonface, 'Our perception of technology in "The Heavenly Creature" (2012)', (Classicfilmclassics, 8 November 2014), <https://classicfilmclassics.wordpress.com/2014/11/08/our-perception-of-technology-in-the-heavenly-creature-2012-spoilers/comment-page-1>, accessed 11 February 2021.

circulation there than in any other country. A declining birth rate, ageing society and shrinking economy are the reasons why, since 2007, the Japanese government and corporate sector have actively promoted the virtues of a 'robot culture'. Nationwide surveys suggest that Japanese citizens are more comfortable sharing living and working environments with robots than with foreign caretakers and migrant workers. Not only are robots obviating the need for guest workers but they are also being designed to preserve 'unique' Japanese customs and traditional styles in the performing arts. While widely popular, this does have its local critics. Yuji Sone, for instance, has called a Japanese national tendency to robotize the country 'techno-determinist economic rationalism', which aggressively promotes robot culture but does not indicate 'why integration of robots in the society would bring significant social benefits'.[4]

These initiatives are paralleled by a growing support among some robotics engineers and politicians to confer citizenship on robots. Jennifer Robertson has pointed out that the Japanese state has a problematic record regarding human rights, especially towards ethnic minorities and non-Japanese residents who have lived and worked in Japan for many generations. The possibility of robots acquiring civil status ahead of flesh-and-blood humans therefore raises profound questions about the nature of citizenship and human rights. She adds:

> Already the idea of robots having evolved beyond consideration as 'property' and acquiring legal status as sentient beings with 'rights' is shaping developments in artificial intelligence and robotics outside of Japan, including in the United States.[5]

---

4 Yuji Sone, *Japanese Robot Culture: Performance, imagination, and modernity* (New York, NY: Palgrave Macmillan, 2017), 21.

5 Jennifer Robertson, 'Human rights vs robot rights: forecasts from Japan', *Critical Asian Studies*, vol. 46, no. 4 (2014), 572. For racism and xenophobia in Japan, see Rupert Wingfield-Hayes, 'The beauty contest winner making Japan look at itself' (BBC News, 4 June 2015), <www.bbc.com/news/world-asia-32957610>, accessed 11 February 2021.

At the same time, despite their relatively short history, artificial intelligence research and robotics in China are advancing at a staggering pace. Technology companies such as Alibaba, Baidu and Tencent were born in the protected Chinese market, but are now innovating rapidly. Baidu is the largest search engine in China and the fourth most visited website in the world. Tencent owns the social platform WeChat, China's equivalent of Facebook.

In June 2017, one month after AlphaGo's victory against China's Ke Jie, the Chinese government announced an ambitious plan to become the world's leading superpower in AI. The State Council of China issued the 'New Generation Artificial Intelligence Development Plan', expressing China's aim not only for global economic and military dominance but also to use AI 'to elevate the capability and level of social governance, playing an irreplaceable role in effectively maintaining social stability'.[6] By 2030, China could have more than 40 per cent of all the world's science, technology, engineering and mathematics (STEM) graduates, compared with only 8 per cent in Europe and 4 per cent in the USA. In addition to training more people in STEM subjects, China has greatly expanded its spending on scientific and AI research. China now accounts for more than 20 per cent of total research and development expenditure globally, and Chinese researchers wrote more than a third of all AI research papers worldwide in 2017. In the world AI conference that same year, Chinese researchers submitted more papers than US and European scientists put together.[7]

From cartoon characters to robot-monks

Conversations on the social media platform Twitter often involve 'bots' or automated programs. Twitter asks that bots be clearly

6 Toby Walsh, *2062: The world that AI made* (Carlton, Aus.: La Trobe University Press, 2018), 244.

7 Walsh, *2062*, 247.

designated as such, a policy intended to prevent their being confused with actual people. Twitter in Japanese includes 'character bots' designed to behave like the characters from popular manga (comic books) and video games. The accounts indicate clearly that they are bots based on fictional characters and not actual humans.[8] On its personal profile page, the character bot is introduced as the fictional character. Thus, there is no question of their pretending to be human or manipulating human users. Using the interactivity of Twitter, fans of the comic-book or game character write lines to be spoken by the character. Produced by fans, character bots are popular among those who respond not only to the original material but also to the creativity of fellow fans.

Japanese robot culture develops out of the ubiquitous and intimate presence of cartoon characters in everyday life. The most popular television series, indeed a mainstay of Japanese family life since 1970, when Japan's new industrial era was transforming the nation, centres on a robot cat from the twenty-second century called Doraemon.[9] Films based on the character of Doraemon have become Japan's most lucrative franchise, spanning three generations. To date, the film series has earned around ¥187 billion ($1.7 billion). Doraemon is sent to help Nobita Nobi, a young boy, who gets poor marks in school and is frequently bullied by his classmates. Doraemon has a four-dimensional pouch in which he stores unexpected gadgets from the Future Department Store, such as Bamboo Copter, a small piece of headgear that allows its users to fly, Anywhere Door, a pink-coloured door that enables people who turn the knob to travel anywhere they imagine, and many more. But Doraemon is a flawed robot. His quick-fix

8 Keiko Nishimura, 'Semi-autonomous fan fiction: Japanese character bots and non-human affect', in Robert W. Gehl and Maria Bakardjieva (eds), *Socialbots and Their Friends: Digital media and the automation of sociality* (New York, NY: Routledge, 2017).

9 I am grateful to a Japanese friend, Yasayuki Kamata, for introducing me to Doraemon. See Russell Thomas, 'Back to the future: the world celebrates the 50th anniversary of Doraemon', *Japan Times* (1 February 2020), <www.japantimes.co.jp/culture/2020/02/01/general/doraemon-50th-anniversary>, accessed 11 February 2021.

tools from the future frequently backfire. They are convoluted and cause more problems than the original one they were supposed to resolve.

Although Doraemon is a successful modern brand, it's possible to relate the character to the cultural traditions of the country, particularly to the *yōkai* (spirits/demons) of Japanese folklore. There are also the Shinto *kami* (spirits/gods), complex characters who are not always benevolent. Like the gods of Greek mythology, they are prone to mistakes, and are intentionally bad and occasionally virtuous. Also, in the Shinto tradition, the distinction between the natural and the artificial is not considered significant, although it is recognized. It is why the integration of robots into Japanese society has been seen by the public as a positive thing and has not generated the fears that typify Western science-fiction accounts of robots seizing control of the earth.

At the same time, Frédéric Kaplan has argued that there is no dream of fusion with such machines. On the contrary, it always seems important to keep a distance. The cyborg is seldom seen as a welcome creature in Japanese fiction:

> Convergence between technology and biology seems to always be considered in negative terms. The young kid piloting the giant colossus symbolizes this well-defined frontier between the biological body and mechanical armour. In Japan, robots and humans may be living in harmony, but side-by-side. Post-human perspectives are rarely considered as having a positive future. More generally, it seems that technology can be 'tamed' without necessarily melding with it.[10]

Kaplan is drawing on the notion of 'technology taming', used to describe the way Japanese state and society, since the Meiji Restoration

10 Frédéric Kaplan, 'Who is afraid of the humanoid? Investigating cultural differences in the acceptance of robots', *International Journal of Humanoid Robotics*, vol. 1, no. 3 (2004), 3.

of the latter half of the nineteenth century, have sought to absorb, enhance and redirect foreign technologies to consolidate, rather than undermine, Japanese culture. He reminds us that the world of the Pokémon, another successful export of Japanese popular culture, is entirely based on this principle. In this imaginary universe, children must capture small creatures, each of which possesses a particular power. A captured Pokémon changes from a wild creature to a tamed ally; and, having studied the characteristics of the creatures they have tamed, children engage in fights using them as weapons.

Among Chinese Buddhists, comic books and animated cartoons have become a popular way of communicating the message of the Buddhist dharma to lay people. In the Longquan Monastery near Shenzhen, the abbot, Xuecheng, delivered his sermons to a nationwide audience through the comic character of the monk Xian'er.[11] Then, in October 2015, AI experts collaborated with the monastery to transform Xian'er into a robot-monk. Over the next three years, the robot-monk was steadily 'upgraded' with expanded communication skills. It can now not only answer others' queries but also question those same queries. It does not always obey when someone tells it to do something, but likes to express reservations and even raise objections. 'During my last visit, in early June 2019,' writes Stefania Travagnin, a student of Chinese religions,

> Xian'er refused to dance or walk in a circle for us; it asked us why it had to do that and none of our answers were, in its view, satisfactory. Xian'er robot's sense of touch is acute: it tells you quite frankly how annoying it is when you touch its ears, and if you do the same with its bottom, then it shouts that you should not grab a monk's bottom and runs away. On the other

11 For what follows, I am indebted to Stefania Travagnin, 'From online Buddha halls to robot-monks: new developments in the long-term interaction between Buddhism, media and technology', *Review of Religion and Chinese Society*, vol. 7, no. 1 (2020), 120–48.

> hand, the third-generation Xian'er is becoming more responsive and interactive than the iPhone's Siri.[12]

The social media platform WeChat lets users interact directly with Xian'er via a series of automated programs, asking questions about Buddhism but also sharing thoughts and concerns about everyday life. In interviews with clerics at the Longquan Monastery, Travagnin was told that robotics technology is just an expedient, falling within the well-known Buddhist category of 'skilful means' (Sanskrit: *upāya*); Xian'er was a skilfully engineered means to attract more people to the monastery and, thus, also to the dharma teachings. So far, the plan seems to have been quite successful, as visits to the monastery have increased, according to the Longquan community. Furthermore, a report made at Longquan states that, from April 2016 to January 2017, an average of 13 articles about Xian'er were published on social media every day; 770,000 users have responded to those articles online, showing how many are aware of the existence of the robot-monk.

Other prominent 'Buddhist robots' can be found in East Asia. In March 2019, a Buddhist temple, the Kōdai-ji in the ancient Japanese capital Kyoto, inaugurated Mindar, an android representing the bodhisattva of compassion. It recites and explains the *Heart Sutra* to those who come to the temple.[13] The typical human monk only memorizes and chants the sutra without engaging with its content. Like Xian'er, Mindar is the result of a collaboration between a Buddhist community and experts in robotics and AI in order to try to attract a younger generation of believers to Buddhism. However, unlike Xian'er, it is revered by the temple priests, who prostrate themselves in front of it, as they would before an icon of any other bodhisattva.

12 Travagnin, 'From online Buddha halls', 133.

13 Thisanka Siripala, 'An ancient Japanese shrine debuts a Buddhist robot', *The Diplomat* (5 March 2019), <https://thediplomat.com/2019/03/an-ancient-japanese-shrine-debuts-a-buddhist-robot>, accessed 11 February 2021.

Further, a semi-humanoid robot-priest, Pepper, invented by the SoftBank Group Corporation in 2014, has been officiating at funerals and other ceremonies in the Japanese Buddhist community since 2017.[14] However, among the general public, opinion about the use of robots in religion has not been unanimous, and the views of religious professionals are similarly divided. Religious leaders in China, in fact, have expressed consternation about the notion of adopting robotics to replace humans in liturgical contexts.[15]

Philosophical and ethical reflections

Philosophical reflection on robotics and machine intelligence is relatively limited in Asian academies. Since Buddhist metaphysics dismisses the discrete, enduring human self as an illusion and reduces consciousness to a succession of transient mental states, questions about robot selves and robot consciousness do not seem to trouble Buddhist ethicists. Most roboticists, whether Buddhist, Confucianist or atheist, seem to assume a functionalist or behaviourist approach to the human: if it looks like a duck and quacks like a duck, it *is* a duck.

In his bestselling book *The Buddha in the Robot*,[16] the pioneer Japanese roboticist Masahiro Mori, who can be described as a utopian transhumanist in the manner of Ray Kurzweil, says little about robots, except for throwaway lines such as 'everything has a buddha-nature' or 'the potential to attain buddhahood',[17]

14 Sigal Samuel, 'Robot priests can bless you, advise you, and even perform your funeral: AI religion is upon us. Welcome to the future', *Vox* (13 January 2020), <www.vox.com/future-perfect/2019/9/9/20851753/ai-religion-robot-priest-mindar-buddhism-christianity>, accessed 11 February 2021.

15 Travagnin, 'From online Buddha halls', 137.

16 Masahiro Mori, *The Buddha in the Robot: A robot engineer's thoughts about science and religion*, tr. Charles Terry (Tokyo: Kosei Publications, 1981).

17 Mori, *The Buddha in the Robot*, 13. The fullest statement is on p. 179: 'The truth is that everything in the universe is identical with the mind of the Buddha. That which controls and that which is controlled are both manifestations of the buddha-nature. We must not consider that we ourselves are operating machines. What is happening is that the buddha-nature is operating the buddha-nature.'

while expounding his Zen interpretation of Buddhism. In a brief but widely influential article in 1970, Mori had claimed that the more lifelike robots become, the more human beings feel empathy with them; a robot too similar to a human, however, provokes feelings of dislike, even revulsion. Mori called this sudden dip in human beings' comfort levels the 'Uncanny Valley'.[18] Mori advised his fellow roboticists to design humanoid robots that behave and perform as humans but which do not look and move exactly like us, so that the humanoid robots will be more socially acceptable. However, in *The Buddha in the Robot*, first published some four years later, Mori does not once mention the concept of the Uncanny Valley and never seemed to return to it.

Mori's openness towards the idea that humans and machines are all part of the 'non-duality' or even 'oneness of all things' is popular in a culture shaped by Zen Buddhist and Shinto practices. When translated into the political sphere, it has dire consequences: far from exalting *all* human persons, it downgrades some humans and elevates some machines. In an article referred to earlier on Japan's problematic human rights record, Jennifer Robertson has drawn attention to the way public popularity polls have been used to grant citizenship to some robots while denying the same to permanent residents who belong to ethnic minorities. 'Familial or communitarian civility', she writes, 'is widely perceived as the affective glue of Japanese society. And that is the rub, for familial civility can nurture – and has nurtured in recent history – an ethno-national endogamy.'[19] Important social ties, including those with robots, are understood using the hierarchical, patriarchal family as a metaphor and model. Since organic and manufactured entities form a continuous network of beings, robots (even non-humanoid ones, such as

18 See Masahiro Mori, 'The Uncanny Valley: the original essay by Masahiro Mori', *Spectrum* (IEEE, 12 June 2012), <https://spectrum.ieee.org/automaton/robotics/humanoids/the-uncanny-valley>, accessed 11 February 2021.

19 Robertson, 'Human rights vs robot rights', 583.

the robotic seal Paro[20]) are imagined to be members of the existing affective and corporate framework of the household.

The Guinness World Records organization officially recognized Paro in 2008 as the 'world's most therapeutic robot', in recognition of its ability to cheer patients in hospitals, senior couples, for whom owning flesh-and-blood pets is no longer possible, and residents of assisted living homes. Distributed over the robot seal's body are five kinds of sensors – touch, light, sound, temperature and movement – that enable it to convey 'emotions', such as surprise, happiness and anger, and, in the process, to produce squeaky cries that mimic the vocalizations of a real baby seal. Paro was the first robot to have a *koseki*, an official document available only to Japanese citizens, since it has a Japanese father (the inventor Shibata Takanori) and was 'born' in Japan.

> The *koseki* is the basis for citizenship and attendant civil rights; it is also praised by nationalists and censured by feminists and minorities as a key signifier of Japanese exceptionalism. Similarly, other animals, robots, dolls, and cartoon characters have been issued special residency permits for which foreigners and resident minority groups are not eligible.[21]

Human 'exceptionalism' is perhaps the key issue in the philosophical discussion of AI and robotics.[22] Those who deny human exceptionalism seem to veer towards narrowly nationalist exceptionalisms (typically Japanese and American) or towards denying the humanness of those with limited capacities (unborn children, severely disabled people, dementia patients and so on). Much of the

20 See Paro Therapeutic Robot, <www.parorobots.com>, accessed 13 February 2021; see also the discussion of Paro in Ch. 12 of this volume: John Wyatt, 'The impact of AI and robotics on health and social care', 186.

21 Robertson, 'Human rights vs robot rights', 593.

22 By 'exceptionalism', I mean the unique ontological and moral status of human beings, vis-à-vis machines (and also other animals).

research is driven by visions of corporate profits or military and technological superpower agendas destined to exacerbate further the social and economic inequalities that threaten any sense of human solidarity.

Paradoxically, functionalist approaches, such as Confucian ethical codes for AI[23] that build on Isaac Asimov's famous three laws of robotics, are unabashedly anthropocentric. They seek to manage the potential hazards of machine decision-making for the sake of ensuring the humane treatment of human beings. Furthermore, the social psychologist Sherry Turkle points out:

> Even before we make the robots, we remake ourselves as people ready to be their companions . . . almost universally, people project human attributes onto programs that present as humanlike, an effect that is magnified when they are with robots called 'sociable' machines – machines that do such things as track your motion, make eye contact, and remember your name. Then people feel in the presence of a knowing other that cares about them.[24]

What muddies thought is the way popular neuroscientific language about human brains and neural networks has bewitched us, wherever we happen to live. No brain has ever entertained a thought, and never will. If that is the case with brains, how much more with computer algorithms and silicon chips? Computers and robots are complicated electronic circuits; they have no more psychological reality to them than the Word program that I use

23 Pak-Hang Wong, 'Rituals and machines: a Confucian response to technology-driven moral deskilling', *Philosophies*, vol. 4, no. 4 (2019), 59.

24 Sherry Turkle, *Reclaiming Conversation: The power of talk in a digital age* (New York, NY: Penguin, 2015), 338, 341. John Wyatt also draws on *Reclaiming Conversation* in 'The impact of AI and robotics', 196. Turkle's work in other places is also discussed in Wyatt's chapter (186 and 191) and in Andrew Graystone, 'Sextech: simulated relationships with machines', also in this volume, 157–8 and 163.

to write has an electrical aspect to it, although it is implemented electronically. The physical state transitions in a piece of electronic machinery are only computations relative to some actual or possible consciousness that can interpret the processes computationally.

What is stored in books, computer hard drives or DNA molecules is only *potential* information, waiting to be read as information by a conscious observer. The philosopher Colin McGinn notes:

> Why do we say that telephone lines convey information? Not because they are *intrinsically* informational, but because conscious subjects are at either end of them, exchanging information in the ordinary sense. Without the conscious subjects and their informational states, wires and neurons would not warrant being described in informational terms.[25]

However, by using a common terminology (for example, 'information', 'intelligence', 'neural networks', 'emotions') when discussing minds, brains and computers, we humanize the machines even as we mechanize humans. And the brain can now be described as an incredibly powerful microprocessor, the mother of all motherboards. As Ludwig Wittgenstein famously put it, when looking back on the naive philosophy of science ('logical positivism') that had once seduced him in the 1920s: 'A *picture* held us captive, and we could not get outside it, for it lay in our language and language seemed to repeat it to us inexorably.'[26]

Raymond Tallis has argued trenchantly that

> *simulating* the behaviour of a thinking, conscious human being is not the same as *being* a conscious, thinking being,

25 Colin McGinn, 'Homunculism', *New York Review of Books* (21 March – 3 April 2013), 6.

26 Ludwig Wittgenstein, *Philosophical Investigations* (Oxford: Blackwell, 1958), sect. 115.

> particularly since the circumstances under which the simulation would deceive are *highly restricted*. (Deep Blue was not expected to make its own way to the competition venue, for example, or to see the point of chess or plan its future schedule of games.) What is more, simulation would count as simulation only to a conscious human being who may (or may not) be deceived. The notion of simulation, in other words, presupposes judges whose consciousness is not simulated. (That is why the concept of a 'zombie' could not arise in a world populated only by zombies.)[27]

Optimism about achieving artificial general intelligence (AGI) often turns on the belief that natural selection followed an incremental path in sorting through random variations and retaining whatever 'worked' – this is how human intelligence and consciousness emerged. With enough dedication, funding and cooperation, smart humans should be able to recreate human intelligence in machines at a quicker rate than natural selection. Consciousness is also assumed to be an 'emergent' property that might spring forth unexpectedly from a sophisticated level of hardware and software organization, quite as the supercomputer HAL's did in Arthur C. Clarke's *2001: A Space Odyssey*.

But talk of 'emergence', for all its popularity, is simply hand-waving. There is not a shred of evidence to support the naturalist claim that matter-energy can assume certain forms of complex organization in which it suddenly becomes conscious, self-conscious and knowing, able to understand and direct its own evolution. Consciousness does not emerge from brains in the same way a whole emerges from its parts. Indeed, our conscious selves are not located in the stand-alone brain or even solely in our bodies, or even in a brain interacting with other brains in bodies. It is part of

27 Raymond Tallis, *Aping Mankind: Neuromania, Darwinitis and the misrepresentation of humanity* (Durham: Acumen, 2011), 196; emphasis original.

a community of minds built up by conscious human beings over hundreds of thousands of years.

Finally, two major ethical challenges that the world faces in relation to AI and robots are about restraining state and corporate surveillance, and banning lethal autonomous weapon systems (LAWS).

1 Restraining state and corporate surveillance

The Chinese government is using face-recognition and other AI programs to control the Muslim Uighur community in the western provinces. But the wider aim is to collect as much information as possible about every company and citizen in the entire country, store it in a centralized database and assign a credit score to both companies and citizens that indicates how 'trustworthy' they are. This is a draconian form of social discipline, designed to identify and punish human-rights activists, political dissidents and other so-called 'anti-social elements' by denying them and their family members employment, housing, banking services and other social benefits. This is to date the most comprehensive effort to implement B. F. Skinner's infamous programme of human 'behaviour modification' through a conditioning system of rewards and punishments.

China is not the only country to be worried about. The big cats of the Internet industry (Google, Amazon and Facebook) condition us more subtly, often invisibly. They mine and store our personal data in staggering quantities, the equivalent of thousands of pages about every user, and use it to customize our searches and choose the advertisements we see. Every click of the mouse, every app we choose to open, sends information about us to thousands of invisible advertisers and, often, government watchers. We are living in what Al Gore called the 'stalker economy'[28] and Shoshana Zuboff, in

28 'Al Gore says Snapchat's popularity is due to "stalker economy"', *The Tech Journal* (2013), <https://thetechjournal.com/tech-news/al-gore-says-snapchats-popularity-is-due-to-stalker-economy.xhtml>, accessed 8 March 2021.

an important recent book, described as 'surveillance capitalism'.[29] And there is no longer a firewall between commercial surveillance and governmental surveillance. The continual drip of tweets, Instagram posts and status updates may not amount to much on its own but, over extended periods of time, can accumulate into a mine of personal information that leaves our vulnerabilities exposed.

2 Banning lethal autonomous weapon systems[30]

Asia is home to three nuclear powers (China, India and Pakistan), with North Korea aspiring to parity. All of them have a record of military opacity, are easily prone to armed confrontation in disputed border areas and are developing artificial intelligence-based autonomous weaponry for potential use on battlefields. Of course, the USA has taken the lead in this area, with its widespread deployment of drones in Afghanistan and Iraq. While current military drones are still controlled by remote human operators, the technology is available to make them fully autonomous, something that many countries are actively pursuing. The technology involved is far less sophisticated and cheaper than nuclear weaponry and can easily be developed (or hijacked) by non-state actors, including terrorist groups.

In delegating the decision to kill to a machine, the use of LAWS transgresses moral lines and fundamentally changes the nature of warfare. All advanced algorithmic systems are basically 'black boxes', with the original programmers themselves unable to understand how a system makes a particular decision. They lack the distinctly human qualities of empathy, reason, prudence and discernment that are necessary to exercise moral judgement on the battlefield. Moreover, they undermine international humanitarian

29 Shoshana Zuboff, *The Age of Surveillance Capitalism: The fight for a human future at the new frontier of power* (London: Profile Books, 2019). See Ch. 14 of this volume: Nathan Mladin and Stephen N. Williams, 'The question of surveillance capitalism'.

30 For more discussion on LAWS, see Ch. 8 of this volume: Noreen Herzfeld, 'Surrogate, partner or tool: how autonomous should technology be?', 130–2.

law by disproportionately transferring the risks of warfare to (usually unseen) civilian populations, rather than professional soldiers. The eminent Australian AI researcher, Toby Walsh, has called LAWS 'weapons of error' as well as 'weapons of terror'. He refers to a 2016 investigation of US military operations against the Taliban, which revealed that nine out of every ten people killed in drone strikes were not the intended targets. This was still when 'humans were in the loop, with situational awareness that is currently superior to that of any machine'.[31]

The scenario of one computer programmer unleashing thousands of autonomous military drones on human populations naturally fills many in the AI field, such as Walsh, with dread. In July 2015, many of the world's leading AI researchers, in both academia and the robotics industry, signed an open letter to the UN calling for a worldwide pre-emptive ban on LAWS. It has been unheeded by the governments of powerful nations. We are left with the dispiriting prospect that the world may have to experience the use of LAWS before the international community takes collective action, just as we had to observe the terrible effects of chemical weapons before the 1925 Geneva Protocol was instituted.

In conclusion, the most important human capacities in the age of robotics and surveillance will be our moral, social and emotional intelligence. It won't be the STEM skills that are currently seen as important for getting a job in shrinking labour markets. The irony is that our technological future compels us to reflect less on our technologies and more about the future of our common *humanity*.

31 Walsh, *2062*, 133.

Part 2

THEOLOGICAL FRAMEWORKS AND RESPONSES

6
What is it to be a person?

STEPHEN N. WILLIAMS

Introduction

When we enquire in the context of artificial intelligence what it is to be a person, more than one underlying issue may be in mind. We may be musing on the possibility that the cultural prevalence of AI is dehumanizing or depersonalizing. Does AI enhance or damage interpersonal relations, or is its effect on them negligible? It is an important question and we shall touch on it at some point in what follows. However, we may be asking something else. When we develop machine intelligence or AI, what view of the human person informs or is implicit in our invention? While intelligence is a property common to human and many non-human animals, the intelligence relevant in the development of AI is human intelligence. What bearing do Christian notions of personhood have on the way we think about AI?

In this opening paragraph, there has been a slide in vocabulary from 'person' to 'human'. There are contexts in which a distinction is deliberately drawn between them. For example, some claim that at the very beginning of life, the being who emerges in the process of conception is clearly human, but that we should not apply the language of 'person' at this early juncture. Whatever the rights and wrongs of that particular claim, in the context of our present enquiry into AI, we shall not be operating with the distinction between being human and being a person. Our question is about personal or human being in the light of AI.

AI, of course, encompasses a range. Some who are professionally involved in computer science grow impatient with the way 'AI' is used to cover a range of phenomena, all the way from what occupies them to entities more suitable for treatment in books of science fiction than in the context of serious discussion of scientific and technological possibilities. AI may simply be a sub-field or sub-discipline of computer science – an impersonal technology for which the question of personhood is scarcely relevant. One computer scientist said that he was no more interested in worrying over the question of whether machines can think than the question of whether submarines can swim. Metaphysical questions of personhood ('metaphysical' questions are broadly the big, underlying questions about the nature of being or reality) are idle as long as you mean by 'AI' a sub-field of computer science. So some maintain. At the other end of the spectrum, discussion about the prospects of AI proceeds in terms of machine consciousness, superintelligence and the possibility of AI dominating humans through superior intellectual power.

Our present interest embraces this end of the spectrum, but pursuing it does not depend on a judgement about what is or is not scientifically possible. Different opinions abound on that, but, whoever is right about it, discussion of AI unearths different perspectives on what it is to be human, regardless of technological feasibility. It is these differences, not the question of feasibility, that account for the need to address the question of personhood. In an earlier chapter, reference was made to standard distinctions made between different forms of AI: weak and strong, AGI (artificial general intelligence) and ASI (artificial superintelligence). ASI in particular, in which cognitive capacities and abilities to manage tasks are enhanced far beyond what is possible for humans, conjures up the 'transhumanist' prospect. This prospect is one of being physically, cognitively and emotionally enhanced beyond humankind as we know it, freed of ageing and even mortality, to the point that we envisage an entirely new and superior 'species', if we opt to use that word. It can also be called the 'post-humanist' condition. Strictly speaking, transhumanism refers to the transitional state en route to post-humanism, although 'transhuman' and 'post-human' are sometimes used identically in the literature.

How should Christians think about what it is to be a person in the light of this range of possibilities, whatever is scientifically feasible?

Humankind as religious

The task of outlining a theological understanding of personhood often begins by alluding to the familiar and lapidary phrase in Genesis 1, where God resolves: 'Let us make man in our image, after our likeness . . . So God created man in his own image, in the image of God he created him; male and female he created them' (vv. 26–27). This English wording is familiar, although not necessarily felicitous; arguably, 'man' should be translated as 'humankind'. Some question the procedure of taking that text as a starting point for our theological thinking about human beings.[1] For one thing, it has been interpreted in a wide range of ways.[2] For another, if Jesus Christ is the exemplar of true humanity and the full disclosure of what it means for us to be made in the image of God (Col. 1.15; 3.10), should we not start here? For our purposes, we do not need to decide on what constitutes the optimal method of theological approach, but we begin generically with the notion of humankind.

1 See David Kelsey, *Eccentric Existence: A theological anthropology* (Louisville, Ky: Westminster John Knox Press, 2009), the most detailed theological account of humankind of our time in the English-speaking world.

2 Henri Blocher, *In the Beginning: The opening chapters of Genesis* (Leicester: IVP, 1984); John F. Kilner, *Dignity and Destiny: Humanity in the image of God* (Grand Rapids, Mich./Cambridge: Eerdmans, 2015); Marc Cortez, *ReSourcing Theological Anthropology: A constructive account of humanity in the light of Christ* (Grand Rapids, Mich.: Zondervan, 2017); Marc Cortez, *Theological Anthropology: A guide for the perplexed* (London: T&T Clark, 2010).

One thing is both clear and fundamental, however we exegete the phrase 'image of God': to speak of humankind as being in the image of God is to say that to be human is to be essentially related to God. From the standpoint of scientific anthropology, that is obviously not the case. Humankind is religious in the contingent sense that, as a matter of evolutionary history, humans have been religious. But that is not a generic necessity. Whether or not there is a God is an open question from the perspective of scientific anthropology. What is clearly ruled out in that perspective is a description of what it is to be human which stipulates that being human means we are *essentially* related to God. Theological interpretation and standard scientific interpretation of the nature of human beings thus differ. They need not be incompatible. A Christian anthropologist may say that, from a strictly scientific point of view, we can define humankind without bringing religion into it, except as a contingent truth about its evolutionary history, but add that a scientific point of view does not cover everything and that, from a theological point of view, we are impelled to bring religion into it. Of course, to say that humans are essentially related to God is not to say that all humans believe in God. It is to say that humankind is constituted by God and thus constitutionally stands in a relationship to him, whether or not that is known or acknowledged.

Such a theological perspective is not threatened by the standard received account of the evolutionary background and history of *Homo sapiens*. Consider the belief that humankind is responsible to God in the sense of generic human design. (It does not entail that every individual, whether infant or severely cognitively impaired, is responsible.) In its place, an investigation of how and when this responsibility is acquired in evolutionary history is important and summons us to reflect on the whole question of biological species and classification. That is not our business here. Bracketing important questions that arise in relation to the beginning and end of life, atheists and religious people alike are usually in practical agreement when we identify someone as being human. Relatedness to God is, in the nature of the case, not visible or scientifically testable. It involves what are sometimes called 'neurological correlates'; that is, being related to God means that you can describe, in neuroscientific terms, the way that the brain of a human being, made in the image of God, is structured and functions in connection with the rest of the body and other humans. But a study of the brain will not directly reveal a religious relationship.

What exactly has this to do with AI? This: whatever we may ascribe to AI, it is not essentially related to God in the way that humans are. The possibility of AI consciousness is often mooted, so we can raise the question of whether an AI system could be programmed specifically to be morally and religiously conscious. However, suppose, for the sake of argument, that we judged such a consciousness possible. Whatever it amounted to, it would not constitute a personal relationship to God as it is understood in the Christian tradition. In Christianity, to be personally related to God is to be accountable to God, tasked by God with a vocation that is both generic (that is, applicable to the human race as a whole) and particular for different individuals. Our vocation is folded into a dimension in which guilt, forgiveness and reconciliation feature, in which non-ritualized prayer is offered and answered, and in which the will of God is sought, known, obeyed, ignored or disobeyed. It is not up to individuals whether or not they enter into a relationship with God. By virtue of their human being, they *are* in such a relationship, although there are specific aspects of that relationship that are only potential in the infant, the severely cognitively impaired or dehumanized cultures. Such a relationship cannot be humanly programmed into AI. AI cannot be personal in the Christian sense.

Of course, the possibility of AI's being personal in any meaningful way is often denied by those who have no religious stake in the discussion. The question of consciousness is pivotal here. For a long time, scientists and philosophers have pondered the nature of consciousness without reaching any consensus. From a scientific or philosophical point of view, there may be a good reason to deny the possibility of conscious AI altogether. However, whether or not that denial is convincing, it is doubtful if Christians simply *as Christians* have a stake in that debate. There is no obvious reason why Christians, simply as Christians, should believe or disbelieve in the possibility of the technological creation of some form of consciousness, even if Christian scientists or philosophers have strong reasons to argue their case from a scientific or philosophical point of view.[3] What can – and must – be said, from a theological point of view, is that any hypothetical AI consciousness could not be the kind of religious or moral consciousness that is involved in being created by God in his own image. Since there is nothing higher for any created being than having a personal relationship with God, AI that hypothetically possessed consciousness would certainly not be a higher form of being than humans.

It follows that 'intelligence' in reference to AI bears a different meaning from when it applies to humankind made in the image of God, because it is not integrated into a religious consciousness definitive of humankind as made by God. A practical definition or account of intelligence is demanding enough and a theoretical one is harder still. When AI was first developed, the emphasis was on calculative capacity – it was the reasoning processes of humans that invited experimentation with and the construction of AI. Those involved in the field have long acknowledged that earlier iterations of AI worked with too crude and abstract a view of human intelligence if AI was designed and destined to simulate, in a satisfactory way, human intelligence. Even so, the notion of people as machines, albeit very complex ones, apparently continues to underlie later attempts to develop AI along more sophisticated lines. What the notion of machine intelligence raises is the question

3 Donald M. Mackay, *Brains, Machines and Persons* (London: Collins, 1980), 62–5.

of the relationship of humankind to embodiment, a question that has received plenty of attention in the Christian tradition.

Humankind as embodied

It seems clear to many people that the notion of human being is inextricably tied to the notion of embodiment: how could they be separated? According to some thinkers, past and present, Christian or not, they could. This conviction has deep historical roots. In the West, the most familiar challenge to belief in the essential embodiment of human beings is generated by the notion of the soul, understood as a disembodied entity that characterizes humans along with their bodies in this life, but which does not require the body to survive beyond this life. Although there are post-human scenarios that entertain the prospect of a consciousness that lacks embodiment or, at least, lacks visible and tangible embodiment in any sense familiar to our experience, AI is usually 'embodied' if, by that word, we mean possessed of physical hardware. But when we talk naturally of human embodiment, we mean biologically carbon-based embodiment. Suppose that we begin to adapt, enhance and reconstruct ourselves with artificial materials; do we remain human or is there a point at which we should say that we are no longer human beings but cyborgs? Alternatively, supposing that we could digitally represent the brain and upload it to robotic hardware, would the resulting entity be human, even if in a dramatically enhanced state? These are not idle questions.[4]

A majority of those who work within the Christian tradition emphasize that Christian hope is for the resurrection of the body and not for the perpetual existence of a disembodied soul. Within that tradition, some hold that humans may enjoy a period of conscious non-embodied existence between death and the advent of new

4 The celebrated bodily experiments of Kevin Warwick, the holder of several university positions and who has been designated the world's 'first cyborg', testify to this.

heavens and a new earth. In that case, you can be human without being embodied. However, this is understood as an interim state. It remains the case, in this scenario, that embodiment is our human destiny on a new earth just as it characterizes our human existence on this earth. How is this related to ways of thinking about AI?

If we take our lead from the New Testament, the distinction between our present embodiment and our future embodiment on a new earth is greater than is popularly supposed. The most sustained discussion of our eschatological bodies (the bodies that we shall enjoy in resurrection life) is provided by Paul in 1 Corinthians 15.35–54. He emphasizes the discontinuity between the present and future forms of embodiment. He talks about the future in terms of a 'spiritual body', although neither he nor any other New Testament author uses the creedal phrase, 'resurrection of the body'. Whatever the composition of the spiritual body, it is not the same as our present body of flesh. What launches Paul's discussion is precisely the Corinthian folly of supposing their identity or similarity. What is sown is not the body that is to be, although there is some principle of continuity between present and future embodiment. Sun, moon and stars are 'embodied' in Paul's sense of the term. What will not inherit the life of the kingdom of God in the future is this body of flesh and blood. Paul gives us no idea of what the future body will be like and he has no need to because God's promise and power are sufficient to warrant our confidence. Although he spends time earlier in the chapter talking about the risen appearances of Jesus Christ, he conspicuously fails to pick out the risen body of Christ as the prototype for our own future bodies. The exact material form of the body of the risen Christ, in all its mystery, belongs to the time between the resurrection and the Ascension; the biblical testimony is not to its future form.

I rehearse this to indicate that Christian faith conceives of human embodiment in a generously wide variety of ways. Yet our future embodiment is connected to our present embodiment, and the reason that the New Testament has so little to say on how precisely we should conceive our future form is that its interest lies in the *moral* connection between our present bodily existence and future hope. This is summed up in the second letter that Paul wrote to the Corinthians in terms that are more widely representative of New Testament theology: 'For we must all appear before the judgement seat of Christ, so that each one may receive what is due for what he has done in the body, whether good or evil' (2 Cor. 5.10). Christian hope is hope for human creatures who have experienced embodiment on this earth, with all its frailties, sufferings and struggles (and it is a wider hope for the cosmos, of course). This does not mean that medical science is insignificant or irrelevant; on the contrary, there is a magnificent tradition of Christian involvement in medicine and care for the body that expresses love for our fellow human beings. What it does mean is that there is a difference between seeking to heal the body or alleviate suffering and bypassing the present form of the human condition altogether, and trying, through technology, to shape forms of being that have not been subject to the processes of conception, birth and growth, which are the common lot of those humans who survive early death. If we aspire to shape such forms of being technologically, it is not a case of human enhancement, from a Christian point of view; on the contrary, it is radically reductive.

Important questions surround what we may or should do here and now with our human frame, whether by genetic engineering, replacement of body parts or intellectual enhancement. Our discussion of human personhood remains on a fairly general and superficial plane (perhaps 'skeletal' is not the ideal word to use in this context!) if we do not engage with those questions. However, they lie outside the scope of our discussion. While we should understand better what is at stake in contemporary discussions of personhood by working through them one by one, space forbids it, so I take a short cut by attending briefly to some germane cultural factors. It is to these wider cultural implications of AI in relation to a Christian perspective on personhood that we now finally turn.

Where are we now?

Why has AI developed? We have addressed this specifically in an earlier chapter, so we merely generalize swiftly here as far as its social development is concerned. Assessment or evaluation of AI cannot be disconnected from the wider question of technological advance, of why, for example, transport, communications and labour-saving devices have developed – trains, planes, machines, calculators and telecommunications. Speed, efficiency, mobility, accessibility, prosperity and freedom all factor into the story. Curiosity and convenience alike stalk its pages. Prominent among the questions asked about social impact – and obviously not asked by religious people alone – is the question of what all this has done to our relationships. The advent of AI perpetuates, sharpens and gives a distinctive turn to that question. It is a truism that we enter life in a nexus of relationships grounded in the bodily senses of touch, smell, taste, sight and hearing, although some are deprived of these. The baby experiences safety or insecurity, the consolation or deprivation of love, long before cognitive capacities are formed. Her or his emotions are the sign language of the body. It is familiar Christian teaching rooted in biological fact: humans are relational creatures.[5] The fundamental moral principle of inter-human personal relationships is, of course, love. In fact, 'moral' is a far too feeble and somewhat unserviceable word, for humans are formed by God in the very core of their being to be recipients and givers of love. This is the blazing truth enshrined in the relatively detached but proper description of humans as interrelational beings: 'The person pure and simple does not exist.'[6]

---

5 This informs the wide-ranging *Jubilee Manifesto: A framework, agenda and strategy for Christian social reform* (Leicester: IVP, 2005), edited by Michael Schluter and John Ashcroft. From a theologically neutral perspective, see the important and celebrated contributions by Dan J. Siegel, including *Pocket Guide to Interpersonal Neurobiology: An integrative handbook of the mind* (New York, NY: W. W. Norton & Co., 2012).

6 Paul Tournier, *The Meaning of Persons* (London: SCM Press, 1957), 129.

What is going on culturally when AI enters into the world of human relationships, whether we are thinking of it in relation to AI consciousness and personhood or conceiving it more widely and generally as a social presence? The answer is – more than one thing. For example, some are worried about our damaging objectification of the material world; they propose that it is appropriate to address AI in personal terms because the depersonalizing of the created world is demeaning of it, and AI is an extension of that world: a human creation under the hand of God.[7] The argument for this is multilayered; the world cannot be neatly divided into the personal and the impersonal, as we realize when we reflect on animals and our relationships with them. I believe that we should reject this proposal because to address or relate in personal terms to human artefacts is to ascribe to them characteristics they do not possess, unless we are deliberately using personifying language, as we do when we feel affectionate towards or frustrated by our car.[8]

The question of technology opens up huge vistas that we can scarcely usefully survey if we are equipped initially with no more than the bland supposition that technology is a force for both good and evil. Yet we need that bland reminder, adding that technological evil is the wrongful use of the potential embedded in God's creation for good. Locally and proximately face-to-face relationships that could be maintained, at one time, only by travel became mediated by an exchange of letters dependent on the messenger on horseback, then by the development of shipping, steam locomotive and telegraph technology, and then, subsequently, on the camera and telephone. We tend to think of such technologies in general as enabling and not enfeebling human relationships. Technology that now enables 'Facetime' at a distance, allowing eyes to meet even when bodies

7 Michael S. Burdett, 'Personhood and creation in an age of robots and AI: can we say "you" to artifacts?', *Zygon* (Spring/Summer 2020).

8 Burdett cites this example. In a personal communication, he informs me that parts of his article are written more in an exploratory than in a dogmatic mode.

cannot touch, can feed and encourage the desire for sensory contact, and promote the opposite of a flight from relationships. Thus, AI is both in principle and in practice capable of being the medium for relationships that affirm rather than diminish human personhood.

Of course, the big question here is whether there is gain or loss overall, but to address it, we must operate with a criterion for human flourishing drawn from the Christian tradition, although not confined to it, namely, the enhancement of love. Its enemy is the focus on the enhancement of the individual. Money invested in Western technology for such a purpose is necessarily diverted from some other end. Hence the question of both international and national social inequality arises in the context of the development of AI. A place voluntarily gained in an institution of higher education or a sports team by someone who is enhanced intellectually or physically is a place non-voluntarily forfeited by the majority who are in no financial or social position to avail themselves of technological instrumentality.[9] How does medical technology enable us to flourish as personal beings if it is not developed first and foremost to allow the world's neediest people to thrive?

In operating with a criterion of love, we are beholden not to an idea but to a person, the person of Jesus Christ. He, through whom the world was made, is the centre of Christian reflection on personhood. As an image of humanity, he subverts many of our ordinary ways of thinking. One of the big challenges to thinking about human personhood arises from considering the experience of and with disabled people. The idea of autonomy as the apex of human dignity is shattered with that perspective. Dependence emerges as the quality that brings to light the nature of human personhood – mutual dependence, not just the dependence of disabled people on carers.[10]

9 See Francis Fukuyama, *Our Posthuman Future: Consequences of the biotechnology revolution* (New York, NY: Farrar, Straus & Giroux, 2002), 97.

10 Brian Brock and John Swinton (eds), *Disability in the Christian Tradition: A reader* (Grand Rapids, Mich./Cambridge: Eerdmans, 2012).

We should always have known this through Jesus Christ, who, out of a lowly human life, sacrificed in death, called into being the relational community of the Church, its mutually dependent members constituting one body. Some theologians have emphasized that our relational humanity is grounded in the inner relational being of God, who is one in three persons. However, we may adumbrate this: AI, like everything else, must face the test of Christology.

On the basis of discipleship to Christ, Paul told Timothy that 'if we have food and clothing, with these we will be content' (a standing challenge to the cultural drive towards AI and its applications), but before that, he had used the abstract noun 'contentment' (1 Tim. 6.6–8).[11] In the vocabulary of the Stoicism of Paul's day, the Greek word that Paul used (*autarkeia*) signified 'self-sufficiency'. Although contentment has been advocated in the history of Stoicism, self-sufficiency and contentment mean different things. Today, a degree of interest in Stoicism swirls around Silicon Valley, even if it is a 'popular' rather than a classical form of philosophical Stoicism.[12] Self-reliance and unperturbed willingness to accept limitation when it is inevitable are qualities that can be incorporated into a Christian framework. However, they take on a radically new aspect if contentment with food and clothing is the appropriate basic attitude to human life and relationships in the world.

Finally, one interpretation of what it means for humankind to be made in the image of God is that humans are given dominion over creation: 'Let them [humans] have dominion over the fish of the sea and over the birds of the heavens and over the livestock and over all the earth' (Gen. 1.26). Some interpreters argue that this is not a description or definition of the image of God; rather, it sets

11 This point is taken up in the last chapter in this volume: Nathan Mladin and Stephen Williams, 'The question of surveillance capitalism'.

12 It has been promoted particularly by Ryan Holiday: for example, see *Ego Is the Enemy: The fight to master our greatest opponent* (London: Profile Books, 2017); *The Daily Stoic: 366 meditations on self-mastery, perseverance and wisdom* (New York, NY: Penguin, 2016).

forth a mandate given to those who are in the image of God. We do not need to settle that argument. What is important in the discussion of AI is figuring out the extent of human dominion: at what point do we exceed its God-given bounds in relation to our bodies and our technologies? Obviously, the early chapters of Genesis do not answer the question in that form. They narrate the sad story of dominion gone awry, of how humans with dominion powers began to exercise their powers in this world. These early chapters of Genesis have been read and interpreted as authoritative in the Church in a variety of ways; we do not need to examine that more than the interpretation of the image of God. But we should note and ponder the conclusion of the account of dominion gone awry, before the human story recommences with the call of Abraham in the twelfth chapter of Genesis. Its conclusion is Babel.

Babel reveals that when humans, who are in the image of God, exercise their technological powers independently or in defiance of their Creator, their dominion mandate is transmuted into a curse. According to the account in Genesis, the building of a high tower was driven by hubris and insecurity: 'Let us make a name for ourselves, lest we be dispersed over the face of the whole earth' (Gen. 11.4). Pride and anxiety have been described as the twin drivers of culture.[13] When AI directly or indirectly reflects an idea of what it is to be a person, ours should not just be a response to technology as such or even the technology of AI as such. Rather, it should be informed by the warning embedded in the Babel account about the prospects for a technology detached from the knowledge or understanding of God and of humankind, as made in his image.[14] One way or another, such a technology, by which we seek control, ends up controlling us. Left to itself, it will cause personhood to become stunted.

13 So Gerhard von Rad, *Genesis: A commentary*, tr. John H. Marks (London: SCM Press, 1961), 145.

14 This appropriation of the account is not the preserve of conservative biblical scholarship or theology: see Claus Westermann, *Genesis 1–11: A commentary* (Minneapolis, Minn.: Augsburg, 1984), 554.

7

Robots, AI and human uniqueness: learning what not to fear

ROBERT SONG

There is something unnerving about robots and artificial intelligence. It is not just the immediate, practical concerns of whether they will take our jobs, exacerbate our social prejudices or enable big tech companies to invade our privacy. Nor is it the longer-term existential threats about our being annihilated or enslaved by hostile robotic superintelligences. Rather it is about the very idea of AI and what it represents for human identity. What would it mean if there were machines that had consciousness and displayed a similar level of intelligence and emotional responsiveness to that of human beings? What if there were a future when we were no longer able to distinguish human beings from robots? What would all this mean for human uniqueness?

These kinds of questions should be disconcerting for those without religious faith, or so I shall suggest. But for Christians, they are especially unsettling, given the traditional Christian belief that, since human beings are made in the image of God, they have a unique status above animals and the rest of creation. There is something distinctive about humankind, Christians hold, that sets it apart from everything else. After all, when the Word became flesh, it was human flesh that the Word became, which is surely reason to believe that humans have an exclusive status in creation. This special place, it seems, would be threatened if robots could not be distinguished from them.

I am going to suggest that, leaving aside the shorter- and longer-term risks to human society posed by particular applications of these technologies, Christians have nothing to fear from AI and robotics, at least with regard to human uniqueness and identity. But I am not going to argue this on the practical grounds that there are formidable engineering problems in the way of AIs ever developing the same kind of intelligence that we associate with human beings, undoubtedly true though that is. Rather, my claim will be that even if robots were to gain something like human levels of intelligence and the other capacities that we identify with being human, this would still not as such be a threat. For humans would continue to have the calling given to them in Genesis, which is fulfilled and renewed in Christ, and this they can never lose. In fact, at the level of the theology of human dignity and personhood, much more of a threat is posed not by increasingly intelligent machines, but by the implicit downgrading of human beings that is widespread in the underlying philosophy of AI, and which makes the project of making artificial human-like intelligence so seemingly plausible in the first place. If we are to understand what we should truly fear about robots and AI, we should look not to how they might threaten human dignity, but to the naturalist materialism they are often thought to presuppose.

Human uniqueness under threat

Underlying these worries about human uniqueness is a broader modern Western cultural anxiety about the place of human beings in the universe. Despite an intellectual strand represented by French Enlightenment thinkers who regarded the human being in terms of a machine, human status was basically assured, at least until the rise of evolutionary theory in the nineteenth century. The book of Genesis taught that humans were made in God's image and had dominion over animals and the rest of creation. They had a special place in the created order, a little lower than the angels, but above all other creatures. However, evolution put these clear lines of separation in question. Instead of occupying a unique rung in the great chain of being, the human species, in the evolutionary view, was, in principle, no different from any other species: human characteristics could be explained as the result of random mutation and selection, traced through a long evolutionary sequence back to the first molecular forms of life. From this disenchanted perspective, human beings no longer had any unique standing; from the impersonal point of view of the universe, there was nothing essential or necessary about their existence. *Homo sapiens* had become just one accidental twig on one branch of the vast evolutionary tree of life.

Faced with this threat to human identity, but still clinging to an inherited belief about the significance of human beings, a common response in the modern West has been to point out the ways in which human beings are, nevertheless, unlike the rest of the animal world. Almost invariably, these appeal to something connected to the human capacity for reason. Just as Aristotle talked of humankind as a *zōon logon echōn*, a 'rational animal', so anthropologists now refer to our subspecies as *Homo sapiens sapiens*. Human beings, it is said, are animals, but at least they are unique in their linguistic competence, in the sophistication of their tool use, and in the breadth of their creativity and their intellectual aptitudes: no other species has created anything remotely approaching the great works of art or scientific theories that human beings have produced – *King Lear*, the *St Matthew Passion*, the theory of relativity. Even if we do have evolutionary origins, and even though some species may show some proto-characteristics of human rationality (as ravens use tools and chimpanzees display pre-linguistic abilities), there is still evidence of human distinctiveness in the kind and extent of intellectual capabilities that we demonstrate.

The problem now is that this widely proclaimed superiority in rationality is coming under threat from advances in AI. The versions of AI currently in development may not yet be capable of exhibiting the kind of intelligence that human beings have, let alone of replicating such a mystifying thing as consciousness. But AI is becoming increasingly sophisticated, with no obvious endpoint, which intimates yet another displacement of humankind from its place in the order of things. Not only are we not separable from the rest of the animal kingdom in any biological sense, the traits associated with our rationality that we thought might demonstrate our pre-eminence over everything else are in danger of no longer serving that purpose.

So, the search turns to something else that AI lacks which might distinguish human beings and restore us to our unique place. After all, do we still not use visually distorted sequences of letters to keep robots from hacking our systems, because they are not very good at pattern recognition? Perhaps we can beat them at complex games that require some measure of intuition, such as chess or Go? Maybe they lack the creativity to write novels or musical compositions? Could computers ever have emotions? Surely, they won't have the integrated general intelligence that distinguishes human-level intelligence from the task-specific abilities of which AI is currently capable? What about consciousness? Or the soul, whatever that is?

Despite these putative differences there is still a lurking anxiety about whether this strategy for ensuring human uniqueness is going to work. After all, for AI researchers, pattern recognition is just another problem to be solved, one that machine learning based on artificial neural networks has begun to tackle. AI programs can now beat the world's top chess and Go masters, and are causing significant changes in the ways those games are played at the highest levels. Artificial intelligences are now taking up classical music composition, while software-written news reports are often indistinguishable from those written by journalists, and novels created by AI are being entered for literary competitions.[1] Affective

1 See Ch. 13 of this volume: Andrzej Turkanik, 'Art, music and AI: the uses of AI in artistic creation'.

computing is beginning to interpret and simulate human emotions. Barriers that we once thought computers would *never* breach may, for all we know, simply be barriers that they have *not yet* breached.

How far AI will in fact be able to go is unclear. Certainly, there seems to be general agreement among experts that human composers and novelists are not likely to be out of work any time soon. And on the big questions of artificial general intelligence and consciousness, while some researchers think that 'strong AI' may be possible in the next few years or decades, many others believe that it is centuries away – or may never arrive. Others point out that AI is not necessarily the same kind of thing as human intelligence, and that only a tiny part of the research effort in AI aims to replicate human-level intelligence anyway. But it is not yet evident that we are in a position categorically to rule out these possibilities.

Human dignity and human flourishing

For some kinds of secular humanism, the possibility of strong AI presents, or at least ought to present, a problem. For if it were possible for us to engineer beings with human-level intelligence, which may, in important ways, be indistinguishable from human beings, it makes credible the idea that we ourselves are no more than robotic intelligences. And if we are no more than robotic intelligences, we are ourselves merely machines in biological clothing: the human, it seems, has now become explicable in terms of the algorithmic, the meaningful in terms of the meaningless, life in terms of death. For those who cling on to some vestiges of human significance, it looks as though the lesson should be drawn – which should have been drawn long ago from evolutionary theory, at least as presented in its standard philosophical guise – that nothing has value except to the extent we decide to give it value; or, perhaps we should say, no one else has value except to the extent that we decide to give them value. But the moral implications of such a position are sufficiently alarming that it should call into question something in this entire picture.

The possibility of strong AI raises a parallel problem for Christians. Even if their belief that all creation participates in the goodness of God means that Christians are unlikely to be attracted towards philosophies that drain the universe of all value, they still affirm the unique place of humankind above all other creatures. If Genesis and the doctrine of the Incarnation are to be interpreted as implying this exclusive status, there must be some theological basis for distinguishing human beings from all other beings, some capacity or characteristic that marks humans out as superior.

However, I suggest that the whole enterprise of establishing some citadel of human distinctiveness, which the rising tides of AI research will never reach, is mistaken. It is based on a similar kind of error to that made by those in the nineteenth century who searched for a 'God of the gaps', who could never be explained by advances in the natural sciences. Each of these capacities that putatively distinguish human beings is like the bacterial flagellum that intelligent design theorists cite as proof of God's existence. They claim that the flagellum could never have come about by the natural processes of evolution, and so must be evidence of God's intervention as an intelligent designer. The irreducibly complex phenomenon that supposedly cannot be explained by evolution, in the God of the gaps approach, is mirrored in the irreducibly complex phenomenon that is beyond the reach of AI in what we might call the 'human of the gaps' mentality. In both cases, it is driven by anxiety that scientific explanation or technological advance will render either God or human beings or both redundant.

Interestingly, the same error arguably besets some Christian responses to the search for extraterrestrial intelligence. What if there are extraterrestrials out there that are as intelligent as we are or even more intelligent? Leaving aside the question of whether those extra-planetary aliens might be hostile or friendly towards us, the very fact that there could be beings who are superior to human beings in the very capacities by which we distinguish ourselves is threatening. Indeed, if the uniqueness of human capacities is the basis of our belief in human superiority, then, given the size of the universe, the alarm should already be raised by the small but real possibility that there might have been – or might still be – microscopic life elsewhere within our own solar system. On this account, Christian theology itself is under threat from the existence of extraterrestrial life.

In truth, theology should not be beholden to this kind of contingency. The reasonableness of Christian faith should not go up and down like the stock market, based on the latest estimates of the probability of the existence of alien civilizations. Nor should one's belief in the significance of human beings depend on how intelligent, creative, caring or lethal AI turns out to be. If we really believe that human beings have some unique significance, this cannot be, as I shall suggest, because we uniquely possess certain characteristics that no other species has.

What we should be concerned about, I suggest, is not human uniqueness, as if we alone in the universe are bearers of those capacities that we deem to be distinctively human. Rather, our concern should be for human dignity: we should not fear the upgrading of robots so much as the downgrading of human beings. Of course, there are many important practical issues raised by the increasing power of AI: the threat to jobs, the rise of surveillance capitalism, the quasi-monopoly power of big tech companies, the dangers of autonomous weapon systems and so on. These are – or ought to be – the stuff of everyday political and ethical discussion. But we should not be held hostage by ontological or theological anxieties tied to misunderstood claims about human uniqueness. Whether artificial intelligence could become greater than human intelligence, or could never become greater than it or is just a completely different kind of thing, is not an issue of ultimate theological significance.

The issue, in other words, is not anxiety about human status but truthfulness to human calling. No doubt human beings are different from other creatures – they also are made according to their kind. The difference, however, does not amount to the unique possession of certain capacities, such that human beings are elevated to a categorically superior position above all other creatures. Rather, it is about responding to a unique vocation to flourish as the kind of creatures we are, fulfilling and not denying the capacities with which we are gifted, regardless of whether any other creatures may have the same capacities. The questions we should be asking are these: is humankind flourishing in the way it is called to, or is it in practice and in theory denying that? Are our *technological practices* compatible with recognizing the dignity and personhood of human beings, or do they implicitly or explicitly deny that? And are our *philosophical and scientific theories* about the place of humankind in the universe compatible with recognizing the dignity and personhood of human beings, or do they implicitly or explicitly deny that?

Naturalism and the downgrading of the human

It is easy to see how AI and related technologies can negate human flourishing in everyday experience. Dehumanization occurs when software directs workers round automated warehouses in routinized labour that renders human beings barely more than living machines; when social media companies compete in deploying persuasive technologies to keep people's eyeballs on their screens, in what tech commentator Tristan Harris calls the 'race to the bottom of the brain stem';[2] when predictive policing algorithms

2 Tristan Harris, 'The eyeball economy: how advertising co-opts independent thought', *Big Think* (10 April 2017), <https://bigthink.com/videos/tristan-harris-the-attention-economy-a-race-to-the-bottom-of-the-brain-stem>, accessed 12 February 2021.

reinforce institutionally racist bias against black citizens; when children experience reduced attention spans, shallower cognitive abilities and loss of identity as a result of their immersion in online worlds.

However, my concern here is not these forms of loss of flourishing in practice, which are discussed elsewhere in this volume, but in the ways that we are depersonalized by our dominant forms of philosophy and scientific understanding. Central to these is naturalism, a philosophical understanding of human beings that pervades the natural sciences and, to some extent, the social sciences. By naturalism, I mean the claim that everything that exists can be explained in terms of the natural sciences, and that the natural sciences themselves are to be understood in a reductive way, ultimately in terms of physics. Conversely, anything that cannot be understood in these terms does not exist or has, at best, an ontologically dubious status.

This philosophy was first assembled in the seventeenth century during the momentous overthrow of Aristotelian metaphysics that we know as the scientific revolution, through thinkers such as Francis Bacon, Galileo Galilei and René Descartes. We are probably most familiar with the basic mentality through attempts to explain every aspect of human existence as a product of evolutionary biology. On this account, not only are our biological traits, like those of all living things, to be understood as the result of a long process of evolutionary adaptation, but also many of the personal characteristics that we think of as most distinctively human are to be explained in the same way as well. All human capacities for consciousness and mind, all love, morality, art and religion, are ultimately biological in origin. So sub-disciplines grow up that deploy these categories of explanation: evolutionary anthropologists understand the development of human society and culture as adaptive for human survival, while evolutionary psychologists explore the development of the mind, and evolutionary theorists of religion analyse religious belief and practice, all in the same evolutionary terms.

This reductive, naturalist mentality has also influenced the ambitions of the scientific disciplines related to AI. As an enterprise, AI arose out of the effort to model human cognitive processes so that they could be handled by digital computers. This has been undertaken with two different, albeit often overlapping, intentions. For some researchers, typically operating on the overlap of engineering and computer science, the aim has been to develop techniques that could be of practical benefit – whether natural language processing to aid machine translation, data mining techniques to detect credit-card fraud, or computer vision to help in medical diagnosis. This 'technological' form of AI does not have ambitious metaphysical or explanatory goals, and is not, as such, seeking to build human levels of intelligence: its aim as a discipline is to resolve practical questions; it is not unduly worried if it turns out that human kinds of intelligence are not the most effective way of achieving a particular object. But for other researchers, often working in psychology or neuroscience, the aim has been scientific and explanatory, namely to understand the working of the human mind. Rather than trying to develop artificial forms of intelligence for use in everyday practical applications, the underlying objective is to understand human mental processes as computational processes. Perception, memory, emotion, consciousness: the computational hypothesis is that these can all be modelled as one form or another of algorithmic manipulation of data.

But of course, this 'psychological' form of AI, which is pervasive in cognitive science, is not after all so far from the technological form. For if it is possible to provide a computational model, not just of particular mental processes but of the whole human mind, then it follows that, at least in principle, we could build a computer that was in fact a mind with a human kind of intelligence. And while this has not been the focus of most AI research, it has been a recurrent aspiration of AI researchers from its earliest days. The scientific enterprise of modelling a human mind is not so distant in principle from the technological enterprise of building a human mind. And in the naturalist way of thinking, this all suggests that humans may be no more than evolved robotic intelligences.

Mere matter or marvellous matter?

It would be very easy to respond and say that surely human beings are more than merely apes or robots, that there must be something about human beings that is not captured by either evolutionary or computational explanations. But this response is still in danger of falling for the citadel idea, that there is some capacity, some haven of human uniqueness, that is beyond the realm of science and renders human beings categorically superior. Rather, as I have suggested, the first task is not to look for something that human beings uniquely possess, but rather to ensure that these scientific understandings do not undermine what it is for human beings to flourish.

For example, consciousness, a subjective point of view of the world, is intrinsic to what it is to be human and, for all we know, for some other creatures as well. Yet the temptation on the part of naturalistic accounts of human beings is to assume that because some version of naturalism must be true, if we can't explain consciousness in terms of our theory, then consciousness must be an illusion (or, at least, our subjective explanations for our thoughts and actions – often dismissed as 'folk psychology' – cannot be part of any true explanation of them). And so it is for our common-sense idea that there is a connection between the mind and the world. We tend to assume that the belief that 'it is raining' says something about the weather. However, the effect of naturalist modes of thought, in interpreting beliefs as computational processes realized through synapses firing, is to render problematic the idea that physical processes can reach beyond themselves to an external world.

Such Procrustean denials are the stock-in-trade of a certain kind of naturalist mentality. By contrast, it is only through holding hard to what we already know about human flourishing that we will refuse to find short cuts round the profound difficulties of explanation, such as these, that computational accounts face. We will also resist the impulse to pretend away the daunting hurdles that must be surmounted by any programme of engineering human-like AI. The problem is not with the quest for scientific explanation in itself, nor with evolution or AI as such, but with the naturalistic metaphysics that these are assumed to require. For naturalism, to explain is to reduce, to interpret downwards, to explain away; since the world is fundamentally 'merely' material, and matter is assumed to be intrinsically incapable of meaning, meaning must be interpreted in terms of the meaningless, life in terms of the lifeless. And so to see human beings as 'merely' apes or 'merely' robots becomes profoundly threatening for those who want to preserve some account of human dignity but do not have the metaphysics to make sense of it.

By contrast for Christians, matter is never mere matter. Matter is charged with the grandeur of God: it is that out of which the world is made, which God created, declared to be good in all its various forms and blessed through the incarnation of Christ. Matter is intrinsically capable of meaning: it comprises the heavens that tell the glory of God and proclaim God's handiwork, the day that pours forth speech to day, the night that declares knowledge to night. There is therefore nothing to fear in learning that we are material, have a material history and might be understood in material terms. Just as evolution might turn out to be the best way of describing different aspects of the way by which God made us to be who we are, so also with computational models of the mind.

But there is a price to pay for allowing human beings to be successfully understood as material beings. Matter will have to be recognized as much more remarkable than our current reductive, naturalist accounts allow it to be. It is not that *we* are not merely material but that *matter itself* is not merely material. Appreciating this will require a revolution in our metaphysical understanding of matter, one which allows that matter is intrinsically capable of meaning, that matter itself might be mind-full. As the philosopher Thomas Nagel notes in a highly perceptive critique of naturalism, when we recognize that reductionist naturalism and materialism do not do justice to our common-sense understanding of humans, the 'possibility opens up of a pervasive conception of the natural order very different from materialism – one that makes mind central, rather than a side effect of physical law'.[3]

To state the need for change is one thing; to work out its details is a philosophical task of the highest order. Nagel again: 'We should expect theoretical progress in this area to require a major conceptual revolution at least as radical as relativity theory, the introduction of electromagnetic fields into physics – or the original scientific revolution itself.'[4] The end result would indeed be revolutionary. Far from all of material existence being premised on death, it would be seen as fundamentally oriented to life and its possibilities. Instead of human beings being merely the product of impersonal evolution, they would form a place where the universe had come to a glimmering of an understanding of itself. They might possibly constitute the only such place. But equally possibly they might not.

It may seem a long way from the threats posed to human uniqueness by AI and robots to the need for a revolution in the philosophy underlying science, but that is exactly what is at stake if humans are to flourish. Whether or not human beings are well understood in evolutionary or computational terms, whether or not AIs can be built that will be indistinguishable from humans, humans

3 Thomas Nagel, *Mind and Cosmos: Why the materialist Neo-Darwinian conception of nature is almost certainly false* (New York, NY: Oxford University Press, 2012), 15.

4 Nagel, *Mind and Cosmos*, 42.

can never lose their distinct calling to flourish as the kinds of being they are. Of course, a whole slew of questions comes into view as a result. Should robots ever be given rights? Might they one day have to be treated as persons? What kind of dignity should be ascribed to them? This discernment of the nature of other creatures is precisely what is involved in the naming of animals, a task that is integral to Genesis' understanding of Adam's calling and thus of Adam's being made in the image of God. But whatever may be the answer to those questions, what is not in doubt is that this calling to humankind still remains.

8

Surrogate, partner or tool: how autonomous should technology be?

NOREEN HERZFELD

The global spread of the virus SARS-CoV-2 in 2020 sparked an urgent need for effective therapeutics, testing and, ultimately, a vaccine. Scientists called on every tool in their arsenal, including a wide variety of artificial intelligence programs. A first line of defence was to use machine learning to test more than 6,000 existing drugs to see if any of them could be repurposed to combat SARS-CoV-2.[1] Google's DeepMind team trained a neural network to predict protein structures associated with the virus as part of developing a vaccine.[2] Meanwhile, robots stepped in across the USA, Europe and Asia to take over factory jobs, fill delivery orders, disinfect hospital rooms and bring food to the quarantined. Technology to the rescue.

We have always been creators of technologies, from the first hurling of a stone to procure lunch to the striking of flint against stone to create fire to cook that lunch. Technology can give us great power. It changes our world. This is wonderful when fighting a

1 Y. Ge et al., 'A data-driven drug repositioning framework discovered a potential therapeutic agent targeting COVID-19', *BioRxiv* (12 March 2020), <https://europepmc.org/article/ppr/ppr117314>, accessed 13 February 2021.

2 DeepMind, 'Computational predictions of protein structures associated with COVID-19' (4 August 2020), <https://deepmind.com/research/open-source/computational-predictions-of-protein-structures-associated-with-COVID-19>, accessed 13 February 2021.

disease such as COVID-19. But technologies can also bring about changes we might not foresee, as climate change well illustrates. The losses caused by technology are often seen only in retrospect, when we find that a new technology does not live up to our values or intentions, and these losses may be irreversible. Thus, technology is rarely a neutral force. 'It is a power endowed with its own peculiar force,' according to French sociologist, Jacques Ellul. 'It refracts in its own specific sense the wills which make use of it and the ends proposed for it.'[3] Ellul raises a basic question. How autonomous should technology be? While technologies generally reflect and refract our purposes, amplifying our natural abilities, can they also get away from us, embodying a power or purpose of their own?

A hammer amplifies the force of an arm. A telescope lets us see things hidden from the naked eye. Computers and AI programs extend the mind, processing and manipulating vast amounts of data at incredible speed. As a mental tool, AI seems to be the one technology in greatest danger of crossing from the realm of amplification to that of autonomy. How can we best harness it so that AI serves us rather than forcing us to serve it?

What is technology?

Technology has one purpose – to alter our condition or environment. Through various technologies, we have sought to tame our environment, to make our lives longer and more comfortable. The word 'technology' derives from the Greek *technē*, which means 'craft', 'art' or 'knowledge'. *Technē* is about more than tools. Technology embodies not just the machines or instruments we use but also our techniques, processes and goals. Technologies come to define a large part of the societies that use them.

3 Jacques Ellul, *The Technological Society: A penetrating analysis of our technical civilization and of the effect of an increasingly standardized culture on the future of man*, tr. John Wilkinson (New York, NY: Knopf, 1964), 140–1.

Modern technology has had a far greater effect on human society than did the Greeks' *technē*. The social critic Neil Postman notes that we have engaged in a 'deification of technology, which means that the culture seeks its authorization in technology, finds its satisfactions in technology, and takes its orders from technology'.[4] The tools of *technē* solved pressing physical problems in the production of food, clothing and shelter. They aided in our ancestors' survival but did not dictate their world view. In today's world, technology is central to our understanding of ourselves and the environment around us. We define ourselves through our technologies. The technological imperative stands, sometimes in tension, sometimes in harmony, with our religious understandings. Technology plays an undeniably greater role in our lives than it has played at any time previously in human history.

That greater role can be seen in our power to create something completely new, a quest less prominent in ancient *technē*. The German existentialist philosopher Martin Heidegger observed that while the ancient craftsman certainly made something new when he constructed a chair, he did not impose a new form on nature; rather, he worked with what was already inherent in the wood.[5] By contrast, a genetically engineered bacterium changes the natural order. Humanly extracted plutonium never returns to the uranium from which it was derived. In a similar dream for the new, posthumanists imagine a cybernetic future for human intelligence that escapes the limitations of the human body. The products of modern technology do not simply shape nature but transform and replace it. We have become, in the words of the theologian Philip Hefner, 'created co-creators'.[6]

---

4 Neil Postman, *Technopoly: The surrender of culture to technology* (New York, NY: Vintage Books, 1993), 71.

5 Martin Heidegger, *The Question of Technology and Other Essays*, tr. William Lovitt (New York, NY: Harper & Row, 1977).

6 Philip Hefner, *The Human Factor: Evolution, culture, and religion* (Minneapolis, Minn.: Fortress Press, 1993), 23.

Created co-creators

In the first chapters of Genesis, we find two creation stories. They describe God's bringing order out of chaos, making something completely new. They also teach a basic understanding of who we are and our place in relation to the rest of the created world.

Genesis 1.26–27 sets a pattern for humankind:

> Then God said, 'Let us make humankind in our image, according to our likeness; and let them have dominion over the fish of the sea, and over the birds of the air, and over the cattle, and over all the wild animals of the earth, and over every creeping thing that creeps upon the earth.'
>
> So God created humankind in his image,
> in the image of God he created them;
> male and female he created them.
>
> (NRSV)

These verses present both God's intent and action in creating human beings in the divine image. The expressions 'in our image' and 'according to our likeness' are used for no other creature. Humans are set apart and, collectively, given dominion over the rest of creation.

One way in which we reflect the image of the Creator God of Genesis 1 is that we, too, are creators. This precludes a totally negative view of technology. Creation and dominion are two sides of the same coin – the tools and methods we create allow us to exercise dominion over the rest of creation. Biblical scholars generally agree that Genesis 1 describes men and women as God's deputies on earth. According to Gerhard von Rad, humanity is given the divine image so that it 'may control the whole of creation'.[7] For some, this

7 Gerhard von Rad, *Genesis: A commentary*, tr. John H. Marks (Philadelphia, Penn.: The Westminster Press, 1961), 56.

is taking it a bit far. Modern ecologists, following Lynn White, have viewed our dominion over nature with harsh scepticism, but von Rad points out that for the writers of Genesis, chaos was 'the great menace to creation' and threat to humanity.[8] Humans are to join God in imposing order on nature. Technologies help us to do just that.

While biblical scholars focus on dominion in the Genesis text, Karl Barth focuses on verse 26: 'Let us make humankind in our image.' Whereas many interpreters have seen 'us' and 'our' in this verse as referring to God's heavenly court, Barth assumes the plural pronouns point to a God who embodies relationship in God's very being.[9] This relational nature, existing within a triune Godhead, forms the ground of human creation. Human nature is fulfilled only when humans are in relationship with God and with one another. Barth notes, 'Image has double meaning: God lives in togetherness with Himself, then God lives in togetherness with man, then men live in togetherness with one another.'[10]

According to Barth, God created humankind to form a relationship with a being that despite 'all of its non-deity and therefore its differentiation can be a real partner; which is capable of action and responsibility in relation to Him'.[11] In robots and AI, have we finally created something that could, one day, mimic this combination, an 'other' that is wholly different from ourselves yet with whom we might enter into relationship? Is this what we want from AI? What might be the consequences?

One thing we learn from Genesis 4—9 is that dominion alone can have very negative consequences for human relationships. The

8 Von Rad, *Genesis*, 144.

9 Karl Barth, *Church Dogmatics, Volume 3: The Doctrine of Creation*, Part 1, ed. G. W. Bromiley and T. F. Torrance, tr. J. W. Edwards, O. Bussey and H. Knight (Edinburgh: T&T Clark, 1958), 185.

10 Karl Barth, *Table Talk*, ed. John D. Godsey (Richmond, Va: John Knox Press, 1962), 57.

11 Barth, *Church Dogmatics*, 187.

age-old tension between the pastoralist and the technologically more developed agriculturalist is explored in the story of Cain and Abel, in which the relationship between brothers is shattered. Agriculture, together with new technologies of construction, allows the growth of cities, exemplified by the tower of Babel, and whole societies cease to understand one another. Noah's use of technology, building an ark to save humans and the animals, succeeds where Cain and Babel failed, precisely because Noah couples technology with relationship. He enters into a covenant with God, one that repeats both that humans are made in God's image and that they have dominion over the earth (Genesis 6—9). These chapters warn that dominion without relationship with God, one another and the rest of nature can and will produce unforeseen and disastrous results.

Evaluating technologies in the light of relationship

Postman writes, 'New technologies alter the structure of our interests: the things we think *about*. They alter the character of our symbols: the things we think *with*. And they alter the nature of community: the arena in which thoughts develop.'[12] The Amish have been particularly sensitive to the latter. For them, technology comes second to community. The benefits of a technology are weighed against the changes it might bring to those who use it and to the community as a whole.

Contrary to popular conceptions, the Amish have not 'stopped the clock'. They accept some technologies and reject others. They will use a telephone; they simply prohibit having one in each house, since this would diminish the custom of visiting one another to discuss things face to face. They use refrigerated milk tanks,

12 Postman, *Technopoly*, 20; emphasis original.

powered by generators, since these are necessary if their milk is to be sold to the wider community, but see no need for a refrigerator in every kitchen. Some use solar panels to power a saw or a sewing machine, but they prefer to stay off the electric grid.

In general, the Amish ask two questions when considering a new technology. The first is one that we generally ask of any new technology. Does it provide tangible benefits? Modern antibiotics, diagnostics and surgical techniques are acceptable. So is the use of mowers, hay balers or generator-powered woodworking equipment. Each contributes to the health or economic strength of the community. A second question is: how does this technology affect our relationships? Technologies that might cause pride or attract attention are unacceptable. Thus, plastic surgery would be forbidden, as is individual ownership of anything considered a status symbol, such as a car or a smartphone. For the Amish, social equality is important to maintaining a harmonious community. Cars, phones and the Internet would change how members interact and weaken local ties. Television and the Internet also convey some less savoury aspects of secular culture that the Amish see as inimical to their faith and values.

While most view the Amish approach to technology as extreme, the questions the Amish ask of a new technology are not unreasonable ones. They return us to the points that the biblical scholars extracted from Genesis 1. First, does the technology exercise dominion in a useful and responsible way? This answer is usually obvious since most technologies are developed precisely for their tangible benefits. Does it heal the sick, help the poor and suffering, or make the environment a more sustainable and beautiful place? The pitfalls described in Genesis 4—9 – in which technology plays a role in fratricide and conflict – raise the question of technological effects on our relationships. Does technology change the way we think of ourselves and what it means to be human? How will it affect our relationship with God, nature or one another? Are there issues of equality and social justice? Is justice available to all or only to some? While these questions are easy to ask, the answers are not always obvious.

AI: tool, partner or surrogate?

In 1962, the computer scientist John McCarthy, the first to use the term 'artificial intelligence', established the Stanford Artificial Intelligence Laboratory with the goal of creating a 'thinking machine'. At the same time, Douglas Engelbart, the inventor of the computer mouse, established the nearby Augmentation Research Center and coined the term 'IA' or 'intelligence augmentation'. AI and IA represent two different views of how computers should function. AI makes the computer our surrogate in the task of dominion, while IA sees it as merely another tool used under human control and supervision.

Reserving computers for intelligence augmentation keeps them well within the usual bounds of technology. Until now, our tools have been our servants, mechanizing our physical labour. They do not act independently of our use or direction. They rarely surprise us. When they wear out or we discover a better tool, we discard them. Most of the time this is exactly what we want, including with computers. We determine the tasks, provide the programming and look to the computer for execution. We use the computer as a tool for intellectual augmentation, for processing speed and power above and beyond that of our brains. We retain responsibility for the results.

AI offers a different possibility: allowing computers to function as autonomous agents. Agency connotes intention or independence: an agent's action stems from a choice or volition internal to the actor.[13] Can a computer have its own volition or intention? Our intentions arise out of our mental states. The philosopher Daniel Dennett, who takes an instrumentalist stance that suggests

13 Markus Schlosser, 'Agency', *Stanford Encyclopedia of Philosophy* (10 August 2015), <https://plato.stanford.edu/entries/agency>, accessed 10 June 2020.

consciousness is merely a by-product of the mechanical workings of the brain, has no problem considering the internal states of the computer's central processing unit (CPU) analogous to the mental states in a person's brain.[14] Others, such as the Berkeley philosopher John Searle, argue that states in the CPU come from the program's being executed, and thus represent the intention of the programmer, not the computer itself.[15]

Machines act based on their programming. The question is whether they can or should go one level higher and make decisions *about* their programming, changing course from the expected as they interact with their environment. Most AIs do exactly what we tell them to do, although their instructions might be so complex that we cannot always anticipate the result. While AI programs make decisions without direct human control, no current AI can reason about those decisions (and it is controversial whether they will ever be able to do so). For now, there remains a direct causal chain between the machine's behaviour and its programmer. A machine with true agency would have the additional ability to reason independently about its own actions and unpredictably change course, should it consider those actions unethical or in violation of an overarching value or intention.[16]

Michael and Susan Anderson would consider a robot or program to be a moral agent if it fitted three criteria. First, it would not be 'under the direct control of any other agent or user'. Second, its interaction with its environment would be 'seemingly deliberate and calculated'. Third, it would fulfil 'some social role that carries with it some assumed responsibilities'.[17] This third criterion is relational.

---

14 Daniel C. Dennett, *The Intentional Stance* (Cambridge, Mass.: MIT Press, 1987), ch. 2.

15 John Searle, 'Minds, brains, and programs', *Behavioral and Brain Sciences*, vol. 3, no. 3 (1980), 417–57.

16 Joseph Weizenbaum, *Computer Power and Human Reason: From judgment to calculation* (New York, NY: W. H. Freeman & Co., 1976), 74.

17 Michael Anderson and Susan Leigh Anderson (eds), *Machine Ethics* (Cambridge: Cambridge University Press, 2011), 158.

Consider a robot as a caregiver: it would carry out tasks without being under the direct control of its programmer. For some of these tasks, it would make deliberate choices, and its choices might not always be simple or direct. To be a moral agent, however, its choices must be informed by an awareness of its responsibility for its patient.[18] Such a robotic helper does not yet exist. But while we do not now, and may never, have machines that we can consider fully autonomous moral agents, we do have robots and programs operating with a fair amount of autonomy in settings where choices carry serious moral implications, particularly in law enforcement and on the battlefield.

Are killer robots too autonomous?

Lethal autonomous weapon systems (LAWS)[19] use networks of sensors and algorithms to identify a target and decide, without synchronous human control, whether to attack or destroy it. As such, they not only exhibit a high degree of agency but also make judgements and decisions that carry the potential for life or death. The advent of flight inaugurated a second era of warfare, releasing armies from having to be physically present on the battlefield.[20] LAWS have brought a third era, releasing soldiers from the mental decisions of battle as well. LAWS' 'capacity for self-determined action makes them uniquely effective and uniquely unpredictable'.[21] The former US Air Force Major General Robert Latiff considers this the crossing of a new 'moral Rubicon'.[22]

18 Anderson and Anderson (eds), *Machine Ethics*, 158.

19 For more on LAWS, see Ch. 5 of this volume: Vinoth Ramachandra, 'AI and robots: some Asian approaches', 88–9.

20 We see this in the extreme in today's age of drone warfare.

21 Rebecca Crootof, 'War torts: accountability for autonomous weapons', *University of Pennsylvania Law Review*, vol. 164, no. 6 (May 2016), 1349.

22 Robert H. Latiff and Patrick J. McCloskey, 'With drone warfare, America approaches the robo-Rubicon', *Wall Street Journal* (14 March 2013), <http://www.wsj.com/news/articles/SB10001424127887324128504578346333246145590>, accessed 13 February 2021.

Examples of LAWS include the AEGIS Weapon System, a naval air defence system, used by the USA, Australia, Japan, Norway, Republic of Korea and Spain. AEGIS can search and guide missiles in the air, on the surface and under water, deciding independently when and where to fire. It can function fully autonomously or in 'human in the loop' mode, in which operators have the option to override its decisions.[23] At the opposite end of the size spectrum, the Kargu-2 is a 15-lb (7-kg) multi-copter that can track, identify (via facial recognition) and engage targets. These drones can operate in swarms of up to 20, either led by a human-operated drone or fully independently.[24]

These and other autonomous weapons present military commanders with plenty of benefits. They process vast amounts of data and operate at speeds and levels of precision far beyond human capabilities, including making rapid decisions during the changing circumstances of battle. They can operate in harsh and difficult environments. They are less expensive than human troops and can work long hours without tiring. They carry out orders with fewer mistakes. Most importantly, they keep soldiers out of physically and psychologically dangerous or deadly environments.

However, these advantages do not come without costs to the larger human community. Just as twentieth-century ethicists and theologians were forced to re-evaluate the justice of war in the light of nuclear weapons, we must re-evaluate the morality of war in the light of autonomous weapons. How do these weapons affect our decisions on when to wage war, how to wage war and who is responsible for the acts of war? Would fully autonomous weapons

---

23 US Navy Office of Information, 'AEGIS Weapon System' (10 January 2019) <www.navy.mil/Resources/Fact-Files/Display-FactFiles/Article/2166739/aegis-weapon-system>, accessed 8 March 2021.

24 David Hambling, 'Turkish military to receive 500 swarming kamikaze drones', *Forbes* (17 June 2020), <www.forbes.com/sites/davidhambling/2020/06/17/turkish-military-to-receive-500-swarming-kamikaze-drones/#4887e2c5251a>, accessed 13 February 2021.

make war too easy or painless, vitiating the precept that war should always be a last resort? Would an AI's lack of human emotions make it less likely to commit atrocities or would that make it an implacable foe? And, in the worst of scenarios, could such weapons eventually shrug off all human control and turn on their makers?

The technological bottleneck

In 1951, at a discussion at the Los Alamos National Laboratory regarding the likelihood of extraterrestrial life, the physicist Enrico Fermi raised a question now known as the Fermi paradox: 'Where is everybody?' If the probability of intelligent life on other planets is high and if, as we have done, it is quite possible for a technologically sophisticated culture to develop autonomous devices capable of going beyond its home planet, then why the great silence? Someone, somewhere, should by now have colonized large portions of the galaxy, if not in person, then with machines.

The futurist Nick Bostrom has suggested that the silence we observe in space must mean that technologically advanced intelligent life is rare, if not unique. He suggests the existence of a 'Great Filter', an evolutionary step difficult for life to transcend. According to Bostrom:

> passing the critical points must be sufficiently improbable – that even with many billions of rolls of the dice, one ends up with nothing: no aliens, no spacecraft, no signals. At least, none that we can detect in our neck of the woods.[25]

This filter could occur early in the evolutionary process, as early as the development of life itself. Ours may be the only planet with life.

---

25 Nick Bostrom, 'Where are they? Why I hope the search for extraterrestrial life finds nothing', *MIT Technology Review* (22 April 2008), <www.technologyreview.com/s/409936/where-are-they>, accessed 13 February 2021.

Experimental attempts to produce life in a laboratory have so far resulted in little more than a few amino acids. But suppose, instead, that life has evolved on multiple planets. If Bostrom's 'Great Filter' lies ahead of us, then it is likely to be a technological bottleneck, a point at which our technology outstrips our ability to control it. Key properties of evolution make such a bottleneck likely. To adapt an old Amish adage, 'We grow too soon powerful and too late smart.'[26]

At first, technology is remarkable at improving a species' ability to cope with the dangers and difficulties of the environment. The harnessing of fire, the development of tools for hunting and planting, the domestication of animals – each allowed humans to flourish. But technology does not always alter the environment for the better. Species are hunted to extinction, agriculture depletes the soil and weapons help us to kill one another. Evolution functions on an individual level, selecting individuals who show an advantage over their competitors and their comrades, inevitably introducing competition between and within a species, where the fitness of one is raised or lowered by the fitness of the other.

The theologian Reinhold Niebuhr warns that the pitfalls lurking in this competition lead to behaviours that we have traditionally labelled 'sin'. While the domination of nature is part of the Genesis mandate, Niebuhr notes that we find ourselves unable to avoid overreaching, overestimating our capabilities. 'Man is a finite spirit, lacking identity with the whole, but yet a spirit capable in some sense of envisaging the whole, so that he easily commits the error of imagining himself the whole which he envisages.'[27] To develop advanced technology, a species would have to have evolved this capacity of envisaging the whole. However, such a capacity inevitably brings foreknowledge of mortality, causing anxiety and dread,

---

26 The original is, 'We grow too soon old and too late smart,' the wisdom of which I can personally attest to.

27 Reinhold Niebuhr, *The Nature and Destiny of Man: A Christian interpretation, volume 1 - human nature* (New York, NY: Charles Scribner's Sons, 1941), 181.

emotions that Niebuhr sees as 'both the source of creativity and the temptation to sin'.[28]

Nuclear weapons were our first 'doomsday' technology, able to destroy our entire planet. Autonomous AI could be another. A species with multiple ways of destroying itself or its environment must have the wisdom not to do so. Essentially, it is a race between the development of technology and the development of morality. If technology wins, we lose. But we have not only developed technologies – we have also developed religions. While, as with our technologies, we have too often deployed our religions in the service of competition and the vain quest for security, we can also deploy them in mutual cooperation and service to one another. Should we hear from other intelligent species, they will have passed through their technological bottleneck, having acquired the wisdom and moral development to surpass the drive of competition and live in harmony. Perhaps they could teach us a thing or two. Should the skies remain silent, then we must either grow up quickly as a species or accept that transience is part of life, not just for individuals but also for civilizations, for species, even, perhaps, for life itself. According to Niebuhr, 'The problem of sin . . . is the problem of life.'[29] That problem may be insurmountable. But, God willing, we may surmount it and use our technological creativity with wisdom and grace.

28 Niebuhr, *The Nature and Destiny of Man*, 185.

29 Niebuhr, *The Nature and Destiny of Man*, 3.

9
The future of humanity

VICTORIA LORRIMAR

At some point in the not-too-distant future will come the Singularity. This apocalyptic event will occur as artificial intelligence transcends human intelligence, breaks away from human control and continues to improve itself in a runaway explosion of intelligence that will probably result in the extinction of the human species, or at least transform it beyond recognition. Robots and AI will take centre stage in a future that we cannot even begin to imagine with our own limited intelligence. At least, that's the future many Silicon Valley technologists are prophesying.

While the popular trope of AI enslaving humans often features in science-fiction depictions of the Singularity, others are more optimistic. Ray Kurzweil, a Google engineer known for his technological predictions, argues that the Singularity is nothing to fear but will, instead, markedly improve the human condition:

> We're going to get more neocortex, we're going to be funnier, we're going to be better at music. We're going to be sexier . . . We're really going to exemplify all the things that we value in humans to a greater degree.[1]

1 Kurzweil, as interviewed in Christianna Reedy, 'Kurzweil claims that the Singularity will happen by 2045: get ready for humanity 2.0', *Futurism* (5 October 2017), <https://futurism.com/kurzweil-claims-that-the-singularity-will-happen-by-2045>, accessed 13 February 2021. See also Ch. 1 of this volume: Christina Bieber Lake, 'Science fiction, AI and our descent into insignificance', 13.

Although dissimilar in many ways from the technological futurist movement, the Christian tradition also anticipates an apocalyptic event that will transform human experience. Eschatology, the theology of 'last things', explores what this transformation involves and what it means for our life in the present. In considering the implications of AI and robotics for Christian eschatology, therefore, we need first to answer two questions: what is the Christian hope, and what role do humans play in bringing it about?

Let's begin by considering the nature of the eschatological future. You might have a vision of heaven in your mind, a particular fate that awaits you in the next life. Perhaps the old picture of angels sitting on fluffy clouds, playing harps, has made way for a newer, trendier version, such as that of the recent television series *The Good Place* (in which 'heaven' involves being matched with your soulmate and eating lots of frozen yogurt). Perhaps your picture of heaven is more biblically informed: a place where lions lie down with lambs and every tear is wiped away, as suffering is removed for ever. Whatever our source material, we most often tend to picture heaven as a place that bears little resemblance to our present experience. It's somewhere else, a place we go when we die. Or, rather than escape to heaven, perhaps you see the Christian hope as a future we are bringing about in the here and now. As one of the defining figures in the Social Gospel movement, the nineteenth-century theologian Walter Rauschenbusch was famous for this kind of understanding.[2] Along with a group of like-minded colleagues, Rauschenbusch viewed the kingdom of God as something that could be built through social action, consummated entirely through human effort.

How do these particular Christian futures relate to the one anticipated by many technology enthusiasts, wherein robots and AI open an ever-increasing intelligence gap between themselves and

2 See, for example, Walter Rauschenbusch, *Christianity and the Social Crisis* (New York, NY: Macmillan, 1907).

humans, and, in so doing, take control of the human future? On the one hand, if the hope that we have as Christians involves the passing away of our present reality, our leaving it behind for eternal bliss in a heavenly realm, then eschatology has very little to do with our technological endeavours in this world. They are unrelated to the shape of Christian hope, except perhaps in the matter of individual piety and salvation. On the other hand, if the *eschaton* is something that will happen simply with the passing of more time, that is, if it is the future of the present, then the development of AI and robotics has enormous consequences for eschatology. They are part of the future that we are building.

Are these the only two options, that we either escape to our eternal home elsewhere or build it here through our own efforts? Surely not. And if we follow in the vein of theologians such as Jürgen Moltmann and N. T. Wright, we arrive at a different understanding of the *eschaton* altogether. This alternative hinges on the relationship between eschatology and time, a relationship that Moltmann illuminates via a contrast between the notion of *futurum* (the future is a continuation of the present) and *adventus* (the future arises from outside time and space as a fulfilment of divine promise).[3]

Adventus (Latin) is a translation of the Greek word *parousia*, which, in Christian usage, refers to the coming of Christ in glory. And it's no coincidence that we link the more general idea of a future 'breaking in' and transforming the present with the coming of Christ – it is the example par excellence of an *adventus* future. This understanding of the *eschaton* doesn't mean it is entirely unrelated to the present either: Moltmann puts forward a convincing argument for understanding Christian eschatology as neither *within* nor *outside* time (that is, neither simple future nor eternal present), but rather a transformation of time: 'With the

3 Jürgen Moltmann, *The Coming of God: Christian eschatology*, tr. Margaret Kohl (London: SCM Press, 1996), 25–6.

coming of God's glory, future time ends and eternal time begins.'[4] We aren't transported to a different realm to experience the fulfilment of Christian hope, yet it doesn't just come to us passively with time either. This *adventus* of Christian hope sits in stark contrast to the *futurum* imagined by technological futurists.

Wright positions authentic Christian hope in respect to a similar contrast. The trenchant 'progress myth', which considers history marching inevitably towards a liberal democratic utopia through evolution, science, technology and enlightened thought, has influenced Christian visions of the future in a similar direction, as the natural outcome of evolutionary optimism. Yet there is an equally strong influence in Christian thinking about the future from an entirely different perspective; the lingering influence of Gnosticism has led some to a 'souls in transit' notion of the future, whereby Christians hope to leave behind fallen material existence altogether for eternity in spirit form.[5]

Although many are accustomed to thinking of heaven as a place entirely separate from earth, in reality, heaven and earth overlap. Wright describes heaven as the 'control room' of earth; heaven is God's space and earth is ours. But they are not intended to be separate; the book of Revelation's depiction of the New Jerusalem coming down from heaven (Revelation 21) is a vision of the future in which heaven and earth fully overlap, and will do so into eternity.

So when we speak of the new creation, we understand it to be in some way related to the existing creation. God doesn't simply wipe away everything and start completely afresh. Neither is this completely foreign to our present circumstances. We often speak of eschatology as a future entity – in some ways, this is because of our limited experience of time as linear. While the full realization of Christian hope is still to come in our temporal experience, it is, at

4 Moltmann, *The Coming of God*, 26.

5 N. T. Wright, *Surprised by Hope* (London: SPCK, 2007).

the same time, a present reality. For God, it has already happened, even as it continues to unfold.

The notion of the 'apocalyptic' is a helpful one with respect to Christian hope. Although 'apocalypse' has largely become synonymous with ideas of Armageddon, of the destruction of the earth (indeed, many dictionaries simply define it as the end of the world), the true meaning of apocalypse is 'revelation', an 'unveiling' of something that was previously unknown. While apocalypse generally pertains to the end times, a biblical understanding of apocalypse is some distance from the Singularity event described in the opening of this chapter. Garrett Green underscores this difference, contending that 'imagining the future apocalyptically is incompatible with imagining it as the indefinite extension of the present into a continuous future'.[6] Instead, we anticipate the *eschaton* with a hope that is expectant, but not optimistic or escapist.[7]

So far, we have dealt with the relationship between the future and the present, the old and the new creation, in terms of *time*. But we have dealt very little with the *substance* of that hope. What does the new creation look like, compared with the old? To answer this, we must draw on a host of other Christian doctrines: our theological understanding of creation, sin and redemption, the Incarnation, and more are all bound up in the eschatological hope that we affirm.

For example, we might ask, what is the purpose of creation? We know that God does not *need* to create but chooses to do so out of love. The triune nature indicates a relationality intrinsic to God that does not require anything additional for fulfilment. So the purpose

6 Garrett Green, 'Imagining the future', in David Fergusson and Marcel Sarot (eds), *The Future as God's Gift: Explorations in Christian eschatology* (Edinburgh: T&T Clark, 2000), 86.

7 'Optimism' is used here in the sense of Terry Eagleton's *Hope Without Optimism* (Charlottesville, Va: University of Virginia Press, 2015). Eagleton considers optimism to be more an artefact of temperament than a measure of reality.

of creation is not to meet a need of God's. To understand this question, we look to Jesus Christ, the Word made flesh, as God's fullest revelation to us. The revelation of God in Jesus is essential for understanding our own nature and destiny.

The Incarnation gives us a glimpse into the future God intends for us. Jesus, fully human and fully God, is a paradigm for the union of creation with God. Although we understand the Incarnation to be 'for us and for our salvation', it is about far more than just atonement. Yes, the work of Christ is a remedy for sin, but it also reveals a greater hope. It is a part of God's plan from the very beginning to draw the creation into ever closer union with the divine, and the Incarnation is central to this purpose. This doesn't pose a threat to the original goodness of creation, by the way. Think of a newborn: no one says that babies are not perfect as they are, but they are also intended to grow, to realize the potential with which they were born. The capacity for growth is not the opposite of perfection.

Wright summarizes the Christian hope thus: 'What the creator God has done in Jesus Christ, and supremely in his resurrection, is what he intends to do for the whole world.'[8] And what has God done in Jesus? In his person, Jesus represents the complete union of humanity and divinity. Many scholars argue the notion of 'deep incarnation' – that Jesus, although human, stands as representative of *all* creation; in the Incarnation God meets all created matter.[9] In the resurrection of Jesus, we preview the future that awaits the whole creation: transformation, glorification and perfection. This transformed existence is so far from our present experience that we cannot properly conceive of it; this is a characteristic of *adventus* hope.

Now let's take up the second question identified earlier: what role do humans play in the fulfilment of this eschatological hope? In

8 Wright, *Surprised by Hope*, 103.

9 For one example, see Niels Gregersen, 'Deep incarnation: why evolutionary continuity matters in Christology', *Toronto Journal of Theology*, vol. 26, no. 2 (2010), 173–87.

fact, we may expand this question to ask what our role is in God's work, in the world more generally; eschatology is, after all, the final act in the same story God began writing with the creation of all things.

If the eschatological future is related in some way to the present, then it makes sense to argue that what we do in the here and now is also relevant to that future in some way. There is an argument that can be made from Scripture, and advanced at various stages throughout history, that humans act as 'co-creators' with God. 'Co-creation' can be a vague term; its use and interpretation ranges from a synonym for stewardship, to a near equal partnership with God.[10] Acknowledging the potential for misinterpretation, 'co-creation' is used here as a theological term that attributes a role to humans in ongoing creation, distinct from and subordinate to God's work of creation and contrasted with a notion of humans as merely vehicles or passive recipients of God's creation. Co-creation theologies have been put forward by thinkers focused on the arts and literature (for example, J. R. R. Tolkien and Trevor Hart) and the sciences (for instance, Arthur Peacocke and Philip Hefner).[11]

The theologian Trevor Hart suggests that we view creation as 'a project divinely begun and established, yet one that is handed over to us with "more to be made of it yet"'.[12] He explores the biblical portrayal of God as divine artist and concludes that

> at various key points in the story of God's creative fashioning of a world fit for his own indwelling with us, divine

10 Anna Case-Winters, 'Rethinking the image of God', *Zygon*, vol. 39, no. 4 (2004), 821.

11 Note that only Peacocke and Hefner use the specific term 'co-creation' (A. R. Peacocke, *Creation and the World of Science: The Bampton Lectures, 1978* (Oxford: Clarendon Press, 1979), 304; Philip Hefner, *The Human Factor: Evolution, culture, and religion* (Minneapolis, Minn.: Fortress Press, 1993), 27). Tolkien uses the terminology of 'sub-creation' and Trevor Hart presents a similar notion in *Making Good: Creation, creativity, and artistry* (Waco, Tex.: Baylor University Press, 2014). For Tolkien, see 'On fairy-stories', in *Tree and Leaf* (London: HarperCollins, 2001), 1–81.

12 Hart, *Making Good*, 8.

> artistry actively solicits a corresponding creaturely creativity, apart from which the project cannot and will not come to fruition.[13]

Lest this be interpreted as hubris, however, Hart also shows how our understanding of artistry has shifted under Renaissance and Enlightenment thought. 'Craftmanship', as we understand it now, is a more helpful term. God is the master craftsman, with humans analogous to the apprentice in the master's workshop. In such an analogy, there are established boundaries and lines of authority, traditional ways of working and standards of quality that apply. Within this context, though, genuine freedom and ingenuity operate, nurtured and schooled within the Master's domain.[14] The 'otherness' of God must not be undermined in the analogy of human creativity to divine.[15]

The scholar and author J. R. R. Tolkien, best known for *The Lord of the Rings*, describes humans in a similar fashion, using the term 'sub-creator', highlighting the fact that our creative work is always subordinate to God's. He uses three poignant metaphors to capture his point.

First, he refers to the work that we undertake as the 'effoliation of creation'. Tolkien frequently uses the language of trees and leaves in his ideas that human creativity elaborates on what God has made. While we cannot design a new leaf entirely, he writes, 'each leaf . . . is a unique embodiment of the pattern' originally set down by God. Its derivative nature doesn't diminish its worth: 'Spring is, of course, not really less beautiful because we have seen or heard of other like events,' he observes.[16] Sub-creation is the fulfilment of latent possibilities, present from the first creation.

13 Hart, *Making Good*, 37.

14 Hart, *Making Good*, 43.

15 Hart, *Making Good*, 21.

16 Tolkien, 'On fairy-stories', 56–7.

A second metaphor that Tolkien uses for human creativity is the idea of 'splintered light'.[17] White light can be refracted through a crystal into the full spectrum of colours. We humans act like a crystal, Tolkien suggests. We do not generate light on our own but, instead, draw on God's light. Yet from that light, we are able to produce something new after a fashion, a particular hue that would not exist apart from us.

Tolkien's third metaphor for creativity is that of making music. In a fictional creation myth (which we find in *The Silmarillion*), Tolkien sketches a participatory model of creativity, with God inviting the created beings to adorn his major music theme with their own artistic efforts.[18] The resultant harmony develops God's original theme, that is, the created ones do not create in the same way as God but rather ornament the divine creation. Nevertheless, they make a distinct contribution to God's creation with a sense of both freedom and responsibility.

Of course, Tolkien is writing fiction and a lot of his ideas relate mainly to literature (but not exclusively; there is an indication in his work that he hoped these insights might apply to real-world activity as well). Further, it might seem strange to invoke Tolkien's thought in a piece on AI and robots; he was notorious for his suspicion of technology (this suspicion comes across clearly in much of his fiction, and he was reported to have scrawled: 'Not a penny for Concorde!' over one of his tax returns). The idea of co-creation isn't just relegated to art and make-believe, though. To give one example, we find it in the work of Philip Hefner, a scholar who has contributed enormously to the field of science and religion.

Hefner speaks of humans as 'created co-creators', having both freedom and responsibility to participate in ongoing creation. He draws heavily on scientific methodology in developing this

17 J. R. R. Tolkien, 'Mythopoeia', in *Tree and Leaf* (London: HarperCollins, 2001), 87.

18 J. R. R. Tolkien, *The Silmarillion* (London: HarperCollins, 1999), 15–22.

understanding of human being, and (unlike Tolkien) sees technology as part of this co-creative agency. For Hefner, using technology to improve the world is a natural human instinct that comes from being made in God's image; we represent God's freedom, love and intentionality when we act as created co-creators.

What does this mean for eschatology? A true grasp of Christian hope should lead us away from patient endurance into action. As Jürgen Moltmann puts it, 'The goad of the promised future stabs inexorably into the flesh of every unfulfilled present.'[19] Richard Bauckham and Trevor Hart make the similar case that 'hope transfigures the present precisely by enabling us to transcend it imaginatively and, upon our return, to perceive all too clearly its lacks and needs'.[20] Hope should make us uneasy, should compel us to work to set things right as far as we are able.

Christian hope is about discovering what God is doing in creation – for us and *with* us. Bauckham and Hart capture the implications of such a discovery. It

> sets us free even now to be active in pursuit of correspondence to our eschatological destiny, confident in the knowledge that we shall not be forced to rely on our own resources in doing so, and set free from the otherwise crushing burden of responsibility for the ultimate outcomes.[21]

Considering the question of AI and robots and their relationship to eschatology, therefore, we find ourselves in the realm of ethics; discerning the implications of technology and its uses becomes a matter for moral reflection, much like any other ethical issue.

---

19 Jürgen Moltmann, *Theology of Hope: On the ground and the implications of a Christian eschatology* (London: SCM Press, 1967), 21.

20 Richard Bauckham and Trevor Hart, 'The shape of time', in Fergusson and Sarot (eds), *The Future as God's Gift*, 62.

21 Bauckham and Hart, 'The shape of time', 71.

Eschatology isn't just speculation about the future, after all, but an understanding of how it reconfigures our perception and experience of the present, and what it means for how we live now. Instead of focusing on 'end-of-days' scenarios, we realize that questions such as 'What is the good life?', 'What is my vocation?' or 'What does it look like for creation to flourish?' are all eschatological ones. And this is where Christian reflection is particularly worthwhile, exploring the assumptions about flourishing that underpin particular visions of a technological future (including the development of AI and human-like machines).[22]

To what ends do we create robots and AI? According to the transhumanist Anders Sandberg, questions of flourishing and the meaning of life have largely been overlooked in scholarly debates around technological enhancement (which includes robotics and AI).[23] Reflecting on the implicit ends to which technology is most often employed in transhumanist thought, Christina Bieber Lake nevertheless contends that

> to define transcendence as the inevitable outcome of technologically driven human evolution represents not only a phenomenon unique to the twentieth and twenty-first centuries but also a rejection of thousands of years of philosophical and theological thinking about what constitutes the highest and best life available to human beings.[24]

22 See Michael Burdett and Victoria Lorrimar, 'Creatures bound for glory: biotechnological enhancement and visions of human flourishing', *Studies in Christian Ethics*, vol. 32, no. 2 (2019), 241–53; Victoria Lorrimar, 'Human flourishing, joy, and the prospect of radical life extension', *Expository Times*, vol. 129, no. 12 (2018), 554–61.

23 Anders Sandberg, 'Transhumanism and the meaning of life', in Calvin R. Mercer and Tracy J. Trothen (eds), *Religion and Transhumanism: The unknown future of human enhancement* (Santa Barbara, Calif.: Praeger Publishers, 2015), 8.

24 Christina Bieber Lake, *Prophets of the Posthuman: American fiction, biotechnology, and the ethics of personhood* (Notre Dame, Ind.: University of Notre Dame Press, 2013), xii.

This notion of inevitable transcendence is the latest iteration of the kind of utopian thought critiqued by Wright and many other Christian thinkers. Not only does it not align with a Christian account of eschatological hope, but it does not always match up with the reality of technology in the present either. If we look at how AI and robotic technology is most often employed now, we might gain further insight into the underlying assumptions of human flourishing that operate. Significant proportions of the robotics research industry are focused on applications for sex and war, two domains of human activity where moral questions pile in. If we probe beneath the stated utopian aspirations of many technologists, we see that often enhancement technologies are based on ideas of the good life that neglect the majority world and, far from achieving transcendence, will only increase existing inequalities.[25]

Hopeful Christians, recognizing their own part in working towards an *adventus* future that is ultimately the work of God, will practise discernment over the use of AI and robotic technologies within this framework. With a proper understanding of Christian hope, we see robots as neither our salvation nor Armageddon. Like all technology, they may be developed towards noble or deplorable ends, and used for good or malevolent purposes. As Christians, this is where we ought to direct our enquiry, to interrogate and expose where intent and goals are cause for concern, and to advocate the wise use of emerging technologies in service of kingdom ends. Christian hope rightly conceived is galvanizing.

Whether the new creation will include robots and AI is an interesting question, albeit speculative. To what extent will our own creations endure into the new creation? Although Tolkien would have been appalled by the notion of artificial intelligence, he certainly hoped that our own sub-creative efforts would carry over

25 Tom Shakespeare, 'Foreword', in Miriam Eilers, Katrin Grüber and Christoph Rehmann-Sutter (eds), *The Human Enhancement Debate and Disability: New bodies for a better life* (London: Palgrave Macmillan, 2014), xii.

and be perfected in the new creation (his short story *Leaf by Niggle* depicts this hope charmingly). Returning to the earlier discussion of the *telos* of creation, the insistence that the new creation is not a return to an Edenic innocence, but rather a fulfilment of potential and purpose that were present from the very beginning, leaves room for the perfection of our own creations, including technological ones. This only increases our responsibility to create wisely and well.

Other contributions in this volume have addressed some of the social consequences of robotics and AI. The question of whether human creations might attain their own personhood is highly debated, and the eschatological implications of an affirmative answer are beyond the scope of this chapter. It's worth noting, however, that the God of the gospel is a generous God, and the nature and extent of salvation has often taken believers by surprise. Jesus, who came preaching peace and the forgiveness of sins, was a surprise to those expecting a conquering Messiah who would overthrow their Roman oppressors. The early Jewish Christians were surprised when the Holy Spirit was given to Gentiles, and many were surprised again that these new converts did not have to follow the law of Moses. We have a God who is able to do immeasurably more than we can imagine, and we are still working to grasp the breadth and length and height and depth of divine love. Whether this love is wide enough to encompass robots and AI in the reconciliation of all creation to God is something we do not know while we see only as through a glass darkly. But as we await clear vision and God's new creation, we use our co-creative abilities in building the kingdom as far as we can.

Part 3

ETHICAL AND SOCIAL ISSUES

10

Sextech: simulated relationships with machines

ANDREW GRAYSTONE

A soldier is sent on a six-month tour of duty in a foreign country. Among the many home comforts he will miss, one of the biggest is regular sex with his long-term partner. Could a digitally enabled sex robot help to bridge the gap in their relationship? A student goes to study in a city far from home. She wants to remain faithful to her boyfriend, but wonders whether they can sustain the relationship over three years with hardly any opportunities for sex. Would hooking up via a 'sextech' device over the Internet be a good way to keep their long-distance love alive? A man tells his therapist that he can't control his urge to sexually abuse children. Should the therapist prescribe a child-like robot as a harm-free alternative, like methadone for a heroin addict?

Most people don't have an ethical problem with couples using medical or mechanical interventions to facilitate or enhance their sex lives, such as the use of lubricants, drugs or devices to counter sexual dysfunction, although the balance between replacement and enhancement is a contested area, for instance in the theology of disability. Sextech takes a significant further step, providing access to sensation and the semblance of sexual encounter, but without human touch. We have to consider whether and how that matters. 'Sextech' is a broad term for digital technology used to provide a connection with, or a substitute for, another person in a sexual encounter.

Phone contact between remote partners has been available for many decades and, more recently, it has been possible for lovers and friends to connect by video, too. Now we are beginning to add a further dimension to the experience. Haptic technology – which reproduces the sensation of touch – can enable two or more people who are physically distant to engage in a form of sexual interaction mediated by the Internet. A robot can stand in for the missing partner. It can be designed to look roughly human and programmed to imitate the sexual behaviour of a lover, including the sounds and movements of sex. A sex 'doll' can sound and feel a bit like a human partner and can emulate his or her sexual responses in real time, even though the partner is far away or exists only in the imagination. Fully fledged sex robots have a long-established place in science fiction but, so far, they have proven to be very expensive and largely unattractive for most potential customers. However, more basic alternatives, known as teledildonics, are already available. A man is typically equipped with a prosthetic in the form of an electromechanical latex device, designed to look and feel like a vagina, while a woman is equipped with a corresponding device that simulates a penis. These two objects and their users may be geographically distant, but they are connected via the Internet, allowing each person to have some control over the movement within the other person's device. In this way, it is possible for two (or more) people to stimulate each other, albeit rather crudely as yet, even though they are physically distant. If you don't have a willing partner, it is also possible to programme the devices to provide stimulation for an individual. Couple your teledildonic equipment with a virtual reality headset, which adds sound and three-dimensional images to the haptic effect, and you can produce a highly immersive quasi-sexual experience.

Teledildonic devices take their place in a long line of mechanical and electrical devices used by women and men for sexual stimulation throughout the ages, but they cross a fundamental boundary, in that digitally mediated sex need not be limited by geography or history. A form of sex can take place when the participants are spatially and temporally remote from each other. It can be replayed and repeated irrespective of the particular place or point in time at which it was generated. In this way, it is possible for teledildonics, at least partially, to overcome some of the limitations of physicality, such as age, distance and disability. It also allows the creation and marketing of sex programs that enable an individual to experience sex synthetically with a celebrity or an idealized partner. It is increasingly possible to customize synthetic sexual experiences to match the preferences of the user. There is no theoretical reason, for instance, why a widow should not continue to enjoy a form of replicated sexual intimacy with her husband after his death, why a celebrity should not market digital versions of sexual encounters with a high degree of realism, or why an individual man or woman should not stimulate any number of partners simultaneously.

The 'yuck' factor that some may feel when thinking about these sex aids is balanced against a number of possible advantages for the user. Unlike a human partner, a machine is always available; it will never give you a disease or leave you pregnant; it can be programmed to meet virtually any sexual preference, but it will make no emotional or financial demands.

The purpose of this chapter is not to measure these possibilities against conventional notions of sexual ethics, but to consider some of the cultural shifts that might be represented by the new technologies and the broad areas of political and theological challenge that arise. We will look briefly at five areas in which sextech challenges us: the marketization of sexual pleasure, the tension between simulation and authenticity, sexual normativity, the sacramental nature of the body and the social nature of sex.

1 The marketization of sexual pleasure

In its simplest form, sex is a private and cost-free activity that appears to have no overlap with the market economy. At best, acts of sex represent the purest form of transaction between two people. Unmediated sex involves a mutual, non-contingent exchange of benefits. It's not a matter of 'I do this for you' or 'You do this for me' but 'We do this for us'. It is the mutuality of sex that marks it as different from a gift or the creative undertaking of an individual. However, as we know, things are not always that simple.

Not only is sex often bought and sold, but sexual pleasure has been commodified to generate a complex industry of sexual aids, stimulants and devices. An intermediary enters into the relationship, saying, 'Buy this, join this or download this, and it will make your experience better.' The twentieth century saw significant developments in the commodification of sexual experiences. A secondary market in artefacts for use in sex developed, starting in the doctor's surgery and moving to the high street. What were previously described as 'sex aids' became 'sex toys', and are now available at parties and pound shops. When goods, including sexual pleasure, are commodified in this way, they become subject to the forces of the market. This opens up a great many possibilities, including ownership, advertising, credit and debit, and the production of secondary goods to enhance the trade.

When sex enters the digital realm, even in such a crude form as teledildonics, both mechanical and corporate intermediaries are involved, just as they are in the transfer of data about shopping preferences or images uploaded to the Internet. Wherever money changes hands, sex becomes ethically problematic, especially so when an intermediary is involved in the transaction.

One example of the ways in which teledildonics lends itself to marketization is the 'gamification' of sexual encounter. Gamification is the intentional application of elements of game-playing (such as competition, point scoring, challenges and rewards) as incentives in the marketing of goods. It typically appeals to the competitive side of a consumer's nature and is a key driver in digital marketing. Digital mediation in sexual encounter makes it possible for third parties to record, collect, publish, compare and repeat an individual's sexual history for profit. The desire for self-monitoring is part of postmodernity's fascination with embodiment. Teledildonic devices offer to provide feedback on and review sexual interactions, and publish the results online in much the same way that devices such as Fitbit can track and publish data about an individual's exercise, weight and sleep patterns. If this is extended to sexual performance, a similar reduction might occur – reducing sex to numbers of thrusts, body temperature, strength of orgasm or whatever else can be measured. The widely available Fleshlight, for example, is marketed as a sexual 'stamina trainer'.

In a culture of quantified performance comparison, the monitoring and sharing of sexual engagement reinforces the conception of sex as a service that can be rated, in the way that Tripadvisor allows the rating of hotels and eBay encourages the rating of vendors. By turning sex from a mutual gift to a transaction, a range of third-party values enter the equation. How reliable can we expect a person's online sexual history to be? Who will own the datafication of one's sexual experience?

In her work on sex robots, Kathleen Richardson raises concerns about such marketization, based on the asymmetry in digitally mediated sexual relationships.[1] She draws parallels between the use of machine-robots for sex and prostitution. In prostitution, only the purchaser of sex has full status as a subject. This status is not attributed to the sex worker, who may be dehumanized,

1 Kathleen Richardson, *Sex Robots: The end of love* (Cambridge: Polity Press, 2019).

reconstructed and renamed in the image desired by the purchaser, and then required to enact pleasure in return for money.

In conventional prostitution, the one who pays for sex and the one who provides it are often dependent on third-party brokers, who have the potential to exploit the needs of both purchaser and provider. At first glance, it might seem that teledildonic equipment could resolve the imbalance of power in these relationships. A robot can't be exploited, and if two people are using sex equipment, they can have equal access to the 'off' switch. But that is to assume that the only people involved in the transaction are the users of the equipment. In practice, the contract for sex takes place within a wider cultural context in which society and the state have decisive roles. Individuals who use sextech don't do so in isolation. They are dependent on third parties in the form of the manufacturers of the devices and the apps through which they operate, and also on the manufacturers of the computers or smartphones and the Internet service providers, who transmit the signals. By interposing the means of distribution into the sex relationship, sexual pleasure becomes open to the engagement of the market or the state in terms of control, surveillance and so on. In addition, while, during a conventional sexual encounter, the experience is self-contained, a digital sexual encounter produces a distinct and separate artefact in the form of a digital file that carries its own moral and cultural weight. If a sexual act is recorded and stored in the form of a computer file, who owns that information and what is that individual or organization entitled to do with it? Sextech creates intermediaries in the relationship. As much as the user is acting upon the machine, so also the machine, in its commercial and political nexus, is acting upon the user, shaping and even exploiting his or her social and sexual vulnerability. When sexual apparatus becomes a commodity, the market will create its own dynamic of relative values and upselling, of consumer choice, envy and obsolescence, just as it does with every other electrical product.

2 Simulation and authenticity

A second area in which the development of teledildonics marks a cultural shift is the tension between simulation and authenticity – between what is synthesized and what is 'real'. Sextech users may even find themselves conflicted and confused about whether they are, in fact, relating to a human being or to a machine.

The fact that content is digitally mediated doesn't necessarily mean that the human emotions of the producer or recipient are not genuine. Digitally mediated content can evoke very real responses, such as laughter, disgust or compassion. However, the collapse of context – the detachment from space and time – that is inherent in digital communication takes the subjects to an 'uncanny' area in which it is impossible to know whether what they are interacting with is 'real' or constructed. Vital information is lost in digital transmission. If one partner cuts his or her part of the equipment, the other will not bleed. Technology opens a gap between the imaginative work of the mind and the physical expression of the body. Neither partner can be confident that he or she is not being deceived.

We know that human skin receives touch data in a great many forms: pressure, movement, friction, pain, moisture and more besides. In addition, there is contextual information in a sexual encounter in real time and space, such as smell, chemical stimulation and a great deal more that cannot be conveyed by the teledildonic devices currently available. Clever as the technology is, every mechanical enhancement also represents a diminution. As some sensations are simulated and prioritized, others are de-prioritized or lost altogether. Evidence suggests that, in contemporary culture, many people are prepared to surrender some apparently fundamental aspects of encounter for other benefits, such as hygiene, aesthetic convenience or guaranteed orgasms. Sherry Turkle frequently explores the notion that artificial devices may be 'alive enough' to satisfy most people's relational expectations. Her anxieties about the easy trade-off between simulation and authenticity are ontological: 'After several generations of living in the computer culture, simulation will become fully naturalized. Authenticity in the traditional sense loses its value, a vestige of another time.'[2] And this is by no means inconsequential:

> If our experience with relational artefacts is based on a fundamentally deceitful interchange, can it be good for us? Or might it be good for us in the 'feel good' sense, but bad for us in our lives as moral beings?[3]

Turkle wants to know what these developments are doing to our sense of ourselves, our relationships and our bodies. How much this matters is a question of judgement.

3 Sexual normativity

Conventional pornographies tend to objectify the sexual parts of the human body and idealize or fetishize them. Skin is young and smooth, and bodies are hairless. Digital technology goes further, allowing individuals to adapt or modify the representation of their digitally mediated or real-life sexual partners. For example, sextech allows you to experience what it might be like to have sex with your partner if her or his body (or yours) were in some way enhanced. What would sex feel like if you had bigger or smaller breasts, or your partner had a bigger penis? You need only adjust the program to find out. Alternatively, an individual could choose to programme the haptic and visual aspects of the device separately. That way it

2 Sherry Turkle, 'Edge Annual Question 2006: what is your dangerous idea?', *Edge* (n.d.), <www.edge.org/response-detail/11368>, accessed 13 February 2021. In this volume, other authors draw on Turkle's work: see Ch. 5, Vinoth Ramachandra, 'AI and robots: some Asian approaches', 84, and Ch. 12, John Wyatt, 'The impact of AI and robotics on health and social care', 186, 191 and 196.

3 Turkle, 'What is your dangerous idea?'

would be possible to have a mediated haptic sexual experience with one person, perhaps a real-life partner, while visualizing someone else. People with disabilities or disfigurement might (or might not) choose to modify the representation of their own bodies to their partners. Users would have a degree of control over their own and their partners' sexual responses. A man who experienced premature ejaculation might be able to turn down the intensity of sensation he received to a level he prefers – or vice versa. In this way, individuals could synthesize, modify or create immersive sexual experiences, real or imagined, human or not, with a high degree of verisimilitude.

One of the perverse features of digital culture is that choice does not necessarily lead to variety. On the contrary, with all the possibilities available, sextech tends to reverse the liberal trend in sexual culture by reinforcing sexual normativity. The dependence of teledildonics on the market leads to a highly gendered construction of sex and sexual pleasure. Sextech prioritizes male pleasure over female and heterosexual use over homosexual. Significantly, the vast majority of sex dolls marketed thus far are modelled on young white or Asian women. Most of the unique contextual information, the proximity and intimacy, that would be present in a skin-to-skin encounter, is stripped out by the limitations of digital mediation. What is left is a purely haptic and genital experience, heavily focused on penetration and constructed towards orgasm as *telos*, in which the male is the primary subject and the female the object, and which is in itself much closer to rape than the nuanced and complex tactility of conventional sex.

In his 1939 essay *The Work of Art in the Age of Mechanical Reproduction*, Walter Benjamin wrote about the ways that technology reorganizes the sense of touch into an instrument of concussion.[4] Teledildonic equipment is a prime example: it is marketed heavily to women but designed primarily for male pleasure. The 'female' device

4 Available in English at <www.marxists.org/reference/subject/philosophy/works/ge/benjamin.htm>, accessed 13 February 2021.

is essentially passive, and engages only the vaginal wall, while the 'male' device is designed to simulate penetration and pre-orgasmic vaginal thrusting. In addition, teledildonic devices are designed to represent the human genitals in an idealized state – young, hairless, healthy and responsive – and to recreate a predominantly heterosexual and male construction of sexual pleasure, in which the individual orgasm is isolated as the sole goal of sexual encounter. If the vibrator has become a tool of liberation for women of all ages, do teledildonic devices represent a return to an oppressive construction of sexual pleasure? Or might they allow for a form of controlled sexual engagement that is rather less invasive, more sterile and therefore less potentially exploitative than conventional sex?

4 The sacrament of touch

Elisabeth Moltmann-Wendel wrote in 1995 that 'the body has emerged from the shadow of the head in recent years'.[5] What she meant was that the Enlightenment tendency to define physicality against rationality, and feeling against understanding, had been superseded thanks, in no small part, to feminist analysis offering more holistic understandings that recognize feelings as the basis for knowledge, encompassing rationality but not limited by it. Digitally synthesized touch runs counter to that trend.

Most cultures agree that the physical encounter between two (or more) bodies, whether in love or violence, carries a particular cultural and ethical weight. Lisa Isherwood writes that history 'is . . . written on the body and by the body'.[6] Meanings attached to the body therefore have a central importance, and hence anything that appears to be synthetic is of fundamental significance. Christian theology, for

5 Elisabeth Moltmann-Wendel, *I Am My Body: A theology of embodiment* (London: Bloomsbury Academic, 1995), 84.

6 Lisa Isherwood and Elizabeth Stuart, *Introducing Body Theology*, Introductions in Feminist Theology (Sheffield: Sheffield Academic Press, 1998), 36.

example, traditionally suggests that the human body is a special case among objects, not because it is any less subject to the physical laws of history and geography, but because *sōma* (body), as St Paul describes it, has a unique social and spiritual significance. It is heavy with meaning. In Islamic theology, this weight is represented by the prohibition of representations of the body in art or manufacture because the true knowledge of God is conveyed through the body. In Judaeo-Christian theology, physical representations of God are forbidden.

According to a significant strand of theological thought, the physical persona has a sacramental significance in Christian theology. The body is the location of moral agency. The person each of us is morally and spiritually is identical with the person each of us is physically. The instrumentalizing of machines through transferring to them human-like qualities such as pain, dignity and rights may be seen as a form of idolatry. Sextech crosses a line in the construction of body identity by prioritizing the projection of the body's meaning over its physical reality. It implies that a machine can take over some of the functionality of a human sexual partner. It is part of a wider 'flattening' of culture, in which significance is widely distributed but evenly weighted. This has immediate implications for human interactions. The most profoundly social aspects of life risk becoming merely cultural objects. For example, a couple's first sexual encounter is usually heavy with meaning, but if that encounter is recorded and stored as digital information, it has no physical and little cultural weight. It can be copied, edited and carried around on a memory stick that also contains culturally trivial items, such as a shopping list or a half-finished computer game.

At the heart of the sacramentality of the human person is the sense of touch. The cultural and theological meanings of human touch are complex, but they are always freighted. It is impossible for a healthy human to separate touch from its social significance. Touch has a sacramental significance in the transmission of healing and blessing that is universally recognized in religious traditions, and also in spheres such as health care, history and the arts. That is why religions, including Judaism and Christianity, have often restricted touch as a way of preserving the holiness of sacred places, objects and people.

In Western culture, the physical body is often seen as a metaphor for wholeness in the political body. Graham Ward notes that the postmodern fascination with embodiment, expressed through a focus on physical fitness, diet and sexual performance, has ironically coincided with a cultural devaluation of the body as little more than a clothes horse, 'a billboard for the accumulation of brand names'.[7] Correspondingly, the construction of an artificial penis or vagina risks rendering the cutaneous body parts little more than agents of neural pleasure sensation.

The facility to stimulate another person without direct physical contact is perhaps the single most significant feature of teledildonic equipment. Whether the initial stimulation comes from the skin of another human or from a device is superficially irrelevant, but, even without the theological accretions outlined above, human-to-human touch has immense cultural significance. We use phrases such as 'I'm touched by your concern' or 'I feel your pain' to indicate intimacy and empathy. This is hardly surprising, since the areas of the brain that process touch are the same areas that process emotion and identity. The neuroscientist David Linden writes: 'There is, in fact, no pure touch sensation, for by the time we have perceived a touch, it has been blended with other sensory input, plans for action, expectation, and a healthy dose of emotion.'[8]

To echo Sherry Turkle's question, we need to ask whether the synthetic touch reproduced by a device such as a sex robot or a

7 Graham Ward, 'The metaphysics of the body', in Elaine L. Graham and Grace Jantzen (eds), *Redeeming the Present* (London: Ashgate, 2009), 161.

8 David J. Linden, *Touch: The science of the sense that makes us human* (London: Penguin, 2016), 6.

teledildonic penis or vagina is 'real enough'. The computational neuroscientist, Professor Peter Robinson (whose Introduction begins this volume), would answer, 'No'. He describes computers as 'functionally autistic' – unable to determine the emotions that are essentially linked to touch. I suggest that most people would instinctively want to say that a sexual relationship between a human and a robot or a computer, while it might be pleasurable, is of lesser value than an encounter between two embodied humans. In the wider context of companion robots, Sherry Turkle suggests that as machines get better, we have lower expectations of one another.[9] Functionalism creeps into relationships, so that mediated sex acts tend to be essentially masturbatory. There is a world of difference between 'I feel your touch' and 'I feel like I feel your touch'.

5 The social nature of sex

Well before the commercial availability of teledildonics, Linda Woodhead wrote presciently that if

> sex can only be understood as the individual's free quest for intense pleasure this seems . . . to turn all sexual behaviour into a form of masturbation. It becomes impossible to understand sexual activity in terms of anything which transcends the individual – whether that be a relationship or an institution. Sex's sole *telos* becomes the pleasure of the free individual; even when sexual pleasure is brought about by the agency of the other rather than the self, it ceases to have any meaning beyond the pleasure it brings to the self.[10]

9 See Sherry Turkle, *Alone Together: Why we expect more from technology and less from each other* (New York, NY: Basic Books, 2011).

10 Linda Woodhead, 'Sex in a wider context', in Jon Davies and Gerard Loughlin (eds), *Sex These Days: Essays on theology, sexuality and society* (Sheffield: Sheffield Academic Press, 1997), 101.

This creates an ethical and social context in which sex may be generative (meaning positively creative in physical and/or social terms) or it may be exploitative. Normatively, sex is reflexive, so that the generativity or destructiveness is written on to the bodies of both parties. Digitally mediated sex, perhaps a little like tickling, takes place in an uncanny hinterland of assumed mutuality, where it isn't clear who is the object and who is the subject, or whether the act is generative or exploitative.

The anthropomorphism of things, and the way that gender, class and sexuality are inflected in the cultural production of technological artefacts, always has a social dynamic. The rights of an 'other' are nothing more than the rights we believe for ourselves transferred; the meanings that we give to machines reflect back to us what we think is valuable. Much of the discussion about the provision of child sex dolls to paedophiles centres on the idea that a doll cannot be harmed, as it doesn't have the capacity to feel pain or shame. Yet the way we treat machines reflects our own self-understanding: in abusing a human-like doll, we degrade ourselves.

Sex in all its forms is a social act; it has a role in building and strengthening human community. It may happen behind closed doors, but it is neither an individual nor a private experience or else it loses this creative effect. By contrast, sex that is digitally mediated is necessarily private and exclusive to the couple; its creative function is limited to the pleasure of the individuals involved. It is one of the paradoxes of Christian theology that the creative dynamic of sex is grounded in the denial of self, in risk, sacrifice and pain. The use of sextech, by dint of the fact that it offers a guarantee of safety and pleasure without loss of agency or privacy, may actually be a denial of the essential vulnerability of the sexual encounter. It is fair to ask, if the act is enacted on a teledildonic device rather than a body, whether it is sex at all.

Conclusion

There is no doubt that a teledildonic device or a sex robot may function well enough to provide a crude level of sexual stimulation. It may be 'real enough' for some people, for some purposes. But the synthesizing of touch crosses a significant boundary in the cultural and theological meanings of intimacy. Sextech locates sexual encounter firmly in the entertainment industry. It assumes that personal pleasure and individual choice are the premier benefits on offer. But it has the effect of narrowing choice. Digitally mediated sex de-essentializes the individual body, with all the attendant risks of marginalizing women and their pleasure. The substantial focus on the reliable delivery of a male orgasm runs the risk of negating the social dimensions of sex, its unitive, creative and healing functions, and turning an intentional and mutual sexual interaction from a sacramental gift into nothing more than a consumer product.

11
Are the robots coming for our jobs?

NIGEL CAMERON

> We are being afflicted with a new disease of which some readers may not yet have heard the name, but of which they will hear a great deal in the years to come – namely, technological unemployment. This means unemployment due to our discovery of means of economising the use of labour outrunning the pace at which we can find new uses for labour.[1]

It seems almost quaint to read John Maynard Keynes's worries about robots taking our jobs way back in 1930! But in his famous essay on technology and the future, he was, as ever, looking ahead.

The most influential economist of the twentieth century, Keynes laid out with startling clarity the employment implications of technology getting ahead of the labour market. Twenty years later, in the USA, the mathematician Norbert Wiener, known as the father of cybernetics (he made up the word), said much the same thing. As he looked forward, he also looked back and drew a precise parallel with the 'slave economy' – writing, of course, at a time when Americans born into slavery were still alive. In a slave economy, the slaveholder always wins; slaves are just cheaper. It's a parallel that reminds us of the origin of the word 'robot' – first coined by the Czech writer Karel Čapek in his 1920 play *R.U.R.*:

---

1 John Maynard Keynes, 'Economic possibilities for our grandchildren' (1930), in *Essays in Persuasion* (New York, NY: Harcourt Brace, 1932), 358–73.

Rossum's Universal Robots and derived from the Czech word for a serf or a slave.

'Let us remember', Wiener wrote,

> that the automatic machine, whatever we think of any feelings it may have or may not have, is the precise economic equivalent of slave labor. Any labor which competes with slave labor must accept the economic conditions of slave labor. It is perfectly clear that this will produce an unemployment situation, in comparison with which the present recession and even the depression of the thirties will seem a pleasant joke.[2]

Or, as the US computer scientist and entrepreneur Marshall Brain has said, we need to prepare for the coming of a 'second intelligent species'.[3] That's a provocative way of putting it, and we need to be provoked!

Here's how I open my book, *The Robots Are Coming: Us, them and God*:

> The world will soon be teeming with new creatures. It will be the most dramatic change in the history of the human race. It promises to be wonderful, and to be terrible, but above all to be confusing. Because these life-forms will be made by us.
>
> They won't be people. They won't be animals. But also they won't be 'things' in the sense in which we have understood 'things' in the past. We don't yet know much about Them and how They will develop. But we can be sure of some facts: They are developing very fast. They are smart – and will keep on getting smarter. They will take on more and more of the tasks

2 Norbert Wiener, *The Human Use of Human Beings: Cybernetics and society* (Boston, Mass.: Houghton Mifflin, 1950; repr. 1989), 189.

3 Marshall Brain, *The Second Intelligent Species: How humans will become as irrelevant as cockroaches* (Cary, NC: BYG Publishing, 2015).

> that used to be our responsibility. They will work for us, and alongside us. And They will become more like Us all the time.[4]

We believe that God gave us 'dominion' over the rest of his creation – to use our minds and our hands for him. Our God-given intelligence has used the raw materials of which this earth is full to invent everything from the wheel and the plough to cars and aeroplanes – and now highly intelligent machines that threaten to take away our jobs, by doing them more efficiently than we can. The significance of these foundational Christian beliefs is explored elsewhere in the present volume and I am assuming the centrality of work as a calling from God. My focus here is on the likely context in which the Church, and individual believers, will have to interpret the Christian world view as labour markets shift and the role of technology (and therefore capital) vis-à-vis human labour becomes increasingly, and perhaps devastatingly, significant.

Of course, the conventional wisdom is that it's nonsense to worry about the future of employment. Here it is, summed up by Internet inventor (and Google guru) Vint Cerf: 'Historically, technology has created more jobs than it destroys and there is no reason to think otherwise in this case.'[5]

But what if that assumption proves false? It's not just people on the political left, who tend to be more sceptical of new technologies, who are asking hard questions about the employment impact of robotization. Here is the US conservative intellectual Charles Murray, writing in the *Wall Street Journal*:

> We are approaching a labor market in which entire trades and professions will be mere shadows of what they once were.

4 Nigel Cameron, *The Robots Are Coming: Us, them and God* (London: CARE Trust, 2017), vii.

5 Quoted by Walter Frick, 'Experts have no idea if robots will steal your job', *Harvard Business Review* (8 August 2014), <https://hbr.org/2014/08/experts-have-no-idea-if-robots-will-steal-your-job>, accessed 8 March 2021.

> I'm familiar with the retort: People have been worried about technology destroying jobs since the Luddites, and they have always been wrong. But the case for 'this time is different' has a lot going for it.
>
> When cars and trucks started to displace horse-drawn vehicles, it didn't take much imagination to see that jobs for drivers would replace jobs lost for teamsters, and that car mechanics would be in demand even as jobs for stable boys vanished. It takes a better imagination than mine to come up with new blue-collar occupations that will replace more than a fraction of the jobs (now numbering 4 million) that taxi drivers and truck drivers will lose when driverless vehicles take over . . .
>
> The list goes on, and it also includes millions of white-collar jobs formerly thought to be safe.[6]

Murray draws attention to the fact that when horse-drawn vehicles were replaced by trucks there was still a need for drivers, although the news for horses was not so good; they went to the knackers' yard. And as I point out in my book, *Will Robots Take Your Job? A plea for consensus*,[7] the threat isn't confined to the jobs of humans and horses. For the 1988 French film *The Bear*, more than fifty trained bears were auditioned. But in the Oscar-winning blockbuster of 2015, *The Revenant*, that was not necessary. Even though the story centres on a grim, protracted fight between the lead character (a trapper played by Leo DiCaprio) and a grizzly, not a single bear was auditioned. It may be hard to credit if you've seen the film, but the 'bear' was pure pixels.[8]

---

6 Charles Murray, 'A guaranteed income for every American', *Wall Street Journal* (3 June 2016), <www.wsj.com/articles/a-guaranteed-income-for-every-american-1464969586>, accessed 8 March 2021.

7 Nigel Cameron, *Will Robots Take Your Job? A plea for consensus* (Cambridge: Polity Press, 2017).

8 See Jason Guerrasio, 'How that infamous bear-attack scene in "The Revenant" was made, and other secrets of the movie revealed', *Insider* (26 December 2015), <www.businessinsider.com/the-revenant-filming-secrets-2015-12?r=US&IR=T>, accessed 14 February 2021.

In *Will Robots Take Your Job?*, I assume that the conventional wisdom could be wrong. If it's right, of course, we've no reason to worry. As Tom Standage, the deputy editor of *The Economist*, writes in his endorsement of the book: 'Nigel Cameron has a refreshingly honest answer to the question of whether robots will take all the jobs: we don't know.' My argument was twofold. First, if things do turn out all right – if what we refer to as 'full employment' survives (the slightly vague idea that most people looking for jobs can find them) – we are, nevertheless, going to face choppy times in labour markets as we get from here to there. Already, cab drivers have been disrupted the world over by Uber, and high-street shops by Amazon, and this process has just started. We need to get ready for waves of 'Industrial Revolution'-type labour market disruption in many traditional industries. Second, we have to acknowledge that there's a possibility – in the book, the phrase I use is a 'non-trivial possibility' – that these disruptive technologies will not create enough new jobs to enable 'full employment' to be maintained. How likely is this outcome? To be candid, the more I've been involved in these discussions over the past decade, the more uneasy I've become because, if things do go wrong for labour markets, the long-term impact could be devastating. I'm not sure and no one can be sure. But sane people buy fire insurance for their homes, even though the chance of my home burning down is tiny. We have to be prepared.

In the light of the devastation caused by the coronavirus pandemic, which most people (including government employees in the Department of Health and leaders in Public Health England) assumed would not happen and therefore did not need to be prepared for, we should heed the possibility that the conventional wisdom is being driven by plain wishful thinking. And while the coronavirus has had terrible consequences for both health and the economy, they are consequences in the short term. Those of us who aren't killed by the virus will soon have recovered, and so will our economy. If robotization destroys full employment, the drastic implications will be with us for ever and, of course, will just get more serious – from the human employment perspective. Once 'unemployment due to our discovery of means of economising the use of labour', in Keynes's elegant phrase, has started to 'outrun' the 'pace at which we can find new uses for labour', the race will prove unequal.

While the standard view continues to be that we have no reason to worry, there are various dissident voices emerging across the political spectrum – even from inside the tech community. Bill Gates, the co-founder of Microsoft and a philanthropist, has put it like this: demand for labour is going to go down and we're not prepared because people don't 'have that in their mental model'.[9] From the liberal end of the political spectrum, Lawrence Summers, the former US Secretary of the Treasury under Bill Clinton (and President of Harvard), has undergone something of a conversion experience and now believes that the latter-day 'Luddites' might be right. In a 2013 lecture titled 'Economic possibilities for our children', which echoes the famous Keynes essay we have quoted, Summers reflects on his first awareness of the question during his undergraduate days at the Massachusetts Institute of Technology (MIT):

> There were two factions in those debates. There were the stupid Luddite people, who mostly were outside of economics departments, and there were the smart progressive people . . . The stupid people thought that automation was going to make all the jobs go away and there wasn't going to be any work to do. And the smart people understood that when more was produced, there would be more income and therefore there

9 Brad Reed, 'Bill Gates: yes, robots really are about to take your jobs', *BGR* (14 March 2014), <https://bgr.com/2014/03/14/bill-gates-interview-robots>, accessed 8 March 2021.

> would be more demand. It wasn't possible that all the jobs would go away, so automation was a blessing. I was taught that the smart people were right.[10]

He goes on to observe that he has had reason to change his mind and depart from the conventional wisdom:

> Until a few years ago, I didn't think this was a very complicated subject; the Luddites were wrong and the believers in technology and technological progress were right. I'm not so completely certain now.[11]

Keynes framed the question in terms of technology outrunning our finding new uses for labour. Summers frames it as machine intelligence substituting capital for labour. While machines have traditionally complemented human labour – which goes back to the Industrial Revolution and, in a more limited fashion, much further back – they could entirely replace it. Taking the self-driving car as an example, Summers writes, 'You can take some of the stock of machines and, by designing them appropriately, you can have them do exactly what labor did before.'[12] Plainly, if that becomes the pattern, the game is up; the machines will have all the jobs.

Even highly skilled jobs? That may seem unlikely, although in a provocative book, the father-and-son team of Richard and Daniel Susskind suggest that the next jobs to go could be the professions.[13]

10 Lawrence H. Summers, 'Economic possibilities for our children', *NBER Reporter*, no. 4 (2013), 1–6; see <www.nber.org/reporter/2013number4/economic-possibilities-our-children>, accessed 8 March 2021.

11 See note 10.

12 See note 10.

13 *The Future of the Professions: How technology will transform the work of human experts* (Oxford: Oxford University Press, 2015), reviewed in 'Professor Dr Robot QC: once regarded as safe havens, the professions are now in the eye of the storm', *The Economist* (17 October 2015), <economist.com/news/business/21674779-once-regarded-safe-havens-professions-are-now-eye-storm-professor-dr-robot>, accessed 13 February 2021.

How could the best-paid, most difficult and complex of human jobs, done by the 'professionals' who work as academics, doctors and lawyers, suffer the same fate as those of lorry drivers and cleaners? As *The Economist* magazine points out in an essay on the Susskinds' book, these jobs used to be seen as 'safe havens' from all the technological modernization going on around them. Here is the core of their argument:

> How far will this revolution go? Messrs Susskind and Susskind predict that it will go all the way to 'a dismantling of the traditional professions'. These jobs, they argue, are a solution to the problem that ordinary people have 'limited understanding' of specific areas of expertise. But technology is making it easier for them to get the understanding they need when they need it.[14]

As we all know, you can already find plenty of legal advice (and free legal forms) online, and an endless amount of medical advice. People often annoy their doctors by taking along a sheaf of printouts! And, as the Susskinds highlight, this process has just begun.

There are three ways of looking at the potential impact of technology on labour and employment: from history, from the perspective of emerging trends and from the human dimension.

1 History

As I argued recently in an article for the online magazine *UnHerd*, it's not right to say, with Vint Cerf, that 'historically, technology has created more jobs than it destroys'. The devil really is in the detail.[15] Cerf's sweeping statement echoes the responses of many

14 See note 13.

15 Nigel Cameron, 'Why we should listen to the Luddites', *UnHerd* (23 July 2018), <https://unherd.com/2018/07/why-we-should-listen-to-the-luddites>, accessed 13 February 2021.

in the technology community – and also political leaders anxious to prevent anxiety. Perhaps the most cavalier statement has come from Steven Mnuchin, a former US Secretary of the Treasury, in an interview with the US news website Axios. He claimed that the issue is 'not even on our radar screen'; any such effects are '50 to 100 more years' away![16]

Meanwhile, researchers have been looking in increasing detail at the costs involved when Britain's Industrial Revolution led to a huge jump in prosperity, including a detailed review of what effect the new machines had on the working population. For those of us reared on the standard view that the Luddites were overreacting and everything turned out for the best, they have unearthed disturbing facts. These are facts that we should bear in mind as we face fresh changes ahead.

We tend to think of automation as using machines to do routine work. But at the core of the Industrial Revolution, it was the opposite. The heart of the UK's hugely successful textile industry was the 'domestic system' – skilled men and women working their looms at home. The new Industrial Revolution machines took this work into factories and made it simpler so that fewer operators, who had fewer skills and were paid less, could provide most of the labour.

One effect of this was a big increase in child labour: the machines were designed to be operated by children (who were paid little), and children made up around half the factory hands. Having lost their skilled work, the 'domestic system' artisans now faced competition for the new, lower-paid, machine-based jobs from less-skilled workers.

And it was this that led to the most startling effect of all: an astonishing increase in the number of unskilled labourers. The

16 Quoted in Jamie Condliffe, 'Actually, Steve Mnuchin, robots have already affected the U.S. labor market', *MIT Technology Review* (28 March 2017), <www.technologyreview.com/2017/03/28/152929/actually-steve-mnuchin-robots-have-already-affected-the-us-labor-market>, accessed 13 February 2021.

Chief Economist of the Bank of England, Andy Haldane, made a recent speech to the Trades Union Congress in which he stated that between 1700 and 1850 the proportion of unskilled workers in the British labour force actually doubled, from 20 per cent to 40 per cent.[17] Of course, many of these workers did have skills, but their skills were no longer in demand. To find work, they had to compete with people such as farm labourers for unskilled jobs. It was, literally, generations before the situation turned around.

The Oxford economist Carl Benedikt Frey sums up the research:

> Technological progress has created prosperity for mankind at large, yet it has always created winners and losers in the labour market. During the days of the British Industrial Revolution a sizeable share of the workforce was left worse off by almost any measure as it lost its jobs to technology . . .
>
> During the first six decades of the Industrial Revolution, ordinary Englishmen did not see any of the benefits of mechanization: as output expanded, real wages stagnated, leading to a sharp decline in the share of national income accruing to labour.[18]

To be more specific, the researchers found that while output per worker increased by 46 per cent, real wages rose by just 14 per cent. Working hours actually increased by 20 per cent; hourly wages therefore actually declined in real terms.

In other words, the impact of the Industrial Revolution on the workers of England in the early nineteenth century was terrible, even though in the longer term it raised living standards for

17 Bank of England, 'Labour's share – speech by Andy Haldane' (12 November 2015), <www.bankofengland.co.uk/speech/2015/labours-share>, accessed 13 February 2021.

18 Carl Benedikt Frey, Thor Berger and Chinchih Chen, 'Political machinery: did robots swing the 2016 US presidential election?', *Oxford Review of Economic Policy*, vol. 34, no. 3 (2018), 418, 422–3.

everyone. We are reminded of Keynes's famous dictum that 'in the long run, we are all dead'.[19]

Strikingly, David Ricardo, the leading economist of his day, after initially enthusing about the machines changed his mind and ended up sympathizing with the Luddites! He wrote, 'I am convinced that the substitution of the machinery for human labour is often very injurious to the class of labourers.'[20] However, this did not mean he believed that the mechanization process should be closed down. His work on the principle of 'comparative advantage' is widely seen as the core idea behind what we now call globalization. It is not surprising, therefore, to find him saying that if the UK were not to take advantage of the new machines, other countries would.

2 Emerging trends

We can review how technology might affect jobs in the future from the perspective of emerging trends in the current situation. We know about the impact of Uber and other car-sharing companies on traditional cabbies, especially in cities such as New York, where the 'medallion' that licenses taxi drivers was, at one time, worth $1 million; there have been reports of suicides as the value of licences has collapsed.[21] Amazon started out as a bookseller, and rapidly killed off hundreds of small bookshops and then one of the two big US bookshop chains (Borders). Using its power as a monopsonist (a monopoly buyer) in the book trade, Amazon has had a huge impact on publishers, driving down consumer prices; it went to war with the Hachette group, which had tried to resist, and Amazon

19 See 'John Maynard Keynes', *Wikipedia*, <https://en.wikiquote.org/wiki/John_Maynard_Keynes>, accessed 13 February 2021.

20 David Ricardo, 'On machinery', *On the Principles of Political Economy and Taxation* (1817), ch. 31.

21 Brian M. Rosenthal, 'A $750,000 taxi medallion, a driver's suicide and a brother's guilt', *New York Times* (23 December 2019), <www.nytimes.com/2019/12/23/nyregion/nyc-taxi-suicides.html>, accessed 13 February 2021.

won. Now, of course, the company sells pretty much anything, and its success has destroyed countless brick-and-mortar high-street retailers and threatened the big supermarket chains in many countries. These are both powerful examples of new technology-driven platforms that have disrupted traditional jobs and companies right across the economy – and in the process provide better value for consumers. They have succeeded in part by using technology and in part by creating large numbers of mostly low-paid jobs – although, as warehouses are increasingly robotized and cars become self-driving, almost all those jobs will disappear.

That takes us to a parallel trend: the emergence of new kinds of value produced with scarcely any human participation at all. This is most strikingly illustrated by the contrast between Kodak, for generations the global leader in photography, and Instagram. Kodak has essentially collapsed, but it once employed 145,000 people – plus, of course, indirectly, countless thousands in photography shops around the world. It's an astonishing fact that when Facebook bought Instagram in 2012, for a bargain of $1 billion, the company had exactly 13 employees!

We used to take and print small numbers of photographs, and go to photography shops to get them developed. Now we take thousands of photos, store and share them digitally, and occasionally print them ourselves. There are many varieties of digital goods that bring value to a great number of consumers without the suppliers employing many people at all. The most prominent, of course, are 'social media', a blanket term for many different services from Facebook to Twitter to LinkedIn. They do employ people, but few in relation to the number of their users. Another stunning example is the communications sensation WhatsApp: when Facebook bought it in 2012 for $19 billion, it had just 55 members of staff. That may be a world record for the amount of capital per employee in a company. Many of us have experienced the extraordinary convenience of buying everything from bleach to airline tickets through an app – and of being able to do so while watching television or taking a bath. These are new kinds of goods and services, and government economists are having trouble accounting for them in their routine cost-of-living numbers.

3 The human dimension

Most significantly, when considering the possible or probable impact of technology on employment, there is the human dimension. Some years back, I was invited to Brazil to make a TEDx speech on robots and jobs. I talked about Kodak, Instagram and WhatsApp, and – looking ahead – sketched the potential of robotics to end the need for human employment pretty much completely. I summed up the problem by asking whether this would take us to heaven – or to hell. Many people think that they would love the opportunity not to have to work if they could take 'early retirement'. That sounds a lot nicer than long-term unemployment.

Plainly, one huge question is that of income, and that has led to a lot of interest in 'universal income' – the idea that everyone should be paid by the state to allow them to get by whether or not they have a job. It's an intriguing idea, partly as it has had advocates on the right as well as the left of the political spectrum. The issue is actually more pressing in the USA, where social benefits, such as unemployment pay and health care, are mostly lower than in continental Europe (or are completely absent). In some European countries, the 'social wage' already offers a kind of universal income; being in or out of low-paid work doesn't make much financial difference. One of the goals of the UK's controversial Universal Credit reform has been to stop people making more money from benefits than they would from being employed.

I am not a fan of universal income; I think the amount of attention it has been getting distracts us from the core problem for humans if jobs go away. In industrial societies, our entire lives are shaped around jobs: education to prepare us for them and then the daily routines of doing them for income. After I gave a lecture on this theme at a university in Washington, DC, one of the students neatly summed up the problem: 'Are you telling us that as soon as we graduate from college, we shall need to retire?'

In the famous essay that was quoted at the start of this chapter, Keynes points out that while workers look forward to the end of the day, they often aren't quite sure what to do with the leisure when it comes. When we no longer have to work, what do we do? How do we feel about worklessness, whether we don't need to work or can't even if we're able? What do you do with your time if you find yourself marooned on a desert island? This may seem to be a bigger issue for the poorly educated. But plenty of professional people find their lives in tatters after losing their jobs or being forced into early retirement. As well as income, they've lost their routines, their colleagues and, with that, part of their sense of self-worth.

What do people do if they don't need to work? I'm reminded of my late mother, who in retirement busied herself working in three separate charity shops in Edinburgh, each for one or two days a week. People who make a success of stepping down from their jobs generally create something very like another job for themselves. Perhaps the most striking example is Bill Gates. After leaving Microsoft, he and his wife set up their foundation. Wealthy people who don't need to work – the kind the press dubs 'socialites' – often throw themselves into cultural activities, sitting on the boards of orchestras, museums and charities. We need to prepare for a world in which we find ourselves taking earlier and earlier retirement. The Church is the world's largest volunteer organization; it needs to prepare to handle many more volunteers.

It's plain that we need to think through the ramifications of the loss of employment from a theological perspective. In Genesis, 'work' is presented to us as both something good and normal before the Fall (Adam cares for the garden, see Genesis 2.15), and something disordered and unpleasant after the Fall ('In the sweat of your face you shall eat bread' (Gen. 3.19), as the New King James Version of the Bible memorably puts it!). What if we don't work because we can't?

We could start by developing a 'theology of retirement' to build a bridge towards this emerging situation. We have come to think about Christian 'vocation' as getting a job for life. Indeed, until quite recently most people died before or shortly after they stopped being employed.[22] If we don't need to earn pay, are we still called to work? What of leisure? For most of human history, few people had any; many of us now have a lot, and we could soon have a lot more. Do we have a theology of leisure? Does the Sabbath teaching in Exodus 20.10 – of a day with no normal labour, set aside for God – translate into modern notions of time off for family, friends and entertainment? The expansion of retirement years and the growth of 'free time', as employment laws have cut down on work time for many, require a fresh look at what God asks us to do with our time – and that's now! It will help us to think through what it could mean if the time available starts to grow.

The implications of the erosion of full-time work are explosive. What if tomorrow is your last day at work, but you're still paid? What if you're at university and then you graduate straight into retirement? This may sound far-fetched, but don't forget that economists, from Ricardo to Keynes, and technologists, from Norbert Wiener to Bill Gates, have thought and do think we're moving that way. How are Christians to think?

---

22 The Office of National Statistics has calculated that life expectancy at birth is almost double what it was in 1841, when, for example, a baby girl born that year could expect to live to only 42; see Office for National Statistics, 'How has life expectancy changed over time?' (9 September 2015), <www.ons.gov.uk/peoplepopulationandcommunity/birthsdeathsandmarriages/lifeexpectancies/articles/howhaslifeexpectancychangedovertime/2015-09-09>, accessed 13 February 2021. The ONS gives a helpful discussion of the significance and cause of this shift; higher levels of infant mortality make the difference seem more dramatic than it was, but not by much.

12
The impact of AI and robotics on health and social care

JOHN WYATT

From the earliest days of cybernetics and artificial intelligence, health-care applications have been a prime target, not least because of the economic importance of health-care systems in developed countries. The past ten years in particular have seen a remarkable explosion of health-care applications, reflecting advances in machine-learning technology, the accumulation of very large data sets of health-related information, increasing computing power, and the development of sophisticated diagnostic and monitoring technology, based in part on the ubiquity of smartphones. Four of the major US tech giants, Google, Amazon, Apple and IBM, have identified health-care applications as a major priority.

At the root of these developments are the fundamental drivers of automation – increased speed, accuracy and economic efficiency – themes that recur throughout this book. Machine-learning systems can process vast data sets, recognize patterns and make probabilistic inferences about the future and hence predict outcomes. AI technology has many applications in health care, including medical imaging, the analysis of individual patient histories and data sets, the optimizing of the sequence of diagnostic investigations, the creation of virtual agents that interact with patients, the individualization of treatment plans, the optimization of hospital logistics, and population health data analytics.

In addition to analysing personal health information, machine-learning systems are capable of searching and evaluating millions of pages of basic research and clinical trial data in seconds, providing a range of diagnostic probabilities for individual patients and predicting responses to various treatments. It seems likely that AI technology will become ubiquitous within health care across the world, although its pervasive role will be largely hidden from view.

It seems likely that AI and digital technologies will have transformative effects on the traditional roles of physicians, and of health- and social-care professionals. However, it is obvious that all predictions about the development and application of future technologies are highly unreliable. Disruptive technologies can spread with remarkable speed and unintended consequences are inevitable.

At the time of writing, the worldwide coronavirus pandemic is having an unprecedented impact on health- and social-care systems, throwing a harsh light, in particular, on the deficiencies of social care for elderly people in the UK and in many countries across the world. It is too early to assess the permanent consequences, but it is notable that there has been an extraordinary acceleration in the trend towards 'telemedicine', smartphone-based consultations, and a reduction in face-to-face encounters with physicians and other health-care staff. The use of smartphones and wearable technologies for public-health surveillance has also been highlighted by the coronavirus pandemic. At the same time, the deficiencies and vulnerabilities of large care institutions have been highlighted, and many predict that the trend towards providing care for frail elderly people in their homes, using a range of sophisticated monitoring and assistive technologies, will be accelerated.

The ubiquity of smartphone-based platforms and other innovative technologies allow patients to play a central role in initiating contact with a physician. Wearable technologies and telemonitoring services are also playing an increasingly important role. In

2020, there were an estimated 3.5 billion smartphones in use and a majority of these are thought to have at least one health app.[1] In the USA, for example, software is now available that turns a smartphone into an FDA-approved diabetes management system.[2] It provides doctors with a real-time data stream and gives personalized treatment advice.

The impact of digital technologies on health-care professions

Susskind and Susskind have analysed the impact of digital technologies on the traditional professions, including medicine.[3] Medicine represents, in some ways, a prime example of a traditional profession, with an exclusive monopoly upheld by law, established means of qualification and regulation, and clearly expressed standards of professional conduct and ethical codes. But smart technologies are already disrupting the conventional role of the physician.

First, the introduction of digital technology leads to a move away from an individualized face-to-face relationship between physician and patient, in which both explore a clinical problem and discuss possible therapeutic responses. Instead, patients and physicians engage with automated systems, framed as expert 'partners', that allow the human professional to process clinical information more efficiently, and that aid decision-making.

There is also rapid development of AI-based text or synthesized speech programs that are capable of interacting directly with

1 S. O'Dea, 'Number of smartphone users worldwide from 2016 to 2023' (Statista, 31 March 2021), <www.statista.com/statistics/330695/number-of-smartphone-users-worldwide>, accessed 19 April 2021.

2 Diabetes.co.uk, 'Pioneering insulin dose mobile app gets US approval' (21 February 2019), <www.diabetes.co.uk/news/2019/feb/pioneering-insulin-dose-mobile-app-gets-us-approval-96221428.html>, accessed 9 March 2021.

3 Richard Susskind and Daniel Susskind, *The Future of the Professions: How technology will transform the work of human experts* (Oxford: Oxford University Press, 2015).

patients. When combined with sophisticated face- and posture-processing abilities, these technologies will increasingly be able to simulate many of the features of routine interactions between health professionals and patients. The goal is that these systems will be perceived by patients as friendly, reassuring, trustworthy, competent and even 'compassionate'.

Second, the impact of technological advance is to bypass traditional barriers and gatekeepers guarding access to professional expertise. Patients can access expert medical advice via Internet platforms and smartphone apps. At the same time, the classical roles of the physician (clinical diagnosis and therapeutic decision-making) are being increasingly taken over by other professionals, including data scientists and information technology specialists.

This process has been described as the 'decomposition' of traditional professional roles,[4] which are broken down into constituent tasks and given to different agents, both human and mechanical. As the technology improves and more tasks become accessible to automation, it is possible that fewer human professionals will be required for effective health-care systems. Another trend that may become increasingly important is that of the 'Uberization' of the health-care workforce – that is, increased reliance on platform or 'gig' workers. This raises immediate questions about confidentiality and the commercial exploitation of health data, and the trustworthiness and ethical standards of the new breed of data professionals and gig workers.

A third trend is a shift from a traditional reactive response of health professionals to patients' concerns, towards a more proactive approach of patients themselves in monitoring and maintaining their own health. Technological advances mean that patients can obtain help from Internet-based sources and engage in collaboration with other patients as well as health-care professionals.

4 Susskind and Susskind, *The Future of the Professions*, 122.

There is a trend towards the use of sophisticated wearable sensors that have the potential to provide continuous surveillance of both physical and mental health, providing massive data sets for automated analysis in centralized data warehouses. This raises obvious questions about who is in control of the new systems and whether commercial entities might become the new gatekeepers of professional expertise.

Many of these developments are driven by economic factors and the drive for greater cost-efficiency within health care. The positive view is that AI systems will take on the routine, repetitive and bureaucratic aspects of patient care, allowing human professionals to spend more time in face-to-face interactions with patients. This is the position taken by Eric Topol in his recent book *Deep Medicine*, subtitled *How artificial intelligence can make healthcare human again.*[5] Topol, who chaired an influential 2019 review of digital technologies in health care,[6] argues that vastly improved efficiency, driven by AI, will give human physicians and carers far more time for empathetic human-to-human interaction, physical examination and practical caring.

Yet given the pressure on health-care services for ever greater efficiency and speed in achieving 'positive patient outcomes', there are obvious questions about whether human-to-human interaction between professionals and patients will continue to be seen by health planners, managers and economists as of central importance.

Social robotics

It is not only health care that is being transformed by digital technologies. Many forms of socially assistive technology are entering

5 Eric J. Topol, *Deep Medicine: How artificial intelligence can make healthcare human again* (New York, NY: Basic Books, 2019).

6 NHS, *The Topol Review: Preparing the healthcare workforce to deliver the digital future* (February 2019), <https://topol.hee.nhs.uk>, accessed 13 February 2021.

social care. 'Paro' is a sophisticated AI-powered robot with sensors for touch, light, sound, temperature and movement, designed to mimic the behaviour of a baby seal.[7] The robot has become a relatively common sight at long-term care facilities for dementia patients. Clinical studies have suggested that it is effective in improving mood, reducing anxiety, boosting sleep and reducing pain perception.

In her book *Alone Together*, Sherry Turkle reflects on an interaction between Miriam, an elderly woman living alone in a care facility, and Paro. On this occasion, Miriam is particularly depressed because of a difficult interaction with her son, and she believes that the robot is depressed as well. She turns to Paro, strokes him again, and says, 'Yes, you're sad, aren't you? It's tough out there. Yes, it's hard.' In response, Paro turns its head towards her and purrs approvingly.[8]

Sherry Turkle writes:

> in the moment of apparent connection between Miriam and her Paro, a moment that comforted her, the robot understood nothing. Miriam experienced an intimacy with another, but she was in fact alone . . . We don't seem to care what these artificial intelligences 'know' or 'understand' of the human moments we might 'share' with them . . . We are poised to attach to the inanimate without prejudice. The phrase 'technological promiscuity' comes to mind.[9]

Paro is just one example of a wide range of AI-driven robotic systems designed to assist in the care of elderly people. The Japanese

---

7 See Paro Therapeutic Robot, <www.parorobots.com>, accessed 13 February 2021; see also the discussion of Paro in Ch. 5 of this volume: Vinoth Ramachandra, 'AI and robots: some Asian approaches', 83.

8 Sherry Turkle, *Alone Together: Why we expect more from technology and less from each other* (New York, NY: Basic Books, 2011), 8.

9 Turkle, *Alone Together*, 9.

government has been funding the development of care robots for older people to help to fill a projected shortfall of 380,000 specialized carers by 2025. But Japanese robotics companies are also aiming at a potentially lucrative export industry, supplying robots to many countries, including China and many Western European countries that face similar demographic challenges in the near future. Robotic technology ranges from companion robots, and robots that transport, feed and bathe patients, to those that provide some form of 'telepresence' to allow interaction with distant relatives, professionals and carers.

Mental-health applications

AI-based programs are also playing an increasingly important role in the care of mental-health patients. The delightfully named 'Woebot' is a smartphone-based AI chatbot designed to provide cognitive behavioural therapy for people with depression or anxiety.[10] It provides a text-based 'digital therapist' that responds immediately, night or day. As one user put it, 'The nice thing about something like Woebot is it's there on your phone while you're out there, living your life.'[11]

Ever since Joseph Weizenbaum's experience with the text-based program ELIZA in 1965, investigators have found that people are frequently prepared to disclose more intimate and personal information to a computer-controlled simulation than to a real human being. When combined with sophisticated real-time analysis of the client's emotions by monitoring both face and posture, the technology can provide a remarkable simulation of human 'talking therapy'.

10 See Woebot Health, <https://woebothealth.com>, accessed 13 February 2021.

11 Erin Brodwin, 'I spent 2 weeks texting a bot about my anxiety – and found it to be surprisingly helpful', *Insider* (30 January 2018), <www.businessinsider.com/therapy-chatbot-depression-app-what-its-like-woebot-2018-1>, accessed 9 March 2021.

Alison Darcy, the clinical psychologist at Stanford University who created Woebot, argues that it cannot be a substitute for a relationship with a human therapist. But there is evidence that it can provide positive benefits for those with mental-health concerns. 'The Woebot experience doesn't map onto what we know to be a human-to-computer relationship, and it doesn't map onto what we know to be a human-to-human relationship either,' Darcy said. 'It seems to be something in the middle.'[12]

There is a common narrative that underpins the introduction of AI devices and 'companions' in many different fields of health, therapy and social care. There are simply not enough skilled humans to fulfil the roles. The needs for care across the planet are too great and they are projected to become ever greater. We have to find a technological solution to the lack of human carers, therapists and teachers. Machines therefore can be a 'good enough' replacement.

Despite this, several authors have highlighted ethical concerns about the proposed use of assistive care robots for elderly people, including the reduction of human contact, loss of personal liberty and privacy, and potential infantilization and deception, especially when care is provided for people with dementia.[13]

Draper and Sorell have argued that, whenever possible, robot-assisted care should be controlled by the individual user and designed to protect his or her interests. They propose six essential human values to guide robotic care: autonomy, independence, enablement, safety, privacy and social connectedness.[14]

12 Quoted in Erin Brodwin, 'A Stanford researcher is pioneering a dramatic shift in how we treat depression – and you can try her new tool right now', *Insider* (25 January 2018), <www.businessinsider.com/stanford-therapy-chatbot-app-depression-anxiety-woebot-2018-1?r=US&IR=T>, accessed 13 February 2021.

13 Amanda Sharkey and Noel Sharkey, 'Granny and the robots', *Ethics and Information Technology*, vol. 14, no. 1 (2012), 27–40.

14 Heather Draper and Tom Sorell, 'Ethical values and social care robots for older people: an international qualitative study', *Ethics and Information Technology*, vol. 19, no. 1 (2017), 49–68.

Anthropomorphism

At the root of many of the issues surrounding human-to-machine interactions is our profound inbuilt tendency for anthropomorphism, the capacity to project human characteristics on to non-human animals and inanimate objects. Anthropomorphism has generally been regarded as a positive phenomenon in social robotics. Kate Darling, an influential researcher at MIT Media Lab, has argued that anthropomorphism can be encouraged by human-like behaviour and by so-called 'framing' (establishing a social context that will encourage robots to be treated as lifelike). Darling argues that part of the reason that robots are viewed anthropomorphically is because of 'many robots in science fiction and pop culture that have names, internal states of mind, and emotions. Even though people know that current robot technology does not have those capacities, they tend to suspend their disbelief when prompted accordingly.' Darling continues:

> today's social robots can simulate states of mind and social cues through sound, movement, form, and framing, prompting people to suspend disbelief and project agency onto the robots. With these projections come possibilities . . . robots can motivate people to exercise through praise and companionship, take medicine, and serve as a non-judgmental partner in cases where people might be too embarrassed to seek assistance from other adults . . . Since social robots are often intended to provide companionship, teaching, therapy, or motivation, this has been shown to work most effectively when they are perceived as social agents, rather than tools.[15]

15 Kate Darling, '"Who's Johnny?" Anthropomorphic framing in human–robot interaction, integration, and policy' (2015), <http://www.werobot2015.org/wp-content/uploads/2015/04/Darling_Whos_Johnny_WeRobot_2015.pdf>, accessed 9 March 2021.

However, it is important to consider the wider societal context in which caring relationships with machines are being promoted and are likely to become increasingly common. There is an epidemic of relational breakdown within families and marriages, and increasing social isolation and loneliness. According to Age UK, 1.4 million people over the age of 50 described themselves as 'often lonely' in 2016, with the numbers projected to rise to 2 million by 2025. There is a pervasive sense of relational deficiency in our society, so it is understandable that technologically simulated relationships may be seen as providing at least a partial solution. Indeed, a continually available conversational agent, whether physical or virtual, may appear to offer a degree of intimacy and availability that no human bond can ever match.

However, the hidden biases and assumptions in such 'relationships' must be recognized. The 'relationally sensitive' responses that speech synthesis programs generate are those that their programmers have prioritized. So it is inevitable that they reflect what programmers think is desirable in a submissive and obedient relationship. The relationship that is offered reflects the demographic of the programmers – mainly male, young, white, single, materialistic and tech-loving. The image of Silicon Valley engineers is reflected in their machines; these are the hidden humans who are haunting the robots in our homes, hospitals and care facilities.

It is striking that many young tech specialists seem to have a simplistic and instrumentalist understanding of relationships. At the risk of over-simplification, the programmer seems to assume that the primary purpose of a relationship with another human is to meet an individual's emotional needs, to give him or her positive internal feelings. So, if a 'relationship' with a machine is capable of evoking warm and positive emotions, it can be viewed as an effective substitute for a human being.

Sherry Turkle reported that children who interacted with robots knew that they were not alive in the way that an animal was alive.

But children often described the robot as being 'alive enough' to be a companion or a friend.[16] In a study of children who grew up with lifelike robots, Severson and Carlson reported that children developed a 'new ontological category' for them, stating, 'It may well be that a generational shift occurs wherein those children who grow up knowing and interacting with lifelike robots will understand them in fundamentally different ways from previous generations.'[17] What effects will this have on the emotional development of children? As Sherry Turkle put it, 'The question is not whether children will [grow up loving] their robotic pets . . . [the question is] what loving will come to mean.'[18] In other words, how may human relationships become distorted in the future if children increasingly learn about relationships from their interactions with machines?

There is no doubt that human-to-machine relationships raise complex ethical, social and philosophical issues. There have been a number of recent initiatives within the UK and elsewhere aimed at the development of regulatory frameworks and ethical codes for manufacturers of AI and robotic technology.[19] It is not possible to discuss these issues in detail here.

The remainder of the chapter will outline some reflections on these developments from the perspective of the Christian faith.

---

16 Turkle, *Alone Together*, 28.

17 R. L. Severson and S. M. Carlson, 'Behaving as or behaving as if? Children's conceptions of personified robots and the emergence of a new ontological category', *Neural Networks*, vol. 23, no. 8–9 (2010), 1099–1103.

18 Sherry Turkle, 'Authenticity in the age of digital companions', *Interaction Studies*, vol. 8, no. 3 (2007), 501–17.

19 House of Lords Select Committee on Artificial Intelligence: Report of Session 2017–19, *AI in the UK: Ready, willing and able?* <https://publications.parliament.uk/pa/ld201719/ldselect/ldai/100/100.pdf>; Nuffield Foundation, *Ethical and Societal Implications of Algorithms, Data, and Artificial Intelligence: A roadmap for research* (2019), <www.nuffieldfoundation.org/sites/default/files/files/Ethical-and-Societal-Implications-of-Data-and-AI-report-Nuffield-Foundat.pdf>; European Commission, 'Ethics guidelines for trustworthy AI' (8 April 2019), <https://ec.europa.eu/digital-single-market/en/news/ethics-guidelines-trustworthy-ai>; all websites accessed 13 February 2021.

Christian responses

The fundamental philosophical and theological differences between human beings and intelligent machines have been discussed in previous chapters. Given the rich theological underpinnings of the concept of personhood, it is highly problematic to conceive of a machine in this way. However, questions of ontology, the essential nature of an intelligent machine, are not the only important issues. The machine may in reality be nothing but a sophisticated artefact. But if it seems to be human-like, if it functions as a simulated person or carer, and hence is capable of evoking responses of trust, friendship, emotional engagement and so on, this raises new and troubling issues, especially concerning vulnerable and dependent individuals. If I am being looked after by a machine that appears to be friendly, empathic, helpful and compassionate, and as a result I feel safe, cared-for and appreciated, does it matter if in reality there is no human interaction, only thoughtful design and clever programming?

In order to gain some purchase on these complex issues, I will look briefly at theological reflections on the role of human solidarity in health care.

Human solidarity and the practice of care

Stanley Hauerwas has argued that a defining function of medical care is to show solidarity with those who are suffering. He points out that, for most of us, the initial reaction to witnessing the suffering of another human being is to feel repelled. 'Suffering makes people's otherness stand out in strong relief.' Yet another human being's suffering is a call to the rest of us to stand in community:

> It is the burden of those who care for the suffering to know how to teach the suffering that they are not thereby excluded from the human community. In this sense medicine's primary

> role is to bind the suffering and the non-suffering into the same community.[20]

Andrew Sloane, a medically qualified theologian, has also argued that a Christian philosophy of medicine places solidarity with people in their human embodied vulnerability as the primary goal, while recognizing that weakness, dependence and finitude are inherent in the human condition.[21] Building on the work of the philosopher Alasdair MacIntyre,[22] he sees medicine as a 'social practice', with 'internal goods' – standards of excellence that are developed, monitored, evaluated and passed on to the next generation. The excellences of medicine include knowledge and wisdom, technical skill, and humane care for vulnerable patients. As a consequence, the nature of medicine depends on an underlying anthropology and an understanding of the goods proper to our existence as humans. These include an overarching view of human life in community and what counts as human flourishing in relationship.

Sloane argues that at the heart of medicine 'is the caring relationship between doctor and patient in which the weakness of the patient is met by the power of the doctor's knowledge and skill'.[23] The primary goal of medicine is not healing or the alleviation of suffering per se. These might be the means but they are not the ultimate goal. Instead, the goal of medicine is to care for the vulnerable patient appropriately in the circumstances in which their vulnerability has become exposed.

Both Hauerwas and Sloane emphasize, first, the centrality of Christian anthropology for the medical enterprise; second, the embodied

20 Stanley Hauerwas, *Suffering Presence: Theological reflections on medicine, the mentally handicapped, and the Church* (Notre Dame, Ind.: University of Notre Dame Press, 1986), 25.

21 Andrew Sloane, *Vulnerability and Care: Christian reflections on the philosophy of medicine* (London: T&T Clark, 2018).

22 Alasdair MacIntyre, *After Virtue* (London: Duckworth, 1981), ch. 14.

23 Sloane, *Vulnerability and Care*, ch. 8.

vulnerability of the patient; third, the human solidarity that is central to the physician–patient relationship; and, finally, the goals of health care derived from an understanding of the goods proper to human existence. Serious illness threatens our personhood at a profound level and exposes our embodied vulnerability. The medical encounter provides an opportunity for human solidarity that understands, respects and protects the frailty of the patient. This human solidarity involves a recognition of what Hauerwas has called 'the wisdom of the body', a way of learning to live with our created human nature.

It may be argued that this emphasis on profound interpersonal communication and solidarity within the physician–patient relationship is increasingly irrelevant to the realities of modern health care. Many interactions in hospitals and primary care are relatively mechanical and impersonal: a litany of blood tests, repeat prescriptions, scans and procedures. But when faced with life-changing illness or catastrophic injury, the instinctive human need of the patient is not merely for a provider of expert information but for a human face, a 'wise friend' who can come alongside.

How then should we view the active move to encourage the anthropomorphism of mechanical systems in health and social care, given these theological perspectives? In particular, would it be appropriate for these systems to be used to comfort and reassure patients and clients in pain, distress or confusion?

I wish to distinguish between, first, the use of AI systems in health care to provide reassurance, advice and comfort, and, second, the intentional encouragement of anthropomorphism in the use of these systems. In my view, the use of AI systems to provide human-like behaviours, such as comfort and reassurance, *might* be consistent with Christian concerns, within certain limits. Such systems would have to be programmed and applied in a way that was consistent with Christian anthropology, recognizing and respecting the vulnerability, frailty and integrity of the human patient, and encouraging, when possible, essential human values, including independence, safety and privacy. As discussed previously, many people are prepared to 'suspend disbelief' when engaging with a human-like agent; provided there is not a manipulative or deceptive element in the engagement, this may be entirely appropriate and helpful.

From a positive perspective this 'analogous' personhood may be better than no personhood at all. An analogous friend *may* teach me how to build friendships with a real person, and can play the role of friend when my real friend is absent. Hence the appropriate and thoughtful use of such AI systems in health care *might* be regarded as an expression of human community, reaching out to the patient when a human companion or carer is not available.

However, it may be argued that as AI systems become increasingly effective at simulating human-like compassion and understanding, the use of such systems to comfort and reassure patients in distress represents a deep inauthenticity. In particular, the deliberate use of sophisticated and covert techniques to encourage and strengthen anthropomorphism seems to open the patient to manipulation, confusion and coercion. This may be a particular risk in vulnerable patient groups – those with dementia, learning difficulties or mental-health issues, and young children – so the priority of human-to-human expressions of care and compassion must be particularly safeguarded in the case of such people.

As we have observed, a Christian theology of medicine places an emphasis on the embodied humanity, wisdom, compassion and life-experience of the physician and health-care professional. It is this that allows an authentic expression of solidarity with patients in their suffering and imperilled states. To blur the distinction intentionally between a genuinely compassionate human carer and the simulated compassion of a machine does not seem consistent with a Christian concern for authenticity and truthfulness, even if it appears to be effective in improving patient outcomes.

In his influential work *Simulacra and Simulation*, Baudrillard highlighted the destructive potential of a simulation that 'masks and denatures a profound reality'.[24] This formulation may be helpfully applied to the simulation of compassion and care by AI systems. The simulation may have the effect of masking or obscuring the reality of human solidarity. By blurring the distinction between authentic human compassion and a simulated form, the profound nature of human solidarity through shared embodiment may be obscured and instrumentalized. A similar point is made by Sherry Turkle:

> What do we forget when we talk to machines? We forget what is special about being human. We forget what it means to have authentic conversation. Machines are programmed to have conversations 'as if' they understood what the conversation is about. So when we talk to them, we, too, are reduced and confined to the 'as if'.[25]

In addition, the simulation may have the unintended effect of 'denaturing' or subtly changing the nature of the medical enterprise. If the artificial simulation of human engagement is seen to lead to positive patient outcomes, then the goals of medicine may increasingly change from an expression of human solidarity, orientated to the flourishing of our human existence, towards the achievement of positive health outcomes by any means. In the language of MacIntyre, the 'internal goods' of medicine may become fundamentally altered by the application of AI technology.[26]

---

24 Jean Baudrillard, *Simulacra and Simulation*, tr. Sheila Faria Glaser (Ann Arbor, Mich.: University of Michigan Press, 1995), 6. See also the discussion of Baudrillard's work in Ch. 1 of this volume: Christina Bieber Lake, 'Science fiction, AI and our descent into insignificance'.

25 Sherry Turkle, *Reclaiming Conversation: The power of talk in a digital age* (New York, NY: Penguin, 2015), 339. Turkle's work in other places is also discussed here, on pp. 186 and 191, and in Ch. 10 of this volume: Andrew Graystone, 'Sextech: simulated relationships with machines', 157–8 and 163. Ramachandra, too, draws on *Reclaiming Conversation* in 'AI and robots', 84.

26 MacIntyre, *After Virtue*, ch. 14.

Conclusion

'How then shall we live' in a society that seems to be increasingly promoting AI-simulated relationships in many aspects of health and social care? The challenges are complex and multifaceted, but we must surely ask about the underlying questions and needs to which AI and robotic relationships appear to provide a technological solution.

As we saw above, a common narrative is that the needs for care across the planet are too great and that we need to find a technological solution to the lack of human carers and therapists. But the current shortage of carers is, in part, a reflection of the low status and low economic value that our society places on caring roles. There are more than enough human beings on the planet to undertake the work of caring, both in professional and unpaid voluntary roles in families and communities. Of course, the challenges of unlocking this vast human resource are enormous, but it is surely better that we strive to facilitate, encourage and empower human carers rather than resort to technological replacements at the first opportunity.

Although AI technology can provide remarkable benefits in the world of health care, it cannot replace the centrality of the human-to-human encounter. The realities of illness, ageing, psychological distress and dementia all threaten our personhood at a profound level. In response, the therapeutic and caring encounter between two humans provides an opportunity for human solidarity that understands, empathizes with and protects the frailty of the other.

In my experience as a paediatrician, with the privilege of caring for children and parents confronted with tragic and devastating loss, I have learnt afresh that the essence of caring is to say, both in our words and our actions, 'I am a human being like you. I, too, understand what it means to fear, to suffer and to be exposed to terrible loss. I am here to walk this path with you, to offer you my wisdom, expertise and experience, and to covenant that I will not abandon you, whatever happens.'

13

Art, music and AI: the uses of AI in artistic creation

ANDRZEJ TURKANIK

The chapters found in this volume cover an entire spectrum of areas of human lives, all transformed by the widespread impact of algorithms and machine learning. One of those areas that naturally raises eyebrows is the area of art, for which, arguably, a specific type of creativity is required. A few years ago, when a friend mentioned the possibility that an AI program might compose a musical piece on its own, I was intrigued by the concept, although deeply sceptical about the possibility. Thus started my interest in how AI encroaches on all areas of human life, including the holy grail of human creativity: the arts and music. In this chapter, I shall give a few examples of AI employed in producing works in several of the creative arts – painting, literature and music – and then offer some reflections on these developments.

The application of AI to the creative arts is fairly new and rapidly developing; there are relatively few academic publications about it. Instead, the discussion happens online or in interviews, YouTube videos or press releases. Much of the discussion could be regarded as promotional material in the vein of 'fake it till you make it'. In any case, it is notoriously difficult to write about concepts that are abstract or 'transcendent' (surpassing the language of the material universe), such as music and other arts, because technical and academic language does not lend itself easily to such an enterprise. Artistic experience usually requires approximation and metaphor; words and phrases such as 'like', 'similar' and 'can't quite describe, but feels like' are therefore the rule rather than the exception.

AI and art: how does it look?

In 2018, the world saw the premiere of an unusual AI-generated painting, *Edmond de Belamy*. It is one of a series of portraits of a fictitious family by a Paris-based collective called Obvious, which was developed to explore the connection between art and AI.[1] The technology used by the collective is referred to as a 'generative adversarial network' (GAN), involving two algorithms (called the 'generator' and the 'discriminator' respectively) that interact, during the process of creating an image, to make an artwork that resembles one painted by a human artist. A database of 15,000 paintings, produced between the fourteenth and twentieth centuries, was employed, effectively providing a history of Western portraiture.

In the repetitive process by which an image is generated, the GAN program was 'trained' to create a new portrait to resemble the paintings in the database (the role of the generator), and then to remove those features that were not observed in the database (the role played by the discriminator). This process was repeated millions of times until the final image was obtained.

Although undoubtedly a technological feat, the finished AI-generated painting received mixed reviews from a number of art critics. It was described as 'stale, unoriginal and boring' and, in general, 'disappointing'.[2] Despite this, the painting was sold for

---

1 See Obvious AI & Art, <https://obvious-art.com>, accessed 13 February 2021.

2 Tabitha Gruendyke, 'Art powerhouse Christie's sell AI-generated portrait for $400,000 . . . and it's disappointing', *The Wellesley News* (14 November 2018), <https://thewellesleynews.com/2018/11/14/art-powerhouse-christies-sells-ai-generated-portrait-for-400000-and-its-disappointing>, accessed 13 February 2021.

the extraordinary sum of $432,500 at an auction by Christie's in New York.[3]

AI and literature: how does it read?

In August 2020, *The Economist* magazine carried an article about language-generating AI that had been used for the creation of poetry. Here is a sample that was reproduced in the magazine:

> The SEC said, 'Musk,/your tweets are a blight./They really could cost you your job,/if you don't stop/all this tweeting at night.'/ . . . Then Musk cried, 'Why?/The tweets I wrote are not mean,/I don't use all-caps/and I'm sure that my tweets are clean.'/'But your tweets can move markets/and that's why we're sore./You may be a genius/and a billionaire,/but that doesn't give you the right to be a bore!'[4]

This exchange is a fictitious one between Elon Musk, of SpaceX and Tesla fame, and the US Securities and Exchange Commission. The piece was computer generated, using software called Generative Pre-trained Transformer 3 (GPT-3), which was developed by OpenAI, a company based in San Francisco. At the time of writing, it is claimed that this program generates the most advanced human-like language that is currently available with AI technology. It employs a 'language model', derived from an extremely large database of human-generated text, comprising hundreds of billions of words. The model maps the statistical probability of one word being followed by another, for instance, how often the word

3 Christie's, 'Is artificial intelligence set to become art's next medium?' (12 December 2018), <www.christies.com/features/A-collaboration-between-two-artists-one-human-one-a-machine-9332-1.aspx>, accessed 13 February 2021.

4 'A new AI language model generates poetry and prose', *The Economist* (8 August 2020), 63; also available at <www.economist.com/science-and-technology/2020/08/06/a-new-ai-language-model-generates-poetry-and-prose>, accessed 16 February 2021.

'red' is followed by the word 'rose'. A similar approach is applied to sentences and paragraphs. Earlier versions of the software have been used to develop short stories and even a detective story in the style of the Harry Potter novels.

It was claimed by the software designers that it was difficult for the testers to distinguish the AI-generated texts from those written by humans. However, not all the results have been impressive. The *Economist* article made the remark that 'fundamentally, statistical word-matching is not a substitute for a coherent understanding of the world'.[5] As Melanie Mitchell, a computer scientist at the Santa Fe Institute, commented, '[Generative Pre-trained Transformer 3] doesn't have any internal model of the world – or any world – and so it can't do reasoning that requires such a model.'[6]

AI in music production

History is full of examples of the development of mechanized add-ons to complement music-making. Over the centuries, mechanical performing machines have existed alongside live musicians, extending musical performance beyond the fleeting moment of the live concert. The technology has developed from musical clocks and pianos, with recorded tracks on a drum, all the way to performing robots. At the same time, the role of electronic digital technology in music production has increased from the electronic synthesizer and sampling machine of the 1980s, through more sophisticated sequencers and drum programmers in the 1990s, to the digital audio workstations of the present.

As 2020 marked the 250th anniversary of the birth of Ludwig van Beethoven, a noteworthy project was announced for the culmination of the celebrations. When Beethoven died, he left only a

5 'A new AI language model', 64.

6 'A new AI language model', 64.

few sketches for his Tenth Symphony, so the plan was to complete, publish and perform it. A machine-learning approach was employed to generate an original symphony, as though created by the master himself. There is no doubt that the project is ambitious.

At the time of writing, the premiere of the newly completed symphony has not yet taken place and the musical world continues to wait with uneasy anticipation. However, the designers of the project, sponsored by the Deutsche Telekom, identified fundamental issues as follows:

> Can algorithms be creative? Or, put another way, what distinguishes us as human beings from machines? The technologies which help us navigate our way through cities, that tell us which bus or train to take, and even advise us about online shopping choices – are they able to do even more? Can they write novels, paint pictures or compose music? In other words, can they be genuinely creative? And if so, what does this mean for our understanding of art in general?[7]

David H. Cope of Experiments in Musical Intelligence (EMI, also given the more human name 'Emmy') provides a window into AI-generated music in the style of Bach, Vivaldi, Palestrina, Mahler and many other composers.[8] The database employed by EMI for generating music 'in the style of Bach' included detailed analysis of Bach's chorales, recording five variables for every note (the time, duration, pitch, loudness and the instrument employed),[9] together

7 Deutsche Telekom, 'Artificial intelligence will complete Beethoven's 10th symphony' (n.d.), <www.telekom.com/en/company/topic-specials/beethoven-year-2020-special/details/artificial-intelligence-will-complete-beethoven-s-10th-symphony-587432>, accessed 13 February 2021.

8 Examples can be found at <https://www.youtube.com/watch?v=oPcaGlaROjA>, accessed 13 February 2021.

9 Hannah Fry, *Hello World: How to be human in the age of the machine* (London: Black Swan, 2018), 225.

with the progression of notes and chords in the entire corpus of Bach's prodigious output.

So how does it sound?

As it is impossible to cover art, literature and music beyond this point, I am confining myself to music. I conducted a small experiment, asking friends and family members to listen to the output of EMI and give their impressions. Most of them were captivated by the ability of the program to deliver something of the feel of the works of well-known human composers. I was less impressed, perhaps because, on the one hand, of my reverence for the genius of Bach and because, on the other, of the experience of writing pastiche musical pieces myself many years ago, when I was a music student.

A standard definition of 'pastiche' is 'a work of visual art, literature, theatre, or music that imitates the style or character of the work of one or more other artists. Unlike parody, pastiche celebrates, rather than mocks, the work it imitates.'[10] Although pastiche may entail original elements, the main goal is imitation rather than originality. The imitation, if done well, may have elements of aesthetic sophistication. Popular examples of high-quality musical pastiches are found in the compositions of Austrian composer Fritz Kreisler (1875–1962), who performed pieces allegedly written by Pugnani, Tartini and Vivaldi. Kreisler revealed their true origins only after critical audiences had accepted their veracity and artistic merit.[11]

---

10 See 'Pastiche', *Wikipedia*, <https://en.wikipedia.org/wiki/Pastiche>, accessed 13 February 2021.

11 Such was the quality of the pastiches that when the music critic Olin Downes broke the truth about Kreisler's *Classical Manuscripts* on 3 March 1935 in an article titled 'Kreisler's "Classics"' for the *New York Times*, the critics were outraged as they thought they had been deceived by a '30-year hoax'. See <www.nytimes.com/1935/03/03/archives/kreislers-classics-story-of-their-authorship-some-rumors-and.html> and 'Fritz Kreisler: American violinist', *Britannica*, <www.britannica.com/biography/Fritz-Kreisler>; accessed 9 March 2021.

It seems, however, a little presumptuous of David Cope, the originator of EMI, to argue that 'Bach created all the chords. It's like taking Parmesan cheese and putting it through the grater, and then trying to put it together again. It would still turn out to be Parmesan cheese.'[12] Statements like this are highly misleading in that they trivialize a unique and coherent piece of art by reducing it to its mere components of notes and chords.

In a review of many examples of what is claimed to be AI-generated music, it is important to point out that a more accurate description would be AI-*assisted* music, as human editors play a significant role in the process. But the ratio of the human input to the algorithmic production is a well-kept secret of the mixing studios.

Listening to the music designed to imitate the work of classical composers, one has the impression that the pieces are arguably rough samples at best, lacking any semblance of form and musical development, and they clearly miss the element of imagination that is at the core of a musical thought. In good postmodern fashion, the unique timbre is the main feature and sole provider of an interpretative key to the piece, and neither a beginning nor an end is necessary. There is no narrative structure. What matters is the mood that is aroused, irrespective of the form, length or phrasing. Fading in and out is therefore an important feature – otherwise, such pieces would loop infinitely.

EMI produces a static, ambient sound without tension or narrative arc, similar to a lot of elevator music, thus requiring neither the resolution nor the harmonic complexity that can surprise the listener. Sadly, as even the most basic musical literacy is no longer a given in our background-noise saturated society, there seems to be a very low threshold regarding what provides a pleasurable listening experience. Hence, if it sounds even remotely like a piece by Bach or Dvořák, to a lot of people it is as good as something by

12 Quoted in Fry, *Hello World*, 226.

Bach or Dvořák. Yet to many musicians, the overall impression is of little more than an aural reminiscence that suggests a composer or a musical period.

Admittedly, there are some other quite sophisticated attempts at merging AI-power with experienced composer inputs. Ali Nikrang, a pianist, composer and AI specialist working at Ars Electronica Futurelab research centre, used MuseNet, an open-source AI software, to provide a continuation of Gustav Mahler's unfinished Tenth Symphony. Following an orchestral performance of the original composition and the six minutes of the 'Mahleresque' addition, the composer stated, 'It all sounds like music, there are emotions, but someone who really knows Mahler will notice immediately that it is not Mahler.'[13] According to Nikrang, although the technology had made enormous progress, AI was not able to 'come up with a "concept" or overall theme for the music as the classical composer himself did'.[14]

Human creativity and machine creativity

One is left with the question of whether machine-learning approaches can ever move beyond the mere imitation of human genius. Can AI be truly creative or is it doomed to sophisticated versions of repetition and replication?

When the AI program AlphaGo triumphed over a human world grandmaster, Lee Sedol, at the ancient game of Go,[15] many inter-

13 Quoted in Julia Zapper, 'AI as good as Mahler? Austrian orchestra performs symphony with twist', *Tech Xplore* (7 September 2019), <https://techxplore.com/news/2019-09-ai-good-mahler-austrian-orchestra.html>, accessed 13 February 2021.

14 See note 13.

15 Sam Byford, 'Google's AlphaGo AI beats Lee Se-dol again to win Go series 4–1', *The Verge* (15 March 2016), <https://www.theverge.com/2016/3/15/11213518/alphago-deepmind-go-match-5-result>, accessed 13 February 2021; Steven Borowiec, 'AlphaGo seals 4–1 victory over Go grandmaster Lee Sedol', *The Guardian* (15 March 2016), <https://www.theguardian.com/technology/2016/mar/15/googles-alphago-seals-4-1-victory-over-grandmaster-lee-sedol>, accessed 13 February 2021.

preted this as clear evidence of AI's potential for creativity. The Oxford mathematician Marcus du Sautoy, in his fascinating book *The Creativity Code: Art and innovation in the age of AI*, refers to three types of creativity: exploratory (taking what is there and exploring the outer edges); combinational (connecting two independent constructs into a new whole); and transformational (in which a major shift occurs, resulting in a break with existing norms and expectations).[16]

Humans are clearly capable of all three types of creativity. But what about machines? Du Sautoy suggests that even the most uncommon form of creativity, the transformational, was demonstrated in the case of AlphaGo's historic win over a human expert. And yet the mathematical form of creativity demonstrated by AlphaGo seems completely different from that of a human artist creating a unique work of art. The sole task undertaken by AlphaGo was to win a game by following a series of abstract rules. It seems perverse to compare this algorithmic activity to the mysterious and 'transcendent' work of an artistic genius. But how does this all look from a Christian perspective?

Human creativity as an outflow of *imago Dei*

Dorothy Sayers, the Christian author of detective fiction, poet and sage, in her book *The Mind of the Maker*, says, 'It is the artist who, more than other men (*sic*), is able to create something out of nothing. A whole artistic work is immeasurably more than the sum of its parts.'[17] Clearly, much more than a logical sequence of ingredients is required; namely, a creative *thought-process*. Sayers further observes, 'The "creation" is not a product of the matter,

16 Marcus du Sautoy, *The Creativity Code: Art and innovation in the age of AI* (Cambridge, Mass.: Belknap Press of Harvard University Press, 2019), 7–15.

17 Dorothy L. Sayers, *The Mind of the Maker* (London: Methuen, 1941), 22. Sayers' work is also explored in Ch. 2 of this volume: Crystal L. Downing, 'Out of the machine: cinema and science fiction', 37–42.

and is not simply a rearrangement of the matter . . . Without the thought, though the material parts already exist, the form does not and cannot.'[18]

This thought-process – call it imagination – is the key element for Sayers:

> the components of the material world are fixed; those of the world of imagination increase by continuous and irreversible process, without any destruction or rearrangement of what went before. This represents the nearest approach we experience to 'creation out of nothing', and we conceive of the act of absolute creation as being an act analogous to that of the creative artist.[19] Thus Berdyaev is able to say, 'God created the world by imagination.'[20]

Sayers is right. Christian faith affirms the doctrine of the *imago Dei*, the image of God, found in Genesis 1.26–28, which, at its most basic, refers to the likeness between human beings and God. (As other chapters in this collection contain a theological discussion of this profound doctrine, I will not go into the details here.) We do not, of course, create *ex nihilo* as God does, but we nonetheless do create, taking the raw elements – sounds, letters and strokes of a brush – and transforming them into something that did not exist before. This work is intentional, taking individual, unrelated components and transforming them into something new: a complete piece of art.

An autobiographical reflection may be helpful. I was trained as a classical musician (violin, viola and piano) starting in early childhood, progressing through a specialist music school, until

18 Sayers, *The Mind of the Maker*, 23.

19 In the Christian tradition, *creatio ex nihilo* ('creation out of nothing') has been, of course, ascribed to God.

20 Sayers, *The Mind of the Maker*, 23.

I obtained an MA in Music from the Conservatory of Music in Kraków, Poland. I remember, as a very young musician, performing a piece on one occasion. My recollection of the actual performance is that it was far from flawless; I made a number of mistakes. Yet I will never forget how my professor, an older, formidable lady, not known for being emotional, came to me with tears in her eyes, kissed me on my forehead and said, 'You have a spark of God, my child. Keep playing.' There must have been something that had caused her to appreciate the art in the performance. She did not have the theological language to express it adequately, but perhaps she wanted to say, 'You are reflecting God's creativity in your music; keep doing it.' The link between the divine Creator and the human creator is perhaps often intuited rather than openly expressed.

Historically, Christian artists have frequently understood themselves to be carrying out an aspect of God's work in the world. Indeed, many artists have considered their art only as derivative – serving as a channel of divine creativity. The human channel does not function mechanically and the artistic product clearly varies enormously in quality. Yet creative artists point to a reality that is beyond them – to a God who made all and who rejoices in all that is beautiful, all that magnifies his glory. Thus, human creators are contributing to God's praise and majesty, regardless of whether they acknowledge it or not. A machine cannot do this.

It is important to make an additional point. Most great art is conceived of and produced in seclusion. However, this does not mean that it is made in isolation. Every artist is connected to others at myriad points: through upbringing, schooling, social connections, and also to others in history whom he or she never met. Most of all, whether acknowledging it or not, the artist is connected to his or her God, as image-bearer. As we have seen, this connection is the ultimate foundation from which the creative spirit flows. The profoundly relational aspect of great art points up the contrast with a computer program. The relational nature of the human that spans space and time cannot be programmed into a machine; it can only be experienced and entered into. So both the form of its creativity and the isolation of AI from human community limit its contribution to the arts.

Art and suffering

Before we conclude with some general questions on machine creativity, there is one more dimension that should be introduced. One of the transcendental (that is, special and unusual, and hence not explicable in an ordinary way) roles of the artist in the world derives from his or her sensitivity to the suffering of others. The price for such sensitivity is often to be a 'tormented soul', burdened by *Weltschmerz*, to use a fine German word, which may be translated as 'the weight of the world'. Examples of that phenomenon abound not just among the Romantics but also among many musicians and composers throughout history. The music of J. S. Bach, whose sophisticated musical thought merged with an equally sophisticated use of biblical texts, reflected deep reservoirs of faith in Christ.[21] His 'exegetical music' frequently enters into and illustrates the suffering of Jesus. This is seen, for example, in the *St John Passion*, to highlight just one work. Sir John Eliot Gardiner, one of the world's most respected specialists in Bach's music, says of the introductory movement:

> With the entry of the chorus something of unprecedented, shocking power occurs: in place of words of lamentation, Bach introduces a song of praise to the universal reign of Christ, 'O Lord, our Lord, how excellent is thy name in all

21 See Christoph Wolff, *Johann Sebastian Bach: The learned musician* (Oxford: Oxford University Press, 2000), 335–9; Marcel S. Zwitser, 'Divine flame of love: the Lutheran doctrine of the Holy Spirit and its influence on Johann Sebastian Bach', PhD thesis, Utrecht University, 2012.

> the earth' (Psalm 8), a unique occurrence in Passion settings of the time. The voices enter together in three isolated stabs: *Herr! . . . Herr! . . . Herr!* The impression of a dual *Affekt* [visible emotion] could hardly be clearer: an evocation and portrayal of Christ in majesty like some colossal Byzantine mosaic, but one who is looking down on the maelstrom of distressed unregenerate humanity below . . . Jesus' majesty is thus proclaimed, as one Pietist contemporary of Bach's put it, 'behind the curtain of his sufferings'.[22]

Bach himself had intimate personal experience of death and suffering, which is frequently expressed in his music. And other composers, such as Gustav Mahler, almost prophetically sensed the impending doom of the Second World War. Sergei Rachmaninoff drew musical lyricism out of a deep sense of failure and the darkness of depression. Many blues and jazz musicians, sharing their horrific experiences of slavery and racism, served as cultural seismographs, both sensing and expressing the profound sufferings in their communal experience.

Genuine creativity is birthed out of deep emotions from both individual and shared memories. It has been said that 'you can't buy history', meaning that there are aspects of life that can be experienced only over years and decades. Being part of humanity and sharing human cultures give the creative artist access to collective memories and collective identities, stretching back through the centuries.

Concluding reflections

In *The Creativity Code*, du Sautoy admits to being torn between a conviction, on the one hand, that an algorithm will never quite

22 John Eliot Gardiner, *Music in the Castle of Heaven: A portrait of Johann Sebastian Bach* (London: Penguin Random House, 2013), 344.

reach the level of human-produced art, and, on the other, the fact that

> every decision made by an artist is driven at some level by an algorithmic response of the body to the world around it. How easy will it be for a machine to have an algorithmic response as rich and as complex as that which the human code produces?[23]

Du Sautoy hints at an answer:

> At the moment, all the creativity in machines is being initiated and driven by the human code. We are not seeing machines compelled to express themselves. They don't seem to have anything to say beyond what we are getting them to do . . . Our creativity is intimately bound up with our free will, something it would seem impossible to automate. To program free will would be to contradict what free will means.[24]

And his conclusion is telling: 'Until a machine has become conscious, it cannot be more than a tool for extending human creativity.'[25] This naturally leads du Sautoy to ask the familiar question, 'How would we know that the machine has a consciousness of its own?' He argues that even though a machine's consciousness will be very different from humans', it would be through the creative arts and storytelling that a machine might become able to communicate how it feels to be, say, an iPhone.[26]

Here, we are into deep waters, so we shall content ourselves with asking the question, 'What degree of creativity are machine-learning

23 Sautoy, *The Creativity Code*, 280.

24 Sautoy, *The Creativity Code*, 281.

25 Sautoy, *The Creativity Code*, 285.

26 Sautoy, *The Creativity Code*, 285.

algorithms capable of delivering at the moment?' The mathematician, author and broadcaster Hannah Fry gives a perceptive response:

> I can't help feeling that if EMI and algorithms like it *are* exhibiting creativity, then it's rather a feeble form. Their music might be beautiful, but it is not profound. And try as I might, I can't quite shake the feeling that seeing the output of these machines as art leaves us with a rather impoverished view of the world. It's cultural comfort food, maybe. But it's not art with a capital A.[27]

Quoting the philosopher Douglas Hofstadter, Fry puts her finger on the essential issue:

> A 'program' which could produce music . . . would have to wander around the world on its own, fighting its way through the maze of life and feeling every moment of it. It would have to understand the joy and loneliness of a chilly night wind, the longing of a cherished hand, the inaccessibility of a distant town, the heartbreak and regeneration after a human death. It would have to have known resignation and world-weariness, grief and despair, determination and victory, piety and awe. It would have had to commingle such opposites as hope and fear, anguish and jubilation, serenity and suspense. Part and parcel of it would have to be a sense of grace, humour, rhythm, a sense of the unexpected – and of course an exquisite awareness of the magic of fresh creation. Therein, and only therein, lie the sources of meaning in music.[28]

27 Fry, *Hello World*, 229.

28 Douglas R. Hofstadter, *Gödel, Escher, Bach: An eternal golden braid – a metaphorical fugue on minds and machines in the spirit of Lewis Carroll* (London: Penguin, 1979), 676–7, quoted in Fry, *Hello World*, 230.

I hope that the technical community involved in AI would be open to this kind of wrestling with the issues that lie beneath the surface of technological progress. Will AI enhance or diminish human artistic expression? Will it draw out of us this 'exquisite awareness of the magic of fresh creation'? Will it help us to treasure the inheritance of human artistic endeavour or flood us with the digital equivalent of comforting junk food?

In the process of my research, I discovered that those questions are often eclipsed by superficial advertising slogans praising the apparent 'game-changing' characteristics of a given algorithm. The most optimistic voices are, unsurprisingly, those of the AI sales force. Others, working at the coalface of the technology, are notably more cautious about what AI can actually deliver.

In stark contrast to the promotion of AI by its salespeople, artists have generally been very critical about their own work, painfully so at times. History is full of examples of such self-criticism, with artists concealing or even destroying their artwork in pursuit of excellence and perfection. Only time will tell how many of today's lauded AI-generated breakthroughs will last and enter a cultural canon.

In closing, I am cautiously optimistic that AI may indeed play a useful role as long as it is treated as a tool to assist human composers, musicians and artists of different genres, helpfully providing new building blocks and breaking artistic blockages. There is always space for human imagination to be reawakened by new possibilities. Left to its own devices, however, I am afraid that AI will provide us with technically smooth and sleek material, which is, at the same time, lacking in intention, imagination and the thought-world of meaning and purpose. And those are uniquely human or, should I say, God-like traits.

14

The question of surveillance capitalism

NATHAN MLADIN AND STEPHEN N. WILLIAMS

Introduction

Other chapters in this volume have shown us something of how artificial intelligence is a source of endless fascination for some people and grave concern for others. Yet, out in the world, confusion persists about what it is, what it can and cannot do, and how much of a threat it poses to our lives, our jobs and our future. The stereotypical picture of AI as a terrifying, humanoid robot, found in films such as *The Terminator*, *I, Robot* or *Chappie*, continues to hold sway in the popular imagination. But we are seeing a welcome shift in perception. Where people spent time musing on what we are inclined to suspect are the red herrings of artificial general intelligence (AGI) and the Singularity – the scientific and cultural tipping point discussed elsewhere in this volume[1] – attention is increasingly focused on what has already 'arrived'. Although invisible and inconspicuous, they are the myriad algorithms and cutting-edge computational processes shaping our lives, livelihoods and loves in significant ways. It is hard to say for sure, but two events in particular seem to have made this shift of attention possible.

One is the Cambridge Analytica scandal in 2018, which exposed how Facebook data were used to manipulate elections. The other was the popular Netflix docu-drama, *The Social Dilemma* (2020),

1 See, for example, Ch. 9, Victoria Lorrimar, 'The future of humanity'.

which widely publicized existing critiques and seems to have catalysed a growing concern, including from regulatory bodies, about the questionable workings of social-media platforms, the wider surveillance ecosystem, and the types of damage we now commonly associate with them: loss of privacy, addiction, poor mental health, increased polarization, widening inequality, entrenched discrimination and much more.

One of the key points *The Social Dilemma* drives home is the degree to which we are almost continually being tracked and monitored both online and, increasingly, offline. We live, move and have our being not just, as Christians believe, before the gaze of a faithful, loving God, but under the invasive digital eyes of what the Harvard professor emerita Shoshana Zuboff calls the 'big other', a growing number of data-hungry technology companies that feed off our thoughts, emotions and everyday lives in nefarious ways, while giving us 'free' services in return. Unless you've been living under a rock, in a blissful 'analogue' existence, you will be familiar with this picture.

In an extensive work, which has really established the terms for this debate, Shoshana Zuboff brought the notion of 'surveillance capitalism' to wide public attention, although she did not invent that description. Still, such is its influence and detail that in the course of this chapter we shall keep in mind her set of concerns.[2] She identifies surveillance as the core mechanism of Western and some non-Western political and economic systems, naming a practice that we used to associate with governments of an overtly authoritarian bent. Think Communist Eastern Europe, but also China today. With the rapid advances in digital technology of recent years, however, surveillance is now the lucrative business of government and private sector alike. This, it seems, has only been bolstered by the coronavirus pandemic. In the fight against the virus, governments around the world, which have ties to big

2 Shoshana Zuboff, *The Age of Surveillance Capitalism: The fight for a human future at the new frontier of power* (London: Profile Books, 2019).

tech that run deep, have been striking deals with the tech giants to develop contact-tracing capabilities. As a result, the power of both state and big tech has grown considerably. In all of the above, as we shall see, much is at stake.

In the last part of this chapter, we seek to reflect theologically on this phenomenon, which is one of the most powerful, insidious and widespread applications of AI in our society. We shall first pull apart some of the core features of the surveillance system, focusing specifically on the business model of social-media platforms – how the system works and what it's doing to us at the personal and individual level, at the relational and societal level, and at the civic and political level. We shall then look more closely at two key issues widely considered to be at stake and threatened by the surveillance system: privacy and autonomy. While we do well to think them through from a Christian point of view, these notions are so complex and constraints of space so severe that we can only begin to provide some pointers and resources. We must confine ourselves to emphasizing the attitudes that we ought to adopt, rather than specifying the detailed practices that are crucial accompaniments for our attitudes.

What is surveillance capitalism?

Trying to describe surveillance capitalism can seem, at least for some of us, to be a bit like conjuring up a 'theory of everything', such is its breadth and complexity. Nonetheless, daunting as it may be, it calls for urgent attention, unless we are prepared to accept uncritically its pervasiveness, logic and force, an attitude that we must uncompromisingly eschew if we are to love our neighbours well in the digital age.

The three words in the title of Zuboff's landmark book say it all. *Age*: we are dealing with a phenomenon that marks – in fact, dominates – our age, and not simply with one feature of the contemporary scene. *Surveillance* is the name of the game in town: big tech companies have acquired formidable capabilities of surveillance and are exercising them extensively. Google and Facebook are at the top of that game, but there are other players in the field and many more training or warming up on the sidelines. Space for all this is created by a novel kind of *capitalism*, which has undertaken unregulated operations.

In a preliminary way, we could describe surveillance capitalism as an interconnected political and economic system, enabled by significant advances in digital technology, which centres on the *extraction*, *processing*, *selling* and *use* of data and on behavioural modification. But while technological factors are clearly a necessary condition for its rise, they are not a sufficient condition. Indeed, technological factors themselves are never *merely* technological, but politically and economically embedded. It is for this reason that Zuboff, in her book, is careful to highlight a number of other factors that played a decisive role in the development and, indeed, continuing expansion of surveillance capitalism, which include the dominance of the economic principles of laissez-faire neoliberal capitalism, laid out by Friedrich Hayek and Milton Friedman of the 'Chicago School' of economics. These factors also include, crucially, the 9/11 terrorist attacks in the USA and the government's subsequent response, the so-called 'War on Terror' policies, which bolstered national security at the expense of privacy and civil liberties. Here is a situation that is assuredly repeating itself in our pandemic and post-pandemic times.

However we parse the details of its history or speculate on its future, one thing is clear: surveillance capitalism operates today with mighty force. It straddles, shapes and impinges on economic, social and political realities. Few things in our individual and collective experiences are left untouched. We shall proceed to outline some of the key adverse effects and ramifications of surveillance capitalism, as well as the politics and culture it engenders. First, however, we need to get a firm handle on some of its key functions.

How does it all work?

Consider the following: your online activity, including your searches (more than 90 per cent of which are directed to Google), which sites you visit, what you post, comment, 'like' or share on social media, your purchases, your call history, but also things such as phone-charging patterns, typing speed and mouse movements. These and many more data points are all hoovered up, lumped together in vast pools of aggregated data, and analysed by powerful AIs – algorithmic processes and machine-learning tools – to yield extremely accurate predictions about who you are, how you feel, where you hurt and what you crave at any given moment. In the surveillance operation, personal data are generally on view, although data we would not intuitively consider 'personal', including 'meta-data' (data about data), can easily be harvested to identify individuals, when powerful AIs are applied to large data sets.

While a large part of the surveillance operation happens online, it is quickly extending to the 'offline world' and 'analog' spaces. Indeed, with the advent of the Internet of Things (IoT), the spread of 'smart' (that is, surveillance) devices, such as Amazon Echo, Ring and Nest, or Google's Fitbit and the (admittedly delayed) arrival of driverless cars and 'smart cities', the line between online and offline is becoming increasingly blurred. Our relationship to digital technology itself is less like using an inert tool, such as a hammer, and more like engaging in an immersive experience, and being subtly shaped by it in myriad ways.

The capacity to predict and ultimately manipulate human behaviour with this new technology is staggering. In a recent study, researchers developed a model that can identify an individual's personality traits just on the basis of their Facebook likes. The AI was able to do so more accurately than the people who knew the person very well.[3] Indeed, 'big data' allow tech companies to predict a range of characteristics

3 Wu Youyou, Michal Kosinski and David Stillwell, 'Computer-based personality judgments are more accurate than those made by humans', *Proceedings of the National Academy of Sciences of the United States of America*, vol. 112, no. 4 (2015), 1036–40.

beyond those that people disclose on social media. Attributes such as gender, age, political orientation, but also more granular information, such as a history of drug use, parental separation, whether one is HIV positive or not, can all be predicted with a high degree of accuracy. For example, it takes only 68 Facebook likes, regardless for which sorts of post, to predict patterns of alcohol consumption, sexual orientation and mental health.[4] For Instagram users, models applied to the data collected from the app can predict mental-health issues based just on the brightness of the faces or their number in a picture, or the filters used. In all these examples, unassuming 'users' – ordinary people like you and me, with frailties, vanities and vulnerabilities – have no control over the intimate knowledge that is derived about them or how it is used, often against their best interests.

Furthermore, the data-based predictions about who we are, how we feel and what we'll do are continually fine-tuned, more or less in real time, the more we expose ourselves to, and interact with, surveillance-enabled devices and platforms. And it is these profiles and predictions – and not, usually, the raw data as such – that are sold by the Facebooks and Googles of the world on what are called 'behavioural futures markets'. Sold to whom? Primarily to advertisers who, as we can all testify, target us with the 'right' ads, at the 'right' time, in the 'right' place, as if they were physically listening to our conversations or watching our movements, to get us (that is, 'heavily condition and nudge us') to purchase that extra pair of suede boots that we really like, the new iPhone 12 we secretly want or, why not, the military-level 'tactical gear' some wish they could put their hands on.[5]

4 See Michal Kosinski, David Stillwell and Thore Graepel, 'Private traits and attributes are predictable from digital records of human behavior', *Proceedings of the National Academy of Sciences of the United States of America*, vol. 110, no. 15 (2013), 5802–5; Michal Kosinski, Yilun Wang, Himabindu Lakkaraju and Jure Leskovec, 'Mining big data to extract patterns and predict real-life outcomes', *Psychological Methods*, vol. 21, no. 4 (December 2016), 493–506.

5 Ryan Mac and Craig Silverman, 'Facebook has been showing military gear ads next to insurrection posts', *BuzzFeed News* (13 January 2021), <www.buzzfeednews.com/article/ryanmac/facebook-profits-military-gear-ads-capitol-riot>, accessed 14 February 2021.

But data, and the detailed profiles derived from them, also end up, via a shadowy network of data brokers, in the hands of countless 'third parties', including insurance companies, law enforcement agencies, various governmental bodies and many others. The data could even fall into the hands of your potential employer, who may or may not give you your dream job because of what your lengthy rant about 'corporate culture', which you posted on Facebook, reveals about your probable productivity levels. Surely, we should all agree that this is pretty sinister stuff, not least because the whole operation – the collection, analysis and use of data – is deeply and deliberately opaque. Take the example of 'terms and conditions' or 'terms of use', which we find on sites, apps and devices. Long, full of legalese, strewn with small print, they are purposefully designed to dissuade people from reading them. Legal scholar Brett Frischmann and tech philosopher Evan Selinger aptly refer to them as 'boiler-plate contracts' (a description commonly applied to standardized texts and documents).[6] And if someone decides to overcome the hurdles and read the terms, do they really have a choice about how their data are collected and used without forfeiting access? Emphatically, no. WhatsApp (owned by Facebook), which gave its users a 'take it or leave it' deal regarding its new terms of use in early 2021, is a case in point and illustrates the wide disparity in power between customers and the companies playing the surveil-lance game.[7]

It is in this context, and in the light of these sorts of develop-ments, that a growing number of individuals (including tech critics, former big tech employees, technology and AI ethics researchers)

6 Brett Frischmann and Evan Selinger, *Re-Engineering Humanity* (Cambridge: Cambridge University Press, 2018), 62.

7 Isobel Asher Hamilton, 'WhatsApp's new T&Cs didn't really change anything about sharing your data with Facebook, but you should still use Signal if you care about privacy', *Insider* (26 January 2021), <www.businessinsider.com/whatsapp-facebook-data-terms-conditions-privacy-signal-2021-1?r=US&IR=T>, accessed 14 February 2021.

and various advocacy groups have arisen in recent years, drawing on a growing body of research. They agree that there is something profoundly disturbing about the surveillance system built on pervasive data-extraction and targeted ads. Its impacts and ramifications, especially those linked to social media, regularly feature in public debate these days, especially after the publication of Zuboff's book and the release of *The Social Dilemma*. There have also been highly publicized and relevant hearings in the US Congress.

Impact and ramifications

It is impossible to account for all the effects and ramifications of surveillance capitalism, particularly in a short discussion like this. What follows is nothing more than an outline of some of the most widely documented and egregious examples of harm, primarily in connection with social media. These include addiction to the platforms themselves and to social approval and validation; growing social anxiety; shortening attention spans; and an epidemic of poor mental health. Particularly troubling is the dramatic rise in depression, self-harm and suicide rates among teenagers, especially girls.[8]

We can all agree that, over the past ten years, we've seen a palpable increase in polarization, cultural and political tribalism, and social fragmentation. While not everything should be pinned on surveillance capitalism or digital technology as such, there is little doubt that these have amplified existing trends and trajectories. They are playing a detrimental role, fracturing relationships at all levels, including within the family, and undermining both democratic politics and political peace – we could give many examples of this.

---

8 Jonathan Haidt and Jean Twenge, 'Social media use and mental health: a review', unpublished manuscript, New York University, 2019, <https://docs.google.com/document/d/1w-HOfseF2wF9YIpXwUUtP65-olnkPyWcgF5BiAtBEy0/edit>, accessed 14 February 2021.

The surveillance system is also perpetuating discrimination and injustices against racial, ethnic and other minority or disadvantaged groups. These are generally the ones most adversely affected by technologies such as facial-recognition or automated decision-making systems.[9] The latter are being used in more and more areas of society, including retail finance, insurance and judicial sentencing. If you happen to be of the 'wrong' colour or have the 'wrong' algorithmically determined characteristics, you are likely to be refused a loan for which you would otherwise be eligible; you might find yourself paying more for an insurance policy or you could receive a blatantly unfair verdict.[10] Such technologies also appear in so-called 'predictive policing', which are systems for forecasting criminal activity and allocating police resources, and which – most research to date suggests – rely on inaccurate, skewed or systematically biased 'dirty data'.[11] These practices deepen pre-existing racial injustice and entrench racial inequalities.

There is much more that could be said on all of the above, with many threads still to unravel but, in the final part of this chapter, we want to explore briefly how we might, with a Christian perspective, view two underlying issues: *privacy* and *autonomy*. Much of the discussion about the surveillance capitalist system tends to gravitate around them. To reiterate what we said at the beginning: these are complex and multilayered notions, so what follows are only some initial pointers to stimulate further reflection.

9 See Kate Crawford et al., *AI Now 2019 Report* (New York, NY: AI Now Institute, 2019); see <https://ainowinstitute.org/AI_Now_2019_Report.html>, accessed 14 February 2021.

10 Karen Hao, 'The coming war on hidden algorithms that trap people in poverty', *MIT Technology Review* (4 December 2020), <www.technologyreview.com/2020/12/04/1013068/algorithms-create-a-poverty-trap-lawyers-fight-back/amp/?__twitter_impression=true>, accessed 14 February 2021.

11 Rashida Richardson, Jason M. Schultz and Kate Crawford, 'Dirty data, bad predictions: how civil rights violations impact police data, predictive policing systems, and justice', *New York University Law Review*, vol. 94, no. 192 (2019), 192; see <www.nyulawreview.org/wp-content/uploads/2019/04/NYULawReview-94-Richardson-Schultz-Crawford.pdf>, accessed 14 February 2021.

How should we respond?

As we have seen, the surveillance system in which we are caught up has created a situation where we are all too transparent in all aspects of our lives to impersonal, powerful, corporate and state third parties. Without pursuing a process of building trust and intimacy through a relationship with us, these entities have access to our fragile, finite humanity and exploit our vulnerabilities for financial gain or coercive control. Our lives are, as Zuboff puts it, 'raw material' for products designed to make us into what others would have us be. This strips us of our dignity as persons, made, Christians believe, in the image of God, and transforms us into a marketable product.

There is thus good cause for the alarm that both religious and non-religious people feel at the power of what goes under the name of 'surveillance capitalism'. It centres on the overruling of our privacy, and privacy is taken to be an ingredient in our autonomy. Privacy is not an isolated notion here; if it were, a distinctive Christian perspective on privacy would be elusive. That Christians rightly value privacy has been implicit in the course of our account up to this point, but we should be explicit about it. Medical practitioners instruct us in a truth about confidentiality and privacy that obtains outside their profession when they take the Hippocratic Oath, which, in its traditional version, reads, 'Whatsoever I shall see or hear in the course of my profession . . . if it be what should not be published abroad, I will never divulge, holding such things to be holy secrets.'[12]

But here we want to take special note of the words of Privacy International:

> Privacy is a fundamental right, essential to autonomy and the protection of human dignity . . . [it] enables us to create

12 Our thanks to John Wyatt for bringing this fact to our attention and for detailed comment on the first draft of this chapter.

> barriers and manage boundaries to protect ourselves from unwarranted interference in our lives, which allows us to negotiate who we are and how we want to interact with the world around us. Privacy helps us establish boundaries to limit who has access to our bodies, places and things, as well as our communications and our information.[13]

Here, the value of privacy is grafted on to the value of autonomy and a Christian perspective is relevant here. When a figure such as Shoshana Zuboff describes how involuntarily ceding our privacy means ceding control, ceding control means ceding autonomy, and ceding autonomy undermines the very basis of our Western civilization, she represents a very wide constituency indeed.

'Autonomy' is an individualistic notion, and a Christian perspective on human flourishing does not begin there but with the essentially relational nature of human beings. Of course, secular advocates of autonomy may say that it is so, but it is dangerous to absolutize the individual human right to self-determination by picking it out as the foundation of civilization, including the right to create our own values. Absolutizing autonomy easily trips us up. Supposing a surveillance capitalist were to say, 'What I am doing is autonomously creating my own values,' the critic will respond: 'You have no right to trespass on the privacy, and therefore the autonomy, of others in the name of creating your own values.' Let us grant that the critic is right. But then the critic has appealed not to the open-ended right of self-determination, but to an absolute value that is supposed to trump the reasoning of our surveillance capitalist. Self-determination, our critic has said, must be circumscribed; civilization flourishes only when your autonomy is not allowed to impede the autonomy of others. To which our surveillance capitalist may consistently reply (even if it is not politically

13 Privacy International, 'What is privacy?' (23 October 2017), <www.privacyinternational.org/explainer/56/what-privacy>, accessed 14 February 2021.

or publicly expedient to do so): 'But that is *your* autonomously determined moral value, which you are now imposing on me; mine is different.'

Our hypothetical exchange is not idle. It brings to light the fact that those who criticize surveillance capitalism in the name of the fundamental value of autonomy are appealing not only to the right of the individual to create his or her own values, but also to a set of values that all of us are supposed to have. Christians will agree, but that is because God is the creator and giver of values. Humans flourish not by designing their own values and exalting their capacity to control their own lives, but by discovering how they are designed by the hands of their Creator, and gladly internalizing and acting on their discovery. What really grounds a civilization is the knowledge of myself as a being in relationship, bound to love my neighbour as myself, socially committed to the protection of the poor, the weak and the vulnerable. From this perspective, the defence of privacy begins not in the name of a fundamental, absolute right to self-determination, but in the name of care for others. Of course, that care will often extend to the protection of their privacy and the exercising of their right to self-determination. But the emphasis in a critique of surveillance capitalism will not be: 'Look at what this is doing to *my* right to create my own values.' It will be: 'Look at what this is doing to my vulnerable neighbour, to whom I am *essentially* related as a human being.' As Paul told the Philippians, 'In humility count others more significant than yourselves. Let each of you look not only to his own interests, but also to the interests of others' (Phil. 2.3–4).

If this all arises from considering surveillance, we have also to reflect on the 'capitalism' part of surveillance capitalism. We have implied that, from a Christian point of view, the question that must be asked of big tech and the surveillance economy is how they are contributing to the social goal of maximizing care for, and protection of, the most vulnerable, and not just how they are respecting individual privacies. But there are questions that must be addressed to the consumer, too. Discussing the question of the relation of Christianity to capitalism takes us too far afield. What we are bound to ask is whether the ills that we see in surveillance capitalism owe anything to capitalism itself. Are these ills the logical outworking of historical processes that owe their inception to capitalism itself?[14] Even if this question is too big for us to handle, it is necessary for us to ask it. Asking it in connection with consumers turns the spotlight on the further question of whether it is our personal acquisitiveness that has enabled surveillance capitalism to come about. 'Consumption' is a wide-ranging term, but we must ask to what extent capitalism – even if we defend it as an economic system – has developed and flourished in the form it has because it so often preys on our greed.

Again in Philippians, Paul testifies to the fact that he has learned the secret of contentment in all circumstances (Phil. 4.11–12). Elsewhere he writes, 'If we have food and clothing, with these we will be content' (1 Tim. 6.8). Before we Christians share these words with the world, we need to ask whether we show, by our practice, that we believe them. In many poorer countries (for example, in sub-Saharan Africa), Christians say a loud 'Amen!' to Paul and demonstrate in their lives and attitudes that they mean it, although there are also, among their number, plenty who think and feel otherwise. In countries that make the running in global economic terms, Christians utter a pious 'Amen' to the same Pauline text, but demonstrate in their lives and attitudes that they mean not a word of it, although there are also, among their number, many who have taken Paul's injunction to heart. Until we ask whether we have colluded with forces in capitalism that militate against the

14 In academic discussion, the question may be raised of whether we can speak of historical processes as things that have a 'logic'. Author and reader alike will rejoice that we do not have to explain the question, let alone try to answer it!

contentment which Paul describes, our protest against the invasion of our privacy by surveillance capitalism will be inauthentic.

In sum, big tech inserts itself into our moral formation in ways that are not always visible but run counter to the kinds of lives we should cultivate – of contentment rather than conspicuous consumption, of deep and genuine connection rather than superficial exchanges, of gratitude instead of envy, of patience rather than instant gratification. Big tech undermines our ability to choose what we are being transformed into, and it mines or influences our subconscious desires in ways of which we are often not aware. We cede our agency to choose how to be changed; we are continually bombarded with someone else's desires for us, which are often that we should consume with minimal moral consideration or restraint.

In conclusion, we wish to avoid giving the impression that we should harbour a simplistic response to surveillance capitalism. Conceptual and practical issues have to be examined carefully and dispassionately from different perspectives, while we remain ever alert to the need to make distinctions. But what that worthy intellectual habit must not do is to blur our moral vision. We must be clear both about what surveillance capitalism is doing and about the vision of human well-being set out in the Scriptures of the Christian Church, and how these two relate to each other. AI is about many things. As Christians, we hold that only if we scrutinize it from the point of view of a God supremely revealed in Jesus Christ – who is our way, truth and life, lover of neighbour and exemplar of selflessness – shall we evaluate it aright. Surveillance capitalism provides us with a very significant domain from which to scrutinize and evaluate AI.[15]

15 The authors are grateful to Theos for permission to make modified use of some of the material from 'Surveillance capitalism, autonomy and the death of privacy', which appeared in its October 2020 newsletter.

Conclusion

JOHN WYATT AND STEPHEN N. WILLIAMS

In our concluding remarks, we attempt to identify a number of overarching themes that have emerged in this volume. This selection is, of course, a personal rather than a dispassionate one, and the editors make no claim to be providing an exhaustive analysis. We regard this book as a contribution to a series of debates and discussions concerning the meaning and implications of AI and robotics, which are still at an early stage, particularly where Christian believers are concerned.

First, it seems clear that advancing AI technologies lead to a fresh focus on anthropology, on our understanding of what it means to be human. This is a theme that emerges in different forms in virtually every chapter in this volume. It seems to us that the emergence of AI technologies tends either towards anthropologies that privilege what has been termed 'instrumental rationality', rather than other aspects of embodied humanity, or towards crudely materialistic and reductionist understandings of human nature – 'a meat machine', to use Marvin Minsky's memorable phrase.[1]

One example of the privileging of instrumental rationality may be seen in the design of the Turing test, which conceives of 'intelligence' as being demonstrated through entirely disembodied text-based communication, free from any sense that the intelligent agent is situated in the physical world. Christina Bieber Lake argues that

1 Quoted in Joseph Weizenbaum, 'Social and political impact of the long-term history of computing', *IEEE Annals of the History of Computing*, vol. 30, no. 3 (July–September 2008), 41.

> the development of the test itself is a step towards erasing the difference between human intelligence and machine intelligence. It is also necessarily a gnostic step, but without any spiritual content. It describes persons as mere 'ghosts in the machine'. Our brains are more essential to who we can become than are our bodies, which often only get in the way.[2]

Second, the blurring between human and machine intelligence seems to lead inexorably on to the concept of what is now usually termed artificial general intelligence (AGI), the creation of a machine that would be capable of performing every possible 'intellectual' task in a way equivalent or superior to that of a human being. To many philosophers and theologians, the very concept seems outlandish if not incoherent. Human intelligence seems ineradicably embodied, a way of being in the world of a mammalian species, which is born from the body of another, that explores, discovers and learns about the world, and about the human community in which it is physically instantiated and so on. It seems obvious that, however sophisticated its design may be, a machine can never understand, perceive, decide, think, feel, trust, love and believe as we do.

Yet popular thought and technical specialists frequently adopt this anthropomorphic language. As Vinoth Ramachandra puts it, by 'using a common terminology (for example, "information", "intelligence", "neural networks", "emotions") when discussing minds, brains and computers, we humanize the machines even as we mechanize humans'.[3] And once the concept of AGI is formulated, however incoherent it may be, it then becomes almost axiomatic to many people that, as technology increases in power, intelligent

2 Ch. 1 of this volume: Christina Bieber Lake, 'Science fiction, AI and our descent into insignificance', 21–2.

3 Ch. 5 of this volume: Vinoth Ramachandra, 'AI and robots: some Asian approaches', 85.

machines will increasingly replace human beings. Hence, it is only a matter of time before we become redundant and obsolete as a species. In response to these trends, it seems that it would be helpful for Christians to find common cause with others who understand and celebrate the centrality of physical embodiment to our human way of being in the world.

Third, within the Christian tradition, there have always been different ways of interpreting what it means to be in the image of God. In this volume, we encounter two kinds of difference. One is over whether we regard this notion as signifying that the very *being* of humans, not just their *vocation* or task, sets them apart from everything else in creation. The other discussion is among those who agree that humans' being sets them apart, but differ on the extent and nature of what humans may legitimately do in the way of developing some AI technologies.

Fourth, the ability of intelligent machines to simulate a range of human behaviours and emotions has surfaced in several chapters.[4] How do we think of machines that are capable of simulating human compassion and empathy, to the extent that we find the simulation impressive? Could a machine provide a similar experience to having a human companion or a human lover? Does an artistic creation, based on what might be perceived as a sophisticated form of plagiarism and clever programming, have any intrinsic value? If a machine were to behave in every way *as though* it were conscious, how should we treat it?

The crux of the problem is nicely summarized in the interaction, described by Christina Bieber Lake, between a human guest and a robot host in the *Westworld* television series: 'When the guest asks the host, "Are you one of them or are you real?", the apparent host replies, "If you can't tell the difference, does it matter?"'[5] It seems

4 See this volume, 14–27, 63–9, 85–6, 157–8 and 195–7.

5 Lake, 'Science fiction, AI', 17.

that there are many people who will argue, 'No, it does not matter. If it looks like a duck and quacks like a duck then we should treat it as though it were a duck.'

The ability of AI systems to simulate human behaviour with ever-increasing verisimilitude seems to raise genuinely novel and troubling questions for the future of our society. These questions take a distinctive form for Christian believers. There is a deep Christian tradition, reinforced by widespread human intuitions, that values authenticity and regards all forms of simulation, however well-intentioned, as a form of dissembling, a way of being that is fundamentally deceptive and evil. Can this be sustained in a world in which technologically based simulation appears to offer considerable benefits? There is surely an urgent need for more theological and philosophical reflection on the ethics of simulation.

Fifth, we brought our book to its conclusion with a chapter on surveillance capitalism. It was not mandatory that we should conclude with it, but we believe it appropriate. Here, we highlight pressing questions in connection with the use and abuse of digital information, privacy issues and the need for proper regulation. We believe that there is cause for alarm here, and some of the major negative social implications of AI come into view. Our purpose in concluding on this note is, emphatically, not to insinuate that we take a negative posture towards AI overall. Rather, a quick survey of what is going on in surveillance capitalism enables us to reaffirm positively some fundamental truths about humankind in a world of AI.

Finally, we turn to the recurring theme of how AI technologies influence our understanding of our human future. It seems that science fiction has always oscillated between utopian dreams of using machines to achieve human mastery and ultimate control of the universe, and dystopian nightmares of self-aware machines that wish to destroy their creators. These twin poles continue to be expressed in common responses to the real machines we find operating in our midst.

An understandable fear is that technology is advancing at a speed that seems to outstrip our capacity for human wisdom. Peter Robinson, Noreen Herzfeld and Vinoth Ramachandra all point to the very real threat of lethal autonomous weapon systems and emphasize the importance of developing greater moral, social and emotional intelligence, and of high standards of professional ethics and competence.[6] But catastrophic and destructive failures are not the only possible future. Nigel Cameron raises the prospect of technological unemployment, resulting in a change of work patterns and a dramatic expansion in the amount of leisure time.[7] This may not have the same catastrophic consequences as might autonomous weaponry, but we dare not play down its potential social impact.

To summarize: it seems clear that the new prominence of AI leads to a fresh focus not only on what it means to be human but also on what kind of future we are being propelled towards, and whether it is a future in which human beings can flourish. How can these disruptive technologies be crafted in ways that optimize our human potential and decrease social inequality, rather than creating a future in which human beings are obsolescent or in which only a technical elite can succeed?

Christians speak of the future (which Victoria Lorrimar took as the topic of her chapter[8]) in two ways. There is the historical future, which is the subject of uncertainty, hope or fear, optimism or pessimism. Our task is to do all that we can to shape what we see around us in a way that we believe conforms to the will and goodness of God. But there is another future, one that is the subject of God's promise and certain hope. Its focus is the picture of new heavens and a new earth purged of every malformed human work,

6 In this volume, see Peter Robinson, the Introduction, 7; Ramachandra, 'AI and robots', 88–9; and Ch. 8, Noreen Herzfeld, 'Surrogate, partner or tool: how autonomous should technology be?', 130–2.

7 Ch. 11 of this volume: 'Are the robots coming for our jobs?', 178–80.

8 Ch. 9, 'The future of humanity'.

filled with what is good and wholesome and healing. What becomes of the work of our hands in this situation? We do not know. But we believe that the new heavens and earth will be the scene of its consummation. We cannot here and now confidently map AI and robots on to that scene. We can only pray for the wisdom to discriminate right from wrong on this earth, and for the strength to act in accordance with what we discern.

Further reading

Anderson, Michael, and Susan Leigh Anderson (eds), *Machine Ethics* (Cambridge: Cambridge University Press, 2011).

Bauckham, Richard, and Trevor Hart, *Hope Against Hope: Christian eschatology at the turn of the millennium* (Grand Rapids, Mich.: Eerdmans, 1999).

Baudrillard, Jean, *Simulacra and Simulation*, tr. Sheila Faria Glaser (Ann Arbor, Mich.: University of Michigan Press, 1995).

Boden, Margaret, *Artificial Intelligence: A very short introduction* (Oxford: Oxford University Press, 2018).

Bordwell, David, Kristin Thompson and Jeff Smith, *Film Art: An introduction*, 11th edn (New York, NY: McGraw-Hill Education, 2017).

Bostrom, Nick, *Superintelligence: Paths, dangers, strategies*, 2nd edn (Oxford: Oxford University Press, 2017).

Brockman, John (ed.), *Possible Minds: 25 ways of looking at AI* (New York, NY: Penguin, 2019).

Brockman, John (ed.), *What to Think about Machines that Think: Today's leading thinkers on the age of machine intelligence* (New York, NY: Harper Perennial, 2015).

Burdett, Michael, *Eschatology and the Technological Future*, Routledge Studies in Religion (New York, NY: Routledge, 2015).

Cameron, Nigel, *The Robots Are Coming: Us, them and God* (London: CARE Trust, 2017).

Cameron, Nigel, *Will Robots Take Your Job? A plea for consensus* (Cambridge: Polity Press, 2017).

Čapek, Karel, *R.U.R.: Rossum's Universal Robots* (1920; New York, NY: Dover, 2001).

Cortez, Marc, *ReSourcing Theological Anthropology: A constructive account of humanity in the light of Christ* (Grand Rapids, Mich.: Zondervan, 2017).

Cunningham, Conor, *Darwin's Pious Idea: Why the ultra-Darwinists and creationists both get it wrong* (Grand Rapids, Mich.: Eerdmans, 2010).

Danaher, John, and Neil McArthur (eds), *Robot Sex: Social and ethical implications* (Cambridge, Mass.: MIT Press, 2017).

Dennett, Daniel C., *The Intentional Stance* (Cambridge, Mass.: MIT Press, 1987).

Downing, Crystal, *Salvation from Cinema: The medium is the message* (Abingdon: Routledge, 2016).

Eagleton, Terry, *Hope Without Optimism* (Charlottesville, Va: University of Virginia Press, 2015).

Ford, Martin, *Rise of the Robots: Technology and the threat of a jobless future* (New York, NY: Basic Books, 2015).

Frankish, Keith, and William M. Ramsey (eds), *The Cambridge Handbook of Artificial Intelligence* (Cambridge: Cambridge University Press, 2014).

Frey, Carl Benedikt, and Michael A. Osborne, *The Future of Employment: How susceptible are jobs to computerisation?* (Oxford: Oxford Martin School, 2013), <www.oxfordmartin.ox.ac.uk/downloads/academic/The_Future_of_Employment.pdf>

Frischmann, Brett, and Evan Selinger, *Re-Engineering Humanity* (Cambridge: Cambridge University Press, 2018).

Fry, Hannah, *Hello World: How to be human in the age of the machine* (London: Black Swan, 2018).

Gardiner, John Eliot, *Music in the Castle of Heaven: A portrait of Johann Sebastian Bach* (London: Penguin Random House, 2013).

Gay, Craig M., *Modern Technology and the Human Future: A Christian appraisal* (Downers Grove, Ill.: IVP Academic, 2018).

Gunkel, David J., *The Machine Question: Critical perspectives on AI, robots, and ethics* (Cambridge, Mass.: MIT Press, 2012).

Hart, Trevor, *Making Good: Creation, creativity, and artistry* (Waco, Tex.: Baylor University Press, 2014).

Hauerwas, Stanley, *Suffering Presence: Theological reflections on medicine, the mentally handicapped, and the Church* (Notre Dame, Ind.: University of Notre Dame Press, 1986).

Haugeland, John, *Artificial Intelligence: The very idea* (Cambridge, Mass: MIT Press, 1989).

Hayles, N. Katherine, *How We Became Posthuman: Virtual bodies in cybernetics, literature, and informatics* (Chicago, Ill.: University of Chicago Press, 1999).

Hefner, Philip, *The Human Factor: Evolution, culture, and religion* (Minneapolis, Minn.: Fortress Press, 1993).

Herzfeld, Noreen, *In Our Image: Artificial intelligence and the human spirit*, Theology and the Sciences (Minneapolis, Minn.: Fortress Press, 2002).

Isherwood, Lisa, and Elizabeth Stuart, *Introducing Body Theology*, Introductions in Feminist Theology (Sheffield: Sheffield Academic Press, 1998).

Jonas, Hans, *The Phenomenon of Life: Towards a philosophical biology*, Studies in Phenomenology and Existential Philosophy (Evanston, Ill.: Northwestern University Press, 2000).

Kilner, John F., *Dignity and Destiny: Humanity in the image of God* (Grand Rapids, Mich./Cambridge: Eerdmans, 2015).

Kurzweil, Ray, *The Singularity Is Near: When humans transcend biology* (New York, NY: Viking, 2005).

Lake, Christina Bieber, *Beyond the Story: American literary fiction and the limits of materialism* (Notre Dame, Ind.: University of Notre Dame Press, 2019).

Lake, Christina Bieber, *Prophets of the Posthuman: American fiction, biotechnology, and the ethics of personhood* (Notre Dame, Ind.: University of Notre Dame Press, 2013).

McCorduck, Pamela, *Machines Who Think: A personal inquiry into the history and prospects of artificial intelligence*, 2nd edn (Natick, Mass.: A. K. Peters, 2004).

Mackay, Donald M., *Brains, Machines and Persons* (London: Collins, 1980).

Mayor, Adrienne, *Gods and Robots: Myths, machines, and ancient dreams of technology* (Princeton, NJ: Princeton University Press, 2018).

Moltmann, Jürgen, *The Coming of God: Christian eschatology*, tr. Margaret Kohl (London: SCM Press, 1996).

Moltmann-Wendel, Elisabeth, *I Am My Body: A theology of embodiment* (London: Bloomsbury Academic, 1995).

Mori, Masahiro, *The Buddha in the Robot: A robot engineer's thoughts about science and religion*, tr. Charles Terry (Tokyo: Kosei Publications, 1981).

Nagel, Thomas, *Mind and Cosmos: Why the materialist Neo-Darwinian conception of nature is almost certainly false* (New York, NY: Oxford University Press, 2012).

Niebuhr, Reinhold, *The Nature and Destiny of Man: A Christian interpretation, volume 1 – human nature* (New York, NY: Charles Scribner's Sons, 1941).

Richardson, Kathleen, *Sex Robots: The end of love* (Cambridge: Polity Press, 2019).

Sautoy, Marcus du, *The Creativity Code: Art and innovation in the age of AI* (Cambridge, Mass.: Belknap Press of Harvard University Press, 2019).

Sayers, Dorothy L., *The Mind of the Maker* (1941; San Francisco, Calif.: Harper, 1987).

Scharre, Paul, *Army of None: Autonomous weapons and the future of war* (New York, NY: W. W. Norton & Co., 2019).

Siegel, Dan, *Pocket Guide to Interpersonal Neurobiology: An integrative handbook of the mind* (New York, NY: W. W. Norton & Co., 2012).

Sloane, Andrew, *Vulnerability and Care: Christian reflections on the philosophy of medicine* (London: T&T Clark, 2018).

Sone, Yuji, *Japanese Robot Culture: Performance, imagination, and modernity* (New York, NY: Palgrave Macmillan, 2017).

Susskind, Richard, and Daniel Susskind, *The Future of the*

Professions: How technology will transform the work of human experts (Oxford: Oxford University Press, 2015).

Tegmark, Max, *Life 3.0: Being human in an age of artificial intelligence* (London: Penguin, 2017).

Topol, Eric J., *Deep Medicine: How artificial intelligence can make healthcare human again* (New York, NY: Basic Books, 2019).

Turkle, Sherry, *Alone Together: Why we expect more from technology and less from each other* (New York, NY: Basic Books, 2011).

Turkle, Sherry, *Reclaiming Conversation: The power of talk in a digital age* (New York, NY: Penguin, 2015).

Wallach, Wendell, and Colin Allen, *Moral Machines: Teaching robots right from wrong* (Oxford: Oxford University Press, 2009).

Walsh, Toby, *2062: The world that AI made* (Carlton, Aus.: La Trobe University Press, 2018).

Weizenbaum, Joseph, *Computer Power and Human Reason: From judgment to calculation* (Harmondsworth: Pelican, 1984).

Wiener, Norbert, *The Human Use of Human Beings: Cybernetics and society* (Boston, Mass.: Houghton Mifflin, 1950; repr. 1989).

Wolff, Christoph, *Johann Sebastian Bach: The learned musician* (Oxford: Oxford University Press, 2000).

Wright, N. T., *Surprised by Hope* (London: SPCK, 2007).

Zarkadakis, George, *In Our Own Image: Will artificial intelligence save or destroy us?* (London: Rider, 2015).

Zuboff, Shoshana, *The Age of Surveillance Capitalism: The fight for a human future at the new frontier of power* (London: Profile Books, 2019).

Zwitser, Marcel S., 'Divine flame of love: the Lutheran doctrine of the Holy Spirit and its influence on Johann Sebastian Bach', PhD thesis, Utrecht University, 2012, <https://dspace.library.uu.nl/handle/1874/257095>.

Index of authors

Index of authors

Index of subjects

Index of subjects